Community,
Religion,
and Literature

Community, Religion, and Literature

Essays by
Cleanth Brooks

University of Missouri Press
Columbia and London

Library of Congress Cataloging-in-Publication Data

Brooks, Cleanth, 1906–
  Community, religion, and literature : essays / by Cleanth Brooks.
  p.   cm.
  Includes index.
  ISBN 0-8262-0993-9
  1. American literature—Southern States—History and criticism.
2. American literature—History and criticism—Theory, etc.
3. English literature—History and criticism—Theory, etc.
4. Southern States—Intellectual life. 5. Southern States—In
literature. 6. Community life in literature. 7. Religion and
literature. I. Title.
PS261.B75   1995
810.9'975—dc20   94-43049
                                                      CIP

∞™ This paper meets the requirements of the American
National Standard
for Permanence of Paper for Printed Library Materials, Z39.48,
1984.

Text Design: Rhonda Miller
Jacket Design: Stephanie Foley
Typesetter: Connell-Zeko Type & Graphics
Printer and binder: Thomson-Shore, Inc.
Typeface: Minion

For acknowledgments of previous publication, see p. 333.

To James D. Kenney, M.D.
Wonderful Physician and Very Good Friend

Contents

Publisher's Note

Cleanth Brooks and I began discussing this edition of his previously uncollected essays toward the end of 1992. I had come upon one or two of these pieces and was prompted to ask whether there might not be enough essays to flesh out a solid book. He was willing to review the possibilities for me, but qualified that willingness with this remark: "I'm 86 years old, and I simply don't want to appear to be an oldster warming over efforts that are too far gone to be worth the warming process."

By mid-1993, he had begun to gather a good number of essays for the collection. Alphonse Vinh was by that time working on an edition of the letters of Cleanth Brooks and Allen Tate. Because Alphonse was working closely with Cleanth on preparing those letters for publication, he was also able to assist Cleanth with gathering, copying, and reviewing the essays to be included in this book.

In October of 1993, Cleanth wrote me to say, "I do not want to take advantage of a kind friend. You must not feel that you are condemned to publish anything that I write." Only Cleanth Brooks could have been so modest as to use the phrase "condemned to publish" when writing to any editor about any of his own writing. But he was just that humble.

I learned of his cancer diagnosis in March of 1994, and in April he called to report that he had sent me about twenty-five essays he thought "might" merit publication. He had arranged them in the order followed by this book, the order he thought presented the essays to their best advantage. Because I knew his time was limited, I read the collection immediately.

On April 27, I wrote to tell him how the book seemed to me to have pulled together the primary themes he'd dealt with throughout his literary life—community and religion, and the role of literature in those areas. I told him I'd even begun to imagine calling the book by a title that included those words. He called to say he "loved" that notion of a title and how glad he was I'd perceived the unifying threads he thought held the book together. On May 10, 1994, he died in his home.

We at the press were able to complete the remaining steps of readying the book for publication without him. The busywork of securing permission to reprint, proofreading, and preparing bibliographical data on each essay's original publication—these were details we could handle ourselves. But the creative work of selecting and arranging the pieces that make up *Community, Religion, and Literature* was done by Cleanth Brooks himself. Although increasingly weak during those final months and weeks of his physical life, he remained lucid and articulate to the very end. Thus, we have here not a randomly thrown together collection of essays, but a rigorously considered and carefully sorted selection of what Cleanth Brooks regarded as his final commentary on understanding literature.

The University of Missouri Press is honored to bring this book to the public that will be enriched by its existence.

Beverly Jarrett
Director/Editor-in-Chief

Community,
Religion,
and Literature

1

In Search of the New Criticism

❧

*L*ike Lewis Carroll's Snark, the New Criticism is not easy to describe or locate. Even when we feel that it is in our grasp, it usually turns out to be just another boojum. Carroll never told us what either a snark or a boojum was; no more circumstantial was the man who, more or less by accident, gave the New Criticism its name.

In 1941 John Crowe Ransom, that marvelous poet and distinguished man of letters, published a book entitled *The New Criticism*. In it he discussed the critical aims and methods of Yvor Winters as the "logical" critic, T. S. Eliot as the "historical" critic, and Ivor A. Richards as the "psychological" critic. He mentions more briefly R. P. Blackmur, William Empson, and a few others. Though Ransom treated all with respect, he put on record his reservations and disagreements. He neither defined an entity called the New Criticism nor did he attempt to promote it. In fact, his last chapter is entitled "Wanted: An Ontological Critic."

Clearly, the ontological critic has not yet appeared, unless he was Ransom himself. When did the "New Critic" appear? None of those discussed in Ransom's book has ever called himself such, and my impression is that none of them is usually thought of today as a New Critic, except, just possibly, Empson. I, who am only incidentally mentioned, may be the exception.

What in fact occurred is that people who had misread *The New Criticism* or had never read it at all (had just seen the movie) assumed that Ransom was the primal New Critic and that his former students and friends were the others; and of those few, I am usually chosen as the representative New Critic. It is not an enviable position, and I sometimes feel like the man who has drawn the short straw or the child who, in the counting-out ritual, has been denominated "it." As quasi-representative, one has not only to answer for his own sins, but also to assume responsibility for the collective sins of a vague, undefined group.

How did all this come about? Specifically, why did the epithet catch on so quickly? And how could it have done so unless the epithet had, after all, a measure of positive content?

The last two questions interlock, and to answer the latter will provide an answer for the former. The one common element that I can discern among those loosely grouped together as New Critics was the special concern they exhibited for the rhetorical structure of the literary text. This emphasis was widely interpreted by traditional scholars and critics as a playing down, if not outright dismissal, of any regard for the author's biography and his place in the culture that nurtured him.

It also implied, many felt, a disregard for the reader and the emotional impact of a given work on the reader's sensibility. Yet was not the reader's experience the real justification of literature? The charismatic professor who hoped to excite the interest of his class by conveying his own excitement felt that both he and his favorite author had been betrayed.

All three critical emphases, let us grant, have their values and uses. Circumstances will determine which is the more pertinent to the case in hand. As far as the traditional emphasis on the writer and his background was concerned, every one of those of us who were tagged as New Critics had experienced such traditional training. Furthermore, all of us were avid readers and rejoiced in the intellectual-emotional experience of reading. Those of us who taught hoped to convey that delight to others.

At any rate, rightly or wrongly, readers, and especially teachers, felt themselves threatened by this new phenomenon. The threat needed a name, and the "New Criticism" was there pat to the purpose. It came to stand for those who disparaged a study of the author and his times. I suspect that this bad reputation of the New Criticism was strengthened by the appearance of a little textbook that Robert Penn Warren and I published in 1938. We had planned to call it *Reading Poetry,* but the publishers insisted on a title that made a stronger claim, *Understanding Poetry.*

Here I must go a little further into personal history. In the early 1930s I and, shortly afterward, Warren became members of the faculty of a rapidly expanding state university in the Deep South. Though we arrived with lively interests in literary criticism, especially that of Eliot, Richards, Ransom, and Santayana—the least of our concerns was to cram the heads of our undergraduates with literary theory. The fact was that we were faced with a practical problem. One of the courses we had to teach was a course designed to introduce students to literature. Our students were bright enough young men and women, but very few of them had the slightest conception of how to read a short story, let alone a poem.

Out of this urgent problem grew our first textbooks, for the current textbooks simply did not address themselves to the real issues. They printed the text, gave some brief account of the poet's life, supplied notes for allusions or difficult words, and usually topped it all off with a dollop of impressionistic criticism. The following quotations from two popular textbooks of the 1930s will illustrate what we found useless and sought to replace.

> The song of the nightingale [in Keats's "Ode"] brings sadness and exhilaration to the poet and makes him long to be lifted up and away from the limitations of life. The seventh stanza is particularly beautiful.

> These lyrics ["Ode to the West Wind" and "To a Skylark"] are characterized by a freshness and spontaneity, beautiful figures of speech in abundance, melody, and an unusually skillful adaptation of the form and movement of the verse to the word and the idea. Their melodiousness is sometimes compared with that of Schubert's music.

In lieu of an introduction to *Understanding Poetry,* we offered a "Letter to the Teacher," in which we stated our purpose as follows:

> This book has been conceived on the assumption that if poetry is worth teaching at all it is worth teaching as poetry. The temptation to make a substitute for the poem as the object of study is usually overpowering. The substitutes are various, but the most common ones are:
> 1. Paraphrase of logical and narrative content.
> 2. Study of biographical and historical materials.
> 3. Inspirational and didactic interpretation.
> Of course, paraphrase may be necessary as a preliminary step in the reading of a poem, and a study of the biographical and historical background may do much to clarify interpretation; but these things should be considered as means and not as ends.

In the first edition of *Understanding Poetry* we deliberately left out most (though not all) biographical and historical material, for we were hard pressed for space and we believed that, since the graduate schools of the day taught little else, the average college instructor could and would supply any necessary biographical-historical material. When the outcry came, as it soon did, that we disparaged such helps, in later editions we supplied them in abundance. But it was too late. The dog had been given a bad name that he was never able to shake off.

By the 1940s the belief in the anti-historical and anti-biographical bias of the New Criticism had fully developed. In any case, it must have been confirmed by my publication in 1947 of a book entitled *The Well Wrought Urn*. In it I discussed ten poems of different cultural periods to discover what, if anything, they had in common. The book apparently confirmed the notions generated by *Understanding Poetry* that the New Criticism was fixated on "close reading" through "analyses" of poems, and it took no account of the biographical and historical matrix out of which every poem comes.

So "close reading" was taken to be the hallmark of the New Criticism. But closeness is a relative matter: how close is close enough for an adequate appreciation of the work? In determining this matter, one has to take into account the difficulty of the text in question. Obviously, "Twinkle, twinkle, little star" requires less of the reader than Donne's "Goodfriday, 1613. Riding Westward."

Another factor that one has to take into account is the ability of a particular reader to handle a particular text. Yet, analysis is not merely a teaching device. Unless two people, disagreeing about the meaning and value of a particular poem, expect to end their debate in a shouting match, how can they hope to resolve the issue except through patiently showing what each makes of the disputed passages?

On an earlier page I stated that a criticism focused on the writer's life and background, a criticism focused on the work that he wrote, and a criticism focused on the reader's response to that work are all legitimate modes of inquiry and are compatible with each other. But I want to add now that they have different degrees of authority when we come to interpret the text.

I must, however, caution the present reader that the position I am to set forth is not necessarily that of others who have been labeled New Critics. The position to be outlined is my own, but it is not original. In arriving at it, I have been much aided by the writings of René Wellek and W. K. Wimsatt. Neither of these men, by the way, ever declared himself a New Critic. But then, as I have remarked earlier, who ever did?

In 1942 Wellek published an essay entitled "The Mode of Existence of a Literary Work of Art." In the course of the essay, he wrote:

> The view that the genuine poem is to be found in the intentions of an author is widespread even though it is not always explicitly stated. It justifies much historical research and is at the bottom of many arguments in favor of specific interpretations. However, for most works of art we have no evidence to reconstruct the intentions of the author except the finished work itself. Even if we are in possession of contemporary evidence in the form of an explicit profession of intentions, such a profession need not be binding on a modern observer.

In 1946 Monroe Beardsley and Wimsatt published an essay entitled "The Intentional Fallacy," followed by "The Affective Fallacy." The former, perhaps because of what many considered to be its polemical title, provoked a great deal of hostility. It was regarded as an attempt to take the work away from the author, its rightful owner. I remember that one provoked reader called it little less than an act of kidnapping.

Beardsley and Wimsatt, making their own approach and adding elaborate illustrations, came to much the same general position as Wellek's. In 1968 Wimsatt returned to the problem with an essay entitled "Genesis: An Argument Resumed." This essay presents his final clarified views on the subject. I recommend it to any reader who is seriously interested in the problem of the author's intentions. Let me try to put the case against "intentionalism" succinctly and in my own terms.

The real issue is the evidential value of such intentions as the author has stated them in letters, diaries, and conversations about his work. The issue was never, as is commonly supposed, a denial that the author has any intentions; or the belief that he is "inspired" and, like Plato's Ion, writes in an irrational frenzy; or that what a work means is best left to the critic to say.

The writer's conscious intentions and designs for his work do matter, but writers sometimes feel that the work has a direction of its own—an inner drive toward its own proper fulfillment that may resist the author's early plans for the work. The intentions that have evidential value for interpreting the work are those that are actually achieved in the work itself. As Wimsatt puts it in his "Genesis": "The intention [as declared by the author] is always subject to the corroboration of the poem itself."

I grant that readers (including even distinguished critics) may fail to recognize fully realized intentions, or may misinterpret them, but so may the author. In a letter commenting on my account of *The Waste Land*, T. S. Eliot reminded me that he was now, as he looked back on the composition of his poem, simply another reader of it.

The author may also sometimes fail to recognize the full import of what he has said in his work. Katherine Anne Porter, in a letter to Warren, wrote that she liked his account (in *Understanding Fiction*) of her "Old Mortality." But she went on to tell him that he had pointed out symbolism in her story that she was not at all conscious of having put into it. Nevertheless, she was now quite convinced that it was really there. Thus, some of our most distinguished poets and writers of fiction have not blenched at the implications of the position here set forth. D. H. Lawrence, in 1923, went so far as to admonish his readers thus: "Never trust the artist. Trust the tale. The proper function of a critic is to save the tale from the artist who created it." No New Critic ever went *that* far.

In "Genesis" Wimsatt made an interesting and useful distinction between what a literary work can tell us about its author and what the author can tell us about his work. It is legitimate to move from the work back to the author, but not from the author to the work. Wimsatt goes on to choose an extreme case by which to illustrate this point, one in which the personality of the author closely resembles the personality of the protagonist of the poem.

Now, we know from sound biographical evidence that Thomas Gray was a man of a rather grave, reserved, and even melancholy cast of mind. Such seems also the mind and personality of the pensive man who speaks an "Elegy Written in a Country Churchyard." Indeed, writes Wimsatt, his poem "does seem to come out of the historic person Thomas Gray much more directly than many other poems come out of their authors. Nevertheless, the *Elegy* is not *about* the historic person Gray. The self-contemplative speaker [of the "Elegy"] remains anonymous. The poem itself, if it were anonymous, would be intact."

I would add that since it would be intact—all of it still there—even though completely detached from its author, it is fair also to call the poem autonomous. The navel string connecting it to its creator has been severed, and it now lives a life of its own. It is more than a mere extension of its author's mind and personality.

I believe that I implied such a claim of autonomy not only for Gray's "Elegy" but for the other poems discussed in *The Well Wrought Urn*. But, of course, I am not using *autonomy* in any absolute sense. No one would deny that every literary work is the product of language, of history, and of a particular culture. Yet great literary works do seem to transcend the particular culture out of which they came and continue to speak to mankind at large.

It would take me too far afield to discuss such interesting items as Eliot's celebrated (and I think badly misunderstood) assertion that poetry is not the expression of a poet's personality but a "continual extinction of personality," or Richards's conception of the poetry of "inclusion," or Allen Tate's claim that poetry provides the "complete" knowledge that science does not provide. Nor can I deal at length with "The Affective Fallacy," except to remark that the real issue in that essay is also that of evidential value—the value of the reader's expression of the ideas and emotions aroused in him by the work in question. Such excitement is natural and proper; but it tells us more about the reader than what he is reading. Even if we value the opinion of someone we regard as a fine critic, we may prefer to know *why* he likes the work. Although all these concepts have much influenced my own criticism, I am far from sure that they ever became common doctrine.

The related concepts of paradox and irony, which occur often in my earlier criticism, did not become common doctrine either. These terms, too, have usually been misunderstood. What I was attempting to get at were rhetorical strategies that seem to me common to all poetry; even the simplest metaphor may be said to involve a paradox. For to assert that A is A ("A is a rose," etc.) is no metaphor, but to assert that A is B ("My love is a rose") is to find sameness in difference.

Irony has its twin in what most people see as its opposite: romantic wonder. Both irony and wonder arise out of a reversal of our expectations. The poet is constantly discovering for us a pattern in what we had taken to be mere confusion, or something exciting in what we had thought banal, or the dark underside of what we had supposed to be innocent and smiling.

Yet I am honestly trying to keep this little history of the New Criticism from degenerating into an *apologia pro vita mea*. I shall return to what I believe is the only common element among the critics I have been discussing: a special emphasis on the literary work as distinguished from an emphasis on the writer or the reader. I believe that a concrete example will be the most useful way to reveal the relations of these three modes to one another.

For the present reader's convenience, I have asked that my discussion of the poem be printed in ordinary roman type; that criticism mainly concerned with references to the author, along with the historical references in the poem and all other such discussion, be printed in italics; and that what has to do primarily with reader response, including what I am conscious of as my own more subjective responses, be printed in capitals and small caps. I have included in the last category little ramblings from the text as I follow some special interest. Critics are inclined to do this all the time. With some of our very newest critics it becomes almost a matter of principle.

If any reader of this article would prefer to shift the categories a bit here and there, I shall not seriously object. Some contemporary critics will certainly argue that every word of this account should be printed in small caps, since it is wholly subjective, as every piece of criticism, they insist, must be; that, consequently, no "true" reading of any poem is possible, since language is by its very nature empty of all reference to reality. But this is a matter that lies quite outside the bounds of this essay.

Channel Firing
Thomas Hardy

That night your great guns, unawares,
Shook all our coffins as we lay,
And broke the chancel window-squares,
We thought it was the Judgment-day

And sat upright. While drearisome
Arose the howl of wakened hounds:
The mouse let fall the altar-crumb,
The worms drew back into the mounds,

The glebe cow drooled. Till God called, "No;
It's gunnery practice out at sea
Just as before you went below;
The world is as it used to be:

"All nations striving strong to make
Red war yet redder. Mad as hatters
They do no more for Christés sake
Than you who are helpless in such matters.

"That this is not the judgment-hour
For some of them's a blessed thing,
For if it were they'd have to scour
Hell's floor for so much threatening. . . .

"Ha, ha. It will be warmer when
I blow the trumpet (if indeed
I ever do; for you are men,
And rest eternal solely need)."

So down we lay again. "I wonder,
Will the world ever saner be,"
Said one, "than when He sent us under
In our indifferent century!"

And many a skeleton shook his head.
"Instead of preaching forty year,"
My neighbour Parson Thirdly said,
"I wish I had stuck to pipes and beer."

Again the guns disturbed the hour,
Roaring their readiness to avenge,
As far inland as Stourton Tower,
And Camelot, and starlit Stonehenge.

The British navy is at gunnery practice in the English Channel, and the sound carries inland past some little church near the coast. *Mrs. Florence Hardy, the poet's second wife, has told us that Hardy had in mind a particular place, Stinsford Church, which is located not far from Ports-*

mouth, an English naval base. The noise awakens the dead, some buried centuries before. They think that the Judgment Day has come. It is important to note that the whole poem is spoken by one of these dead men. A popular expression, still current, runs: "The noise was so loud that you would have thought it would wake the dead." So a well-worn expression is, along with the dead men themselves, waked into a grotesque but arresting life.

Another threadbare expression comes to life in the description of other responses to the noise. We say "as poor as a church mouse," for most churches would yield precious little provender for a creature even so tiny. Hardy's little church evidently does have a resident mouse, one who has managed to find a crumb, but is so frightened that he lets it fall. THE VICAR OF THIS CHURCH IS EVIDENTLY A VERY LOW CHURCHMAN AND CARELESS TO BOOT, IF BITS OF THE CONSECRATED HOST LIE ON THE FLOOR.

Why all this circumstantial detail about the reactions of the hounds, worms, the mouse, and the glebe cow? The demands of realism, for one thing. If we are to suppose for even a moment that the noise was such that the dead would be aroused, surely the living creatures would be roused.

Hardy's anthropomorphic God does not speak in the language of the King James Version. His speech is colloquial and earthy as he voices his irritation at the doings of these incorrigible beings he has created. They are all as "Mad as hatters." Again, a well-worn simile, THOUGH MOST OF THOSE WHO USE IT ARE PROBABLY UNAWARE OF HOW IT ORIGINATED. IN AN EARLIER DAY, THOSE WHO FASHIONED FELT HATS WERE EXPOSED TO MERCURY, WHICH GAVE THEM THE JERKS AND MADE THEM APPEAR TO BE CRAZY. IN *ALICE IN WONDERLAND*, THE CELEBRATED TEA PARTY INCLUDES A HATTER AND A MARCH HARE. HARES WERE REPORTED TO GO CRAZY IN MARCH, BUT TO TELL YOU WHY WOULD BE TO RAMBLE TOO FAR FROM MY MAIN SUBJECT.

Jehovah has plenty of provocation for his anger. Man's propensity to threaten and roar his "readiness to avenge" is a direct usurpation of God's prerogative. In Holy Writ we read: "Vengeance is mine; I will repay, saith the Lord" (Romans, 12:19).

In the sixth stanza God finally breaks out in a bitter laugh, "Ha, ha." *In the earliest version of the poem (published in* The Fortnightly Review *for May 1914), God says, "No, no." Having him give a sarcastic laugh instead is a much bolder stroke. "Ha, ha," by the way, does occur in the Bible, but in only one place, and there it does not come from the mouth of Jehovah. It is tempting to speculate on how "Ha, ha" got into Hardy's poem. In Job 39:25 the war-horse "saith among the trumpets, Ha, ha; and he smelleth the battle afar off, the thunder of the captains, and the shouting." Did the thunder of the naval guns practicing for battle recall this passage to Hardy? And did he then decide to take the joyous laughter out of the mouth of the war-horse and assign it—though of course with a very different tonality—to Jehovah?* However the poet came by it, "Ha, ha" is a great improvement over "No, no." It admirably fits the emerging tone of sarcasm.

The idea for the concluding lines of this stanza, I suggest, was borrowed from Jonathan Swift's "The Day of Judgement." The first lines of the poem are spoken by Jove (here, of course, an eighteenth-century euphemism for the God of the Christians; after all, Swift was an Anglican parson).

> *"The World's mad Business now is o'er*
> *And I resent these Pranks no more.*
> *I to such Blockheads, set my wit!*
> *I damn such Fools?—Go, go, you're bit."*

The last clause may be translated into colloquial twentieth-century American as "Come, come, you've been had." But whether or not Hardy is echoing Swift is not of much importance. The matter of great importance in Hardy's poem is the deity's shift from hot anger to pitying contempt.

The poet has the dead men take their dismissal calmly. They lie down again, but like little children put to bed, they continue to talk awhile before they resume their everlasting sleep. One of them wonders whether the world will ever improve: apparently the dead man had entertained some vague hope that it might. *In the last line of the seventh stanza, "indifferent" may need a gloss. In this context it would seem to mean "neither good nor bad; of neutral quality"* (Oxford English Dictionary, 7). *In short, the skeleton who speaks here believes that his century was neither better nor worse than any other.*

IN THE EIGHTH STANZA WE ARE TOLD THAT "MANY A SKELETON SHOOK HIS HEAD," WHICH WOULD SEEM TO BE A RATHER DARING ENTERPRISE FOR A SKELETON. BUT IF WE SMILE AT THE NOTION, IT IS NOT, I SHOULD THINK, BE-

CAUSE OF ANY SLIP ON HARDY'S PART. HE IS IN COMPLETE CONTROL: THE SKEL-
ETONS, SOMEWHAT AMUSINGLY, ARE SHAKING THEIR HEADS—CAREFULLY,
ONE WOULD GUESS—LIKE ELDER STATESMEN LAMENTING PAST POLICIES
NOW REVEALED AS MISTAKEN.

In this eighth stanza, the speaker is finally, after a fashion, identified:
he is the neighbor of Parson Thirdly, lying in an adjoining grave. Not
much of an identification, to be sure, but then, the poet does not want to
particularize him. His chosen speaker is anonymous. He is any man, even
Everyman.

*Parson Thirdly's name is another matter. Professor J. O. Bailey has pointed
out that a Parson Thirdly does occur in Hardy's novel* Far from the Mad-
ding Crowd; *but Bailey apparently has been unable to find any person with
such a name in the parish records or other records of Dorsetshire, and in
view of the thoroughness that he manifests throughout his book, if Professor
Bailey could not find the name, nobody else is likely to do so.* BUT I WOULD
THINK THAT BAILEY HAS LOOKED IN THE WRONG PLACE. SURELY, HARDY
GAVE HIS PARSON SO CURIOUS A NAME BECAUSE THIRDLY WAS THE OLD-
FASHIONED PARSON WHO BEGAN THE EXPOSITION OF HIS TEXT WITH "FIRSTLY,"
FOLLOWED THAT UP IN DUE TIME WITH "SECONDLY," WENT ON TO "THIRDLY,"
AND SO ON—AD INFINITUM, SOME OF HIS PARISHIONERS MAY WELL HAVE
THOUGHT.

Thirdly laments what he now considers a misspent life. But his list of
sinful delights is a modest one. He does not mourn the fact that he did
not lead a dashingly wicked life—no glamorous highwayman, no Byronic
lover. His needs would have been fully served by more tobacco and beer,
fewer prayers and sermons.

The poem ends as it began with another peal of thunder from the naval
guns. But this time we are told that their reverberations carry far past the
churchyard, miles inward. *Bailey has calculated that Stourton Tower is
twenty miles north of Portsmouth Harbor; South Cadbury, which he thinks
is the most likely site for Camelot, is twenty-eight miles north of Portsmouth;
and Stonehenge, forty-five miles northeast.*

This is all very interesting and possibly helpful. But for a full appreciation of the poem, it is more important for the reader to note that as the
sound of the guns penetrates farther in space, the names of the places to

which it penetrates take us back in time, deeper and deeper into British history. Stourton Tower is a memorial to King Alfred's victory over the Danes in 878; Camelot was the capital of the British Prince Arthur in the fifth century; and with Stonehenge, the great monoliths on Salisbury Plain, we have passed beyond the bounds of recorded history.

Professor Bailey says that Stourton Tower, Camelot, and Stonehenge "represent civilizations that rose through battle and perished as dynasties." But this comment simply will not do. In the first place, it is at odds with history: for instance, what has Stonehenge to do with the rise of a civilization through battle? And how does Alfred fit into this scheme? He was a king who inherited a civilization and defended it successfully against invaders who meant to destroy it. Most of all, Bailey's remark seems at odds with the tone of the concluding stanza.

The tone of this last stanza is not frenetic or bitterly satiric or pityingly contemptuous. The present incident is being seen against the backdrop of a remote time. The tone is not indignant or scornful, but brooding and tragic. Man apparently from the dawn of history has been a fighting animal, but some of his wars have been fought for better causes than mere loot, and some have involved noble spirits like the historic Alfred and the possibly fabulous Arthur.

The adjective "starlit" makes its own contribution to the sense of grandeur. In choosing the adjective, Hardy may have had in mind the theory that *Stonehenge had been designed as a prehistoric celestial observatory.* In any case, the stars are associated with the remote and the eternal— entities utterly detached from the quotidian affairs of humankind.

Even the metrical variations of this last stanza are used to strengthen the effect of solemnity. Consider the last line. The poet has so cleverly managed matters that the reader has to stress every one of the last five syllables. (Read it aloud and see, or rather hear, for yourself.) Thus Hardy has ensured that in any natural reading the line has a slow and stately movement.

Since the entire poem is imagined to have been spoken by the dead man who is Parson Thirdly's "neighbour," we learn, especially from this last stanza, something about what manner of man he was. Clearly, he was a person of imagination and some learning. He impresses me as wise, rather philosophical, and a profound observer of human nature. HE MAY EVEN RESEMBLE AT POINTS HIS LITERARY PROGENITOR, THOMAS HARDY HIMSELF.

One must be grateful to Professor Bailey for having provided so many facts about Hardy and about Hardy's countryside. They are bound to be interesting to anyone who admires Hardy's poetry and fiction. Some of them may be necessary for a full understanding of Hardy's literary work, but biographical and historical facts as such are not to be confused with literary criticism. Even a worthless poem or a fourth-rate novel may generate its own spectrum of biographical and historical facts, facts that may go far to explain how the work came about. But our mastery of these facts will not necessarily change our views of its value as *literature.*

Hardy dated the composition of "Channel Firing" April 1914—it was published in May—and four months later the firing of the guns in World War I had begun. Did Hardy, then, prophesy the coming on of that great war? *He has told us that he did not foresee it.*

What was his attitude toward that war? *Evidently much like that of other Englishmen at the time: he was saddened, shocked, especially unhappy that the enemy was the German people, whom he regarded as a race akin to his own. But he wrote a number of war poems. They are not very good as poems go, but they are intensely patriotic and justify the British participation.*

Let me make it plain that I do not argue from Hardy's subsequent war poems that he repudiated the sentiments expressed in "Channel Firing." Poets write out of different periods of their lives and out of different states of mind. Sometimes, like other men, they radically change their views. My point, however, is different. I argue that the evidence for believing that "Channel Firing" is not a simple anti-war poem is to be found in the poem itself. In order to make the point, one does not have to cite Hardy's subsequent poems defending Britain's entrance into the war. The attitude expressed in "Channel Firing" is complex, not focused on a single issue, not a special pleading for a particular cause.

BECAUSE "CHANNEL FIRING" IS MORE THAN PROPAGANDA FOR A PARTIC-ULAR IDEA, I DOUBT THAT IT HAS EVER BEEN READ BY A PACIFIST AT A PEACE RALLY. GOD'S BITTER OUTBURST, ENDING IN A CONTEMPTUOUS DISMISSAL OF MANKIND, SCARCELY COMPORTS WITH A CALL TO PROTEST AGAINST OR TO RESIST THE WARLORDS. NOR DOES THE CONCLUDING STANZA, THE NOTE

OF WHICH IS TRAGIC—AS IF ONE WERE DEALING WITH PERMANENT AND IRREMEDIABLE THINGS.

Yet what should the reader make of this fascinating poem? Even those of us who believe we have the answer will be chary of forcing it on the reader. For one thing, forcing will do no good. The reader will ultimately make his own judgment.

Each reader will have to make up his own mind, but he might properly be asked at least to read the work with due attention; to consider the meanings of the words themselves; to treat the figurative language as also meaningful, not merely as idle embellishment; to note the tone established or modulated and shifted; and to consider that even the rhythms may support the total effect. Such, in sum, seems to me to be the burden of what the badly named New Critics have said. In that case, they would appear to be in fact not new at all, but among the most old-fashioned and practical critics that we have.

2

The Primacy of the Linguistic Medium

∾

I have long been concerned with what happens to our conception of
literature if we allow biography and history to encroach on its just do-
mains, or if we allow a preoccupation with what various readers make of
it to determine its meaning and value. I believe, however, that the most
destructive encroachment of all comes from the overweening claims made
by some of the new experts in linguistics. It would be wrongheaded, of
course, to oppose the study of language as such, but I am not alone in
being concerned about the impact of some developments in the linguistic
theories which have been offered by people whose primary interest seems
to lie not in literature but in philosophy.

I have in mind here the structuralists and the deconstructionists. Naturally, I have no pithy, simple definition of "structuralism" to offer you,
but I can offer a sketch of some of its aims. Structuralism, as we know,
originated in a concern for the structure of language, but soon extended
its analysis to take in myths and the social organizations of primitive
societies; its debt is anthropological as well as linguistic, and structuralist
analysis can be applied to all sorts of human activities, for structuralism
holds that all patterns of social behavior are "codes" having the characteristics of a language. I, however, shall be concerned here primarily with
the impact of structuralism on literature. Since the structuralist regards
literature as a part of language, and since he holds that language is by its
very nature an arbitrary system—and therefore committed to no reference to reality—literature has for the structuralist no cognitive value.
"Poetry and literature," as René Wellek has put it, ". . . have disappeared.
There remains only a disembodied methodology."

Other critics have made similar observations, some arguing that the structuralist literary critic is much more interested in his *method*—in his analytic tools—than he is in any given literary work. Michael Lane, for example, who edited *Introduction to Structuralism,* acknowledges that "much that is exciting and illuminating [has been] written about the tools of the structuralist criticism," but regrets that there has been "so little application of these tools to classic literature." Lane made these remarks many years ago, but the actual fruits of structuralist literary criticism still seem meager. Lane goes on to make another point: the artistic value of a work is also of relatively little importance to the structuralist, for "there is no a priori reason to believe that the system of signs in *Superman* is any less coherent than that in *King Lear.* Values"—including literary values—"are a function of ideologies, not methods." I will also mention deconstructionism here, if only for the sake of Jacques Derrida, the contemporary French critic who has probably made the most powerful impact on current American criticism. Deconstructionism, we understand, is an outgrowth of structuralism, but whereas structuralism attempts to reveal the deep structure that underlies the surface meanings of any literary construct, deconstruction, using a more radical analysis, deconstructs *that* very structure, revealing its lack of any relation to anything beyond itself. But upon one point both structuralism and deconstruction come to the same conclusion: namely, that literature is a self-enclosed system, referring to nothing outside and beyond itself. The consequences of any such conception of literature seem to me to be devastating to any concept of its humanistic value.

Wellek, too, calls into question the applicability of any merely linguistic model "to the totality of literature." Granting that the linguistic element is obviously very important in literature, he nevertheless insists that linguistics is far from constituting the whole of literary study. He points out that

Motifs, themes, images, symbols, plots, and compositional schemes, genre patterns, character and hero types, as well as qualities such as the tragic or the comic, the sublime or the grotesque, can be and have been discussed fruitfully with only a minimal or no regard to their linguistic formulations. The mere fact that the great poets and writers—Homer, Dante, Shakespeare, Goethe, Tolstoy, and Dostoyevsky—have exercised enormous influence often in poor and loose translations which hardly convey even an inkling of the peculiarities of their verbal style should demonstrate the comparative independence of literature from language.

This is an argument, I think, which constitutes a powerful refutation of any tidy attempt to force logic beyond the bounds of common sense, and Wellek goes on to say further that

> The whole doctrine of man's imprisonment in language should be doubted: we must assume that language itself is in an ontological relation to reality, as all older philosophers of language and even Heidegger assert. There is, after all, a perceptual life of man: personality and self . . . cannot be reduced to language relations. Even deaf-mutes find their way around the world. [This] does not deny that civilization as we know it is possible only because of the development of language or that linguistics can throw light on many questions of literature. It only denies the view of the prison house of language with the nihilistic consequences drawn by the prophets of the death of literature.

In an article in the *Partisan Review,* M. H. Abrams addresses the same issues:

> In these new writings about reading . . . the author deliquesces into writing-as-such and the reader into reading-as-such, and what writing-as-such effects and reading-as-such engages is not a work of literature but a text, writing, *écriture.* In its turn the text forfeits its status as a purposeful utterance about human beings and human concerns, and even its individuality, becoming simply an episode in an all-encompassing textuality—dissolved, as Edward Said has remarked, into "the communal sea of linguisity."

Abrams proceeds to a careful and, I believe, fair-minded exposition of Derrida's position, in the course of which he points up its relation to that of Friedrich Nietzsche, who proclaimed the death of God and invited the adventurous soul to step fearlessly out into a realm beyond good and evil. Abrams interprets Derrida as an absolutist who can find no absolute, nothing upon which to ground the human enterprise. Even language itself cannot be grounded in the reality of human experience, for language refers to nothing outside itself. Abrams eventually sums up Derrida's philosophy of language in these two sentences:

> [Derrida] agrees that language works, then asks, "But is it possible that it really works?" He concludes that, lacking an ultimate ground, it is abso-

lutely not possible that it works, hence that its working is only a seeming—
that, in short, though texts may be legible, they are not intelligible, or
determinately significant.

That is to say, texts do not indicate any one definite and unambiguous
meaning. Abrams concludes his account of Derrida with the sardonic
observation that, despite Derrida's conviction in the inherent deceptive-
ness of language, Abrams himself can, like Hamlet, "tell a hawk from a
handsaw"—or, to shift to a modern idiom, that he can warn somebody to
get out of the way of an onrushing truck. Ordinary language *does* work,
and ordinary language bears *some* resemblance to the language used in
literature.

Of the various commentators on the present scene in which literary
theorists are contesting with one another, one of the very shrewdest, I
think, is David Hirsch, whose reviews and essays have appeared regularly
in the *Sewanee Review.* In one of these essays, Hirsch makes the interesting point that the new literary theorists always move away from the
literary "text," the verbal construct, to talk about something else:

> [They] are not concerned with such questions as "What does a poem
> mean?" or "What is a particular poet or novelist saying?" or "What makes
> a great work of art?" or "How are the great works different from mediocre
> [works]?" Instead, theorists have turned their attention to such questions
> as "What is meaning?" and "What is language?" Is language (mind you,
> *language,* not merely poems) self-referential? Is "meaning" to be equated
> exclusively with "differences" (oppositions?) within language systems, i.e.,
> the signifier "table" is not a designation for a physical entity: it is a sound
> designating a concept which achieves its value from the fact that it is unlike
> other sounds within the same system that designate other concepts. The
> questions are not new, nor is the radically skeptical mind-set that generates
> them. What is new, I believe, is the insistence with which these questions
> have come to occupy the center of literary-theoretical concerns. More and
> more the theorists lean toward classically trained philosophical thinkers;
> they move further and further from poems, stories, novels, and any other
> works of literary and aesthetic merit.

I would add: their aim would seem to be to effect a revision of philosophy
and the elimination of metaphysics. Their concern for literature seems to
be quite secondary. Thus, it is not surprising that they have no interest in

a work as an aesthetic object. Some of them seem to deny that it even exists. The poem, for example, is simply another example of writing, of *écriture*. Indeed, the attempt to defend the aesthetic object as something worthy of careful examination and thoughtful contemplation has clearly worsened since 1946, when W. K. Wimsatt and Monroe Beardsley first published their "Intentional Fallacy."

I must not, however, give the impression that these new critics are living in some realm of shadows completely removed from the world of everyday affairs in which most earthbound mortals live. However remote from practical, everyday affairs the more extreme structuralists and deconstructionists may seem to be, there is evidence that they are fully in the spirit of our times. The best statement of this last point that I have come upon is the conclusion of a short but pithy article by Alvin Kernan, who makes the point clearly in the concluding paragraph of an article published in *New Boston Review:*

> But the world may learn something about its own future from the effects of structuralism on literature. For structuralism is not merely one of the many critical squabbles which enliven a small institution, but the working out, in the area most suitable to the issue, of a view of man which is already having profound effects. What once was character is becoming a role or a life-style: advertising has replaced goods with media messages; television "theatricalizes" the news; and politics has become the art of image making. Structuralism did not cause these changes—but it is the philosophy which justifies and explains a world in which the center can be and is thought of as a deficiency.

The signs are clear enough. Each morning as I shave, for example, and listen to the news on the radio, a certain men's clothing house in New York warns the city's corporations that their success depends upon how their executives are dressed—on whether or not they project the image of the proper businessman. And, again, in the beautifully acted and photographed *Brideshead Revisited,* the voices of the actors from time to time become inaudible. The background music simply won't stay in the background, and I have to conclude that the director doesn't think that the spoken words really matter. The stunning imagery on the screen and the technological ingenuity of the voice-over become everything.

In short I think that Kernan's indictment is just, and we can plainly see that it is if we ask ourselves whether structuralism gives any support to the humanistic endeavor. It gives almost none at all. And what, in this respect, about the criticism of Harold Bloom? Although he has made it plain that he is not a structuralist or a deconstructionist, it is becoming more and more difficult to associate his criticism with humanistic values. He has declared, for example, that

> the living labyrinth of literature is built upon the ruin of every impulse most generous in us. So apparently it is and must be—we are wrong to have founded a humanism directly upon literature itself, and the phrase "humane letters" is an oxymoron. . . . The strong imagination comes to its painful birth through savagery and misrepresentation.

The basic philosophy behind so much of these movements, whether those promoted by Derrida or those adumbrated by Bloom, is a deep skepticism, and such skepticism can do little more than lend some further structuralism to the voice that invites the vigorously adventurous soul to step out boldly into some realm beyond good and evil, to find some satisfaction in some free and joyous Nietzschean affirmation of his own life. The doctrine that language is a closed system, referring finally to nothing beyond itself, would seem to render null any notion that literature can nourish a humanistic education. For if literature is simply a game of words, a game played for no life-and-death stakes—played for no stakes at all, in fact—it would appear to most of us to be quite empty. True, we could learn from it how agile and supple language is, and what a marvelous thing is this instrument that human beings have been clever enough to invent. (Unless, of course, it's true that language has invented the human being.) We could learn also from such a study of literature much about the history of taste and what men at various periods of history have conceived mankind to be, but the true-blue structuralist would deny that literature could throw any light on values as such.

The underlying goal of Derrida has been to destroy metaphysics itself— to demonstrate that none of our intellectual systems rests on any firm substratum of reality. I have wondered sometimes whether the new literary critics really understand this philosophy that they have attempted to apply to literature. David Hirsch has gone further and made a judgment on the matter:

> More and more literary theorists are playing philosophers' games that they do not understand, and dabbling in philosophers' discourse that they do not control. Until literary critics move away from these anti-humanist discourses and return to what they presumably do best—help others to understand the discourse of literature—we seem to be in for a long siege of tortured logic and muddled thinking.

The anti-humanist quality of the critics scolded by Hirsch derives in part from their relativism. If the meaning of a text *is* radically indeterminate— if there is no way to pin down a specific meaning—then there is in fact no way of making judgments of value about the text.

Why do I make such an issue of relativism? Because I believe that relativism is inimical to humanism. The point has been made quite forcefully by Wellek: "Logic, ethics, and, I believe, even aesthetics," he writes, "cry aloud against complete relativism. It would lead to a dehumanization of the arts and a paralysis of criticism."

In logic, the case is obvious. A logical demonstration that is good in America must also be good in China, and if it is true in the twentieth century, it has to be true in the fourth century B.C. Ethics, too, aspires to security in universal principles: there can't be ethically one law for the rich and another for the poor, or one law in the twentieth century but not in the eighteenth. (That customs and laws have, from the beginning of time, differed from tribe to tribe and from nation to nation is another matter.)

The case for the objectivity of aesthetic judgment is much harder to make; yet pure subjectivity obviously means chaos, and it is easy, I believe, to show that such relativism leads to the dehumanization of literature. The literature of the ancient world, for example, is indeed very different from our own, reflecting a world possessed of different technologies, social and political organizations, and habits and customs. Nevertheless, you and I *can* participate in the classic literature of ancient Greece.

Consider, for instance, Sophocles' *Antigone*. Some of you will remember that in this play Antigone's brother dies fighting against his native city, Thebes, and that Creon, the ruler of the city, has decreed that no one, under pain of death, shall bury the body of the rebel. Antigone neverthe-

less dares to do so and is made to pay the penalty. Now, to understand
fully what is at issue here, the twentieth-century reader may need the help
of the scholar and, perhaps, the help of the literary critic as well. Unless
he knows classical Greek as well as his own native language, he will
obviously have to have the help of a translator. In addition, the scholar
may need to tell the reader how important it was in Greek belief for the
dead to have a proper burial, and he may also need to inform the reader
of the importance of a man's loyalty to his city-state. Such historical information may help the modern reader to realize how intense were the
pressures felt by Antigone, the conflicting claims of the blood-tie and
those of loyalty to the state. Yet such is only an intensification of the
conflict that any human being possessed of a heart might feel. Laws,
attitudes, and burial customs have changed, and yet the dilemma in
which Antigone is caught is certainly not incomprehensible to us. Indeed,
in our own day, William Faulkner has reminded us that the universal
theme of great literature is "the human heart in conflict with itself."

I do not mean to minimize the differences that exist between cultures
of the past and those of the present. But these alien worlds are not
completely sealed off from each other. A stable human core persists from
age to age and from culture to culture. There is a basic continuity: if this
were not so, the past would indeed be completely meaningless to us.
Obviously, it is not. Ernst Gombrich, the great art historian, approaches
the matter with basic but firm common sense:

> To the humanist concerned with distant ages or distant lands [the local
> traditions in which each of us grows up] present a challenge. But I have
> never had much patience with the claim that the challenge cannot be met
> and that we are forever imprisoned in our own language and outlook. . . .
> Even though he may know that he will never be able fully to respond, the
> humanist will welcome the opportunity of transcending his limitations and
> widening his imaginative sympathy.

What we can learn from the literature of the past, from other cultures, and
from our own lives is essentially something about mankind itself. I have
already mentioned a faith in man's continuity: Homer's heroes and his
heroic women, for example, represent human types with which we are
familiar—the brave but sometimes petulant and self-absorbed Achilles; the

wily and sagacious Odysseus; the powerful but not terribly intelligent Ajax. So with Shakespeare's characters; so with Molière's. The costumes that they wear may seem bizarre, the social conditions in which they live strange, but we can nevertheless see our lives and hearts reflected in theirs.

A good friend of mine, a poet and novelist, once remarked that we Americans had a greater contempt for the past than any other people who had ever lived. Perhaps he put it too strongly, but we are indeed a future-oriented people. Literature, therefore, renders us a palpable service if it reminds us that, in view of the fact that the men of the ancient past are recognizably our brothers, we can learn from man's past experience. And if it can remind us of our kinship with men from the past, literature can certainly perform an even more palpable service if it reminds us that the people of other countries and cultures are our brothers, too—in spite of differences in languages, customs, and institutions. Finally, literature can help us to understand ourselves: if we cannot articulate our thoughts, if they remain half-formed, inaccessible to reflection and meditation, they can never be fully available to us. In short, literature, ancient and modern, can play a most important part in a humanistic education. It has done so for centuries.

And if someone should ask why literature rather than philosophy and history, a convincing answer is at hand. Literature portrays human beings in *action*. Its method is not that of direct exhortation or the statement of philosophical generalizations. It is concrete and dramatic. It does not appeal to the intellect alone, but to the imagination as well. Thus we find ourselves humanly involved in Macbeth's temptation to gain the crown that he so much covets, or in Don Quixote's fully committed but outrageously foolish deeds of derring-do, or in Keats's musing on the challenge and the charm that the voice of nature, expressed in the nightingale's song, presents to the reflective human being.

It has been argued that some of us (I being perhaps one of the chief sinners) had already years ago questioned the ability of words to say anything about reality—that in intimating that a poem was a kind of well-wrought urn, I was insisting that a poem is a self-enclosed system, a static object, spatial and not auditory. This is probably very late in the day for me to attempt a clarification—and almost certainly too late to catch up with what I have to regard as a serious distortion of my views. Nevertheless, let me make a few remarks on the subject.

I have said before that the Beardsley-Wimsatt article "The Intentional Fallacy" does not argue that a writer lacks an *intention,* nor does the article on "The Affective Fallacy" argue that we are not *affected* by literary works: poems, novels, and plays certainly affect *me,* but I believe that it is more useful to discuss the makeup of a literary work than to talk about any particular emotions of my own that may be aroused by it. I do have emotions, but I like to find grounds for them in what the author has presumably created for me and for other readers.

Literature tells the *truth,* but, as Emily Dickenson says in one of her poems, it tells it at a "slant." It tells the truth through a *fiction,* but it is the truth nonetheless. Literature has something to say about *reality,* and is in fact one of the clearest available windows for looking out on to reality.

It is true that literature does not typically deal with that world of abstraction beyond the human senses—the world opened up by a modern science, predicated on a system that can be accurately described only in the language of mathematics. But then literature does not—and ought not—try to compete with science. Nor does literature compete with philosophy or with theology. Nevertheless, literature has much to say about the *human* world that we can know more directly and through our senses. If someone objects that mystics sometimes write poems that open into a transcendent world beyond the senses, my reply is that, in order to give the rest of us some notion of what their vision is, they properly resort to analogies drawn from the familiar world of the senses that we all know. Thus in *Four Quartets,* when T. S. Eliot attempts to tell us what dwelling in *eternity* might be like, he makes use of references to the world of *time:* spring, winter, summer, the "short day" of a midwinter month like February, the "dark time of the year." He describes a day of windless cold but of special brightness, and the description provides him with his basic image for the "zero summer" which lies outside the world of time. How could it be otherwise? The poet's readers, we time-bound human beings, can be afforded a glimpse of eternity only in some such way.

The truth provided by literature is not asserted or stated, but *rendered,* and the mode, I repeat, is essentially *dramatic:* we are asked to listen to someone speaking to someone else (if only to the speaker's deeper self) in the context of a particular situation. We have to make of it what we can. It is usually fatal for the author to preach at us or to make assertions which we must accept on his own say-so. The speaker in the poem, of course, may do this, and so can various characters in a novel or play, but it is *we* who are permitted to make the judgment: *we* will judge whether what is being said is profound or poppycock. This is the essential situation in both the tiniest lyric and *Paradise Lost*.

The privilege of interpretation accorded the reader or hearer may also be looked upon as an obligation. In either case, the work is literally *delivered* into his hands. He has the *privilege* of responding to its invitation to use his own imagination to invest it with a fullness, with a *richness,* gleaned from his own experience. And yet the work has its own *dynamic;* it is not simply inked characters on paper. Think of the musical score of Beethoven's Seventh Symphony. The symphony is "present" in the form of signs that are to be realized in musical tones. Granted that music is an art far more auditory than poetry, the analogy with a literary work is a just one. To say that a conductor's close study of the musical score is treatment of the symphony as mere "spatial form" is nonsense.

Yet if the reader has the privilege of realizing the literary work as a full human experience, I repeat that he also has an obligation to respect the text that the writer has prepared for him. To feel that he can read into it or out of it anything that he fancies is, at the least, an act of egotistical pride. The reader is indeed an all-important part of the literary transaction, but it is willful of him to try to take the place of the author.

I want to return, finally, to the issue of the *referentiality* of literature— to the claim that, in spite of its understanding of the use of fiction and analogy, literature nevertheless provides us with *knowledge*.

I have earlier sought to take such knowledge out of competition with the knowledge that the hard sciences provide or with the kinds of speculative knowledge which are the matter of philosophy and theology. Furthermore, the knowledge gained from literature is not, I have said, to be confused with the circumstantiality and factuality of history. Nevertheless, the fictional worlds contrived by the literary artist have a very real relationship to the familiar world in which we live.

A test case is provided by those two minor classics of the Victorian period, Lewis Carroll's *Alice in Wonderland* and *Alice through the Looking*

Glass. In spite of the obvious elements of fantasy—a March hare drinking tea from a china cup, a white rabbit wearing a waistcoat and consulting his pocket watch, the pieces and pawns of a chess set coming to life and walking about—the Alice books tell us a great deal about Victorian life, customs, and opinions on all manner of subjects. Austin Warren has published a charming and thoroughly convincing account of how the Alice books reflected Victorian life and, more specifically still, the manners and attitudes of one special segment of Victorian society, the world to which Charles Dodgson, mathematician, priest of the Church of England, and Fellow of Christ Church College, Oxford, belonged. I have, however, more sizable game in mind than the historical and sociological lore provided by literature. The Alice books can also provide us with universal truths about human nature. Little Alice's direct and uncluttered vision of the world penetrates the conventions and disguises behind which we grown folk live. The satire is not bitter; it is disarming. But it often reveals things about ourselves that we usually fail to perceive. To mention only a few instances: the hypocritical Walrus and Carpenter, who weep over the fate of oysters as they devour them; the White Knight, who bubbles over with quixotic schemes which he will never put into operation, for he is so impractical that he cannot even manage to keep his seat on his horse; the rhetorician Humpty Dumpty, who uses language in a way of his own and boasts, "When I use a word, it means just what I choose it to mean—neither more nor less."

Indeed, one special motif in the Alice books is an exposure of our absurdly fatuous civilities. In the Alice books, polite expressions are shown to be almost invariably illogical. The characters in the book constantly "deconstruct" courteous expressions if not other aspects of the language. There are also the devastating parodies of some nineteenth-century poems that take themselves a little too seriously—even the great William Wordsworth is caught off-guard. Victorianism is assumed to be dead, but the Alice books are very much alive, and among other things, they show how much of Victorianism still lives on in *us*.

As a concluding example of the humanistic uses of literature, I choose to use a poem. It is William Butler Yeats's little masterpiece called "Long-Legged Fly":

That civilization may not sink,
Its great battle lost,
Quiet the dog, tether the pony
To a distant post;
Our master Caesar is in the tent
Where the maps are spread,
His eyes are fixed upon nothing,
A hand under his head.
Like a long-legged fly upon the stream
His mind moves upon silence.

That the topless towers be burnt
And men recall that face,
Move most gently if move you must
In this lonely place.
She thinks, part woman, three parts a child,
That nobody looks; her feet
Practice a tinker shuffle
Picked up on a street.
Like a long-legged fly upon the stream
Her mind moves upon silence.

That girls at puberty may find
The first Adam in their thought,
Shut the door of the Pope's chapel,
Keep those children out.
There on that scaffolding reclines
Michael Angelo.
With no more sound than the mice make
His hand moves to and fro.
Like a long-legged fly upon the stream
His mind moves upon silence.

I shall not try to deconstruct this poem, but I shall attempt a simpler and more modest task, that recommended by David Hirsch: "to help others to understand" Yeats's discourse here.

The plan of the poem is simple. There are three scenes: the first shows Caesar planning his next battle; the second concerns an incident in the girlhood of Helen of Troy; in the third, Michelangelo is painting the ceiling of the Sistine Chapel. We could describe the three as representing, respectively, military and executive power, love and beauty, and the creation of heroic art. The voice that speaks the poem cautions us in each instance to keep quiet: "Quiet the dog, tether the pony / To a distant post"; "Move most gently if move you must / In this lonely place"; "Shut the door of the Pope's chapel, / Keep those children out." Why the need for silence? Because an act of contemplation must not be disturbed. Genius is at work.

This emphasis on the need for—and the value of—solitude on the part of the man of action, as well as on that of the artist, is clearly made—the poem could not be more emphatic on this point. But if you must appeal to something beyond the poem itself, read Yeats's essays and his biography. He believed that all great work needed to be gestated in solitude. If someone is now muttering to himself, "Aha, Mr. Brooks is himself committing the intentional fallacy here," I demur. At most, I am simply testing what Yeats says in his essays and memoirs against what is to be found in the poem. In any case, the need for quiet contemplation is scarcely a peculiar and esoteric doctrine. We all experience the need for it. You don't want a hi-fi bellowing rock-and-roll music when you're studying for a difficult examination, do you? I appeal to your own experience.

What about the second stanza, however? Why does Helen of Troy need solitude? Clearly, Yeats puts her need for quiet on a par with Caesar's and Michelangelo's. Such seems to me to be stated here in the poem. But again, in his prose writings and in at least two of his other poems, Yeats makes it plain that he regards the truly beautiful woman as an artist. Her beauty is not merely nature's casual gift, something bestowed randomly, but a discipline to be mastered. She has to work at it. The idea, of course, is not an odd notion: cosmetics advertisers proclaim every day that you, too, can be beautiful if you will only work at it. Again, I appeal to your own experience.

I notice that, in his book on Yeats, Harold Bloom does not mention any "anxiety of influence" in his discussion of this poem, and surely he is correct not to do so, for if there ever was a confident poet, a poet absolutely certain of himself, the Yeats of his middle and late periods was that poet. Nevertheless, I believe that Bloom misunderstands the poem when he says that "Caesar prepares for the great battle . . . by aimless reverie." To Caesar's orderly or to a centurion who may have just entered his tent to ask what was to be the disposition of his own contingent in the battle line, it might have appeared that "Caesar's eyes [were] fixed on nothing," but what Caesar is doing in his head will have everything to do with how the battle will turn out tomorrow. He is using simply the "inward eye" which Wordsworth called the "bliss of solitude."

The whole poem stresses the importance of the mind moving upon silence. Look at what Yeats says three times in the refrain:

> *Like a long-legged fly upon the stream*
> *His mind moves upon silence.*

Indeed, to neglect or mistake the refrain is to miss the meaning of the poem. What *is* Yeats's long-legged fly, and how *does* it "move upon the stream"? Recourse to reference books won't help much. We would learn that the insect belongs to the family *Gerridae,* is hemipterous, and has "elongate middle and hind legs adapted for darting over the *surface* of the water." This last phrase is in fact the important one: the insect is supported on the water by surface tension—it can literally walk on the water. The American species is called a water-strider, and when I lived in the country, I used to stand on the bridge over a little stream and watch the striders at their antics. The insect is not swept down the stream but is able to hold his chosen position with an occasional short dart upstream. Yeats is being very accurate here: he does not say that the fly *floats* on the stream or *swims* in the stream, but that it *moves* upon the stream.

Bloom, in arguing that Caesar and Helen abandon "their minds to the stream's movement," implies—mistakenly, I think—that the fly is swept downstream. I suggest that Yeats uses the figure of the stream to suggest the stream of time. The flowing stream is, of course, an age-old symbol for the passing of time. Heraclitus, Samuel Johnson, Sir Walter Scott, Wordsworth, and many another used the analogy, and the eighteenth-century hymn writer Isaac Watts has made it familiar to millions of church-goers—"Time like an ever-rolling stream / Bears all its sons away." No, not all of them: not a Caesar or a Helen or a Michelangelo. They have not been wholly swept away. Their names linger in our minds.

Yet what I want particularly to stress is the apt analogy that the long-legged fly, with its marvelously delicate tread, provides for the mind's noiseless but powerful pressure on actions and events. The mind exerts a force that can actually reshape the world of human affairs. It can alter history. The salvation of civilization will tomorrow depend not nearly so much upon the clashing of sword and javelin on breastplate and shield as upon what is going on now in the head of Caesar. Michelangelo's hand, moving his paintbrush upon the ceiling of the great chapel, makes "no more sound than the mice make," but the artist's mind, the mind that conceived the great design and which is now guiding the brush that executes it, makes absolutely no sound at all.

Like a long-legged fly upon the stream
His mind moves upon silence.

3

The Crisis in Culture
as Reflected in Southern Literature

❧

*I*n an essay entitled "Romanticism Re-examined," René Wellek has described the common endeavor of the great romantic poets of England, Germany, and France as an attempt "to overcome the split between subject and object, the self and the world, the conscious and the unconscious." Such has also been the endeavor of later generations of literary artists, including some of the most distinguished writers of our present century. The crisis in culture to which my title refers is precisely the split described.

Some of the twentieth-century writers would not, to be sure, be thought of as romantics. They are usually called symbolists or modernists, and at least one of them has called himself a classicist. But the cultural situation with which they have been concerned is essentially that encountered by the great romantics of the nineteenth century.

William Wordsworth had seen the problem as primarily having arisen from man's alienation from nature. He became gravely concerned over the distance that had opened up between the poet's way of perceiving reality and the way in which the scientist or the man of affairs perceived it. The heart found itself more and more in conflict with the head. In one of his sonnets Wordsworth mourns that "Little we see in nature that is ours" and insists that men have given their hearts away. His brother poet, Samuel Taylor Coleridge, urged that it was necessary to keep the heart alive in the head. Let me hasten to say that the rift between heart and head was becoming visible long before the date of Wordsworth's birth. But it is not my purpose here to go back as far as René Descartes, who, someone has said, had cut the throat of poetry by limiting the poet's exercise to a purely subjective realm, whereas the scientist took over the great outside world of objective fact.

Nor am I here particularly concerned with what happened after the time of Wordsworth and Coleridge—with such figures as Charles Darwin, T. H. Huxley, John Ruskin, John Henry Newman, and Matthew Arnold. I shall be concerned with some of the more special forms that the problem has taken in the twentieth century and with how the twentieth-century writers of the southern states have addressed themselves to it.

Yet, before turning to the southern writers we might consider briefly how some of the writers of the first third of our century have responded to the situation. William Butler Yeats reacted sharply against what he saw as an increasingly secularized and industrialized world. Ireland had remained agrarian and traditional well into the twentieth century, and, in spite of an official Roman Catholicism, somehow pre-Christian—at least Yeats wished to think that the legends of ancient Ireland had not been utterly forgotten. He brought the ancient gods of Ireland into his poetry; he retold Irish fairy tales; and he involved himself in astrology, Hermetic lore, and spiritualism. The impact of applied science and its effect on human beings worried Yeats quite as much as the influence of theoretical science. He carried on a lifelong quarrel with the bourgeoisie; the country gentleman, the peasant, the saint, and the artist possessed, in their rather different ways, the virtues that he admired.

D. H. Lawrence's reaction was nearly as extravagant as Yeats's, though it attached itself to a different sort of primitivism and developed a different mythology, one dominated by the dark gods of the blood.

T. S. Eliot very early faced up to the contemporary world and addressed himself to writing poems based on life in the modern city. But the cultural crisis underlies nearly every one of his earlier poems, and his way of coping with the problem fairly soon became a restatement of the orthodox Christian "solution."

The influence of Eliot on the writers of the twentieth-century South has been profound, but even writers on whom he early made a sharp impact devised their own responses to the cultural situation in which they found themselves. After all, they had deep commitments to a cultural province that had its own special history, customs, and even, to a limited degree, language.

John Crowe Ransom of Tennessee early became concerned with the fissure that had opened between man's inner and outer life. Just how early, one does not know, but a poem written by 1926 has as its theme the plight of such a fragmented man. Ransom, however, states the problem not as one of fragmentation but of loss of orientation; for he has titled his poem "Man without Sense of Direction."

This creature of modernity is, as Man should be, a microcosm, a little world, but in this particular world "There is no moon . . . that draws / His flood of being." He does not lack abilities and potentialities; what he lacks are purposes to be achieved. Without "direction" he is simply a mechanism, and Ransom describes him so:

> He flails his arms, he moves his lips:
> "Rage have I none, cause, time, nor country"
> . . . .
> So he stands muttering; and rushes
> Back to the tender thing in his charge
> With clamoring tongue and taste of ashes
> And a small passion to feign large.

He cannot give himself totally to a loved one any more than he can give himself to a cause. One further line in the poem summarizes his total situation: he is a creature "Who cannot fathom nor perform his nature." In an earlier day, man did have some sense of what he was and so could fulfill himself. But this typical man of our age cannot do so.

A poem written in the same general period, "Persistent Explorer," suggests why he cannot. The world that he inhabits has become strange and unknown. Nature, in short, has been neutralized, and the sensitive observer feels somehow betrayed by that fact. Thus, when Ransom's explorer comes upon a mighty waterfall, the sight leaves him unsatisfied. He notes that "Water is falling—it fell—therefore it roared. / But he cried, That is more than water I hear." In an earlier age the great cataract might have been the proper setting for a theophany, its "cloud of froth" a fit vesture for a goddess revealing herself to some mountain shepherd. But to the explorer in question, no goddess appears and he must remind himself that such beings as "fierce faun" and "timid" water nymphs do not exist—must remind himself that the descending substance is only "water—the insipid chemical H_2O."

Neither the poet nor his explorer reproaches the scientist for his non-animistic account of the situation. Ransom has moved far, far beyond Wordsworth's taunting reference to the "fingering slave" who would "peep and botanize / Upon his mother's grave." It is folly to dismiss as false the scientific description of nature. Nevertheless, the explorer refuses to accept as a valid account of reality the neutralized nature that the modern scientist has described and analyzed. This "persistent explorer" means to go beyond such a world in the hope of finding one that will satisfy the human spirit. But no one, least of all the poet, can promise that even the most persistent exploration will reveal another more meaningful world.

So much for the cause of the modern disease—Arnold's "sick hurry and divided aims"—and its typical effects on the human being, whose life in a reduced and de-animated world loses purpose and direction. Ransom's most brilliant account of the division within modern man is to be found in his sonnet sequence "Two Gentlemen in Bonds." The gentlemen in question are twin brothers between whom man's full being is divided. Their dead father, speaking from the grave in the final sonnet, puts matters in this wise: "My manhood halved and squandered, two heads, two hearts, / Each partial son despising the other's parts."

The paired opposites, clearly, cannot be neatly tagged as "heart" and "head." They are more properly seen as the "intellectual" man, who tries to live by abstractions, and the sensual man, who revels in his appetites. Paul is the sensual, pragmatic man-in-the-street; Abbot is the intellectual and idealist—though these definitions are not wholly satisfactory, either. Abbot, for instance, has something of the sour ascetic in his nature. He scorns the flesh:

Vainglorious he may have been, stiff-necked;
His stars conspired together to deject
Him from conspicuous glories; he lived on air
And would not taste earth's sweetness; great and spare
And pale, his ghost still haunted the slight girl
Who, husbanded now with her fair lord the churl . . .

Ransom tries to be impartial in describing these opposed half-men: Paul is frankly the churl, though successful in love and fortune, and Abbot's pride—"he clung to his cold and poverty and night / And leaned in the rain"—is essentially a self-destructive folly. The last phrase is not too strong.

Ransom is an artist, and the artist allies himself with the whole man—man as a total and harmonious being. Art rests upon the life of the senses. This point comes clear in Ransom's fine late poem "Painted Head." "Beauty is of body," the poet insists. The "head" needs all of the help that the body can give it.

One might observe that neither Paul nor Abbot represents the poet. Neither of these half men is capable of writing a poem: Paul is too deeply immersed in the flesh to be able to rise above it; Abbot despises the flesh too much to give it its due regard. For Ransom, as for Wordsworth, one suspects, the poet must succeed in holding in fruitful tension both body and mind.

Duality is thus at the core of Ransom's aesthetics. In 1927 he wrote to his fellow southern poet Allen Tate: "Give us Dualism, or we'll give you no Art." In the same letter he told Tate that it was necessary for the artist to accomplish three things: to "find the Experience that is in the Common Actuals," to have "this experience" carry as its precious freight "the dearest possible values to which we have attached ourselves," and finally "to face the disintegration or nullification of these values as calmly and religiously as possible." His program is as ambitious as it is austere.

I assume that the disintegration of which Ransom writes here is the inevitable erosion of "our dearest possible values" as we become distracted or forgetful or tired and old, and that he is making no special reference to the breakdown of values in our contemporary civilization. But in either case, Ransom's recommendation would surely be the same. His *God without Thunder* spells out these issues in detail with special reference to those who have been brought up in the Christian values. But small wonder that few Christians could accept his transformation of Christianity into the kind of nature religion that *God without Thunder* essentially sought to effect.

Though Ransom joined his friends in an Agrarian Manifesto, *I'll Take My Stand* (1930), and seemed for a time to take seriously the formation of a practical program for an agrarian economy, in his later years he wrote that he had come to feel that Agrarianism was a diet too rich for his blood. Yet his attitude toward man's plight remained basically unchanged: to face the disintegration of these (and even dearer) values "as calmly and religiously as possible."

Such quiet detachment reminds one of the philosopher George Santayana's attitude toward Christian and traditional values generally, though of course there was nothing of Santayana's Mediterranean Catholicism in Ransom's personal background. In this general connection, I remember Ransom's once saying to me that the younger men, confident of building a new and better civilization, would, of course, fail to achieve their aims. Nevertheless, one had to allow them to make their attempt. The tone of the remark was not bitter or cynical; it was spoken with what I can only call a rather kindly detachment.

The reader will find a somewhat early stage of Ransom's personal religion spelled out in his *God without Thunder*. Again, it reminds one of Santayana's position with reference to religion. The poet Robert Lowell referred to Santayana as that "free-thinking Catholic infidel." He would never have applied these terms to his old mentor John Crowe Ransom. He would have felt, if not seen, important differences, but I am confident that there are resemblances, too.

To face the loss of our traditional values "as calmly and religiously as possible" did not and does not appeal to Allen Tate. Yet the difference between Tate and Ransom was only in part a matter of temperament and personality. Basically, it amounted to their differing interpretations of religion. Ransom's was an attitude of acceptance of the natural world, and was, in the deepest and least frivolous sense of the word, "aesthetic." He had shorn away from Christianity its supernatural elements and preferred to stress the nurture, through liturgy and meditation, of the life of the spirit. His set of values deserves to be called a "religion," if we take seriously the etymology—a "binding back" of the individual to nature and to past history. But it was a religion that was nondogmatic, without any of the accouterments of ecclesiastical organization or acceptance of supernatural beliefs.

I have said that Ransom's position would not have appealed to Allen Tate, who had very early—and long before he came to accept orthodox doctrinal Christianity as embodied in Roman Catholicism—rejected as wholly inadequate the naturalistic account of man. But his essential diagnosis of the distemper of modern man may have close affinities with Ransom's own. Both men agreed that man required more than a purely scientific account of reality. Otherwise, values and facts become detached from each other, the realms of ends and means are without relation, and as a consequence man is not a whole being but becomes a fragmented creature.

Tate's essays record the developing stages of his philosophical and religious position even more thoroughly and in more detail than do Ransom's, but to sense the special timbre of alarm and concern in Tate's observations, one has to turn to his poetry. Perhaps the classic example is his celebrated "Last Days of Alice." Like the little heroine of *Alice in Wonderland* and *Alice through the Looking Glass,* modern man finds himself in a strange and perplexing world in which objects that had for generations past been regarded as stable and solid have become "empty as the bodiless flesh of fire." Man himself, a creature of flesh and blood, turns out to be no more than a "mathematical shroud," being "all infinite, function depth and mass / Without figure," something that can be accurately described only in mathematical terms. Modern man is "blessèd without sin," not because his sins have been forgiven, but because the concept of sin has been explained away.

The desperate man who speaks the poem is in no way comforted by such a state of blessedness. Indeed, at the end he calls upon the "God of our flesh" to return man to His wrath. To be damned is somehow better than being immersed in antiseptic nihilism, and in his desperation the speaker even begs to be evil. But in the context of the total poem, his meaning becomes plain: better to fail morally in a world of good and evil than to inhabit a realm where the terms *good* and *evil* are meaningless. Baudelaire would have had no trouble in making out what the speaker is praying for. (My reference to Baudelaire is probably apposite: as a very young man Tate was attempting translations of some of Baudelaire's poems.)

In his novel, *The Fathers,* Tate refers the malaise that he has earlier treated only in general terms to a historical context, that of the Old South on the verge of the War Between the States. The character in this novel who represents modern man is a disoriented southerner. He is the attractive young George Posey, who marries into an extremely conservative Virginia family. Posey turns out to be Ransom's "man without sense of direction." He fits such a description in almost precise detail; for he has neither "cause, time, nor country." "Rage," too, he lacks: for he is thoroughly detached, an almost entirely cold-blooded character. True, under stress, he is capable of shooting his brother-in-law; but he acts on sudden impulse, almost automatically, for Posey is a spasmodic man. Lacking any coherent code of conduct and ill at ease in any ritual designed to confirm such a code, he is at the mercy of whim and impulse. The manners and morals that are instinctive to the life of his father-in-law, Major Buchan, turn into absurdities under Posey's skeptical gaze. Indeed, an unwary reader, himself a man of the twentieth century, may come to think of Posey as the one "rational" character in the novel. But Posey's skepticism is simply an instrument for debunking any claims that the older tradition may make upon him. It has no positive force. Posey clearly does not lead Santayana's recommended life of reason.

By choosing as the setting for *The Fathers* the area around Washington, D.C., at the time of the outbreak of the War Between the States, Tate has adopted the perfect historical setting for his purpose. In these critical years men living on the uppermost borders of the Confederacy are driven back upon their most deeply held political beliefs and their ultimate loyalties. Posey, a citizen of Georgetown, Maryland, married to a Virginia girl, finds it impossible to decide what his true country is. He has difficulty in associating himself with either cause. Actually, he ends up by working for both sides, buying war supplies from the Union forces in order to get them through the lines into the Confederacy. He tells himself that he is actually aiding his Virginia friends and relatives, but the result of his endeavors is that he makes a great deal of money for himself. It is appropriate that this should be so, for money is the one commodity that knows no country.

Tate has been very shrewd in his accounting for Posey's disabilities. Posey had grown up in a family that had lost any sense of community. His cantankerous father had died early. His uncle was an eccentric freak, his mode of living much like that of Edgar Allan Poe's Roderick Usher. He isolates himself in the upper room of the ancestral house, completely absorbed in the fancies and aberrations of his own mind. George Posey's mother and his aunt were "peculiar ladies," as self-absorbed and self-indulgent as was their brother. Any sense of genuine family relationships has completely disappeared—perhaps it had never made an appearance throughout George's childhood.

George's wife, Susan Buchan, on the other hand, had grown up in a family that was, if anything, too cohesive, too tightly bound to one another. The transplantation of Susan from the family world of Pleasant Hill in Virginia to the Posey establishment in Georgetown eventually brings her to madness: she succumbs to what for her has become a radically disordered world.

Tate, however, does not set forth the virtues of the good and honorable "southern" Buchans against the wrongheaded, neurotic, and "Yankeefied" Poseys. In the first place, the Poseys are by birth and breeding southerners, too. Of course, merely being southern guarantees nothing. If the Buchans do typify some of the virtues and pieties that we associate with the Old South, they also suggest the dangerous rigidities of a traditional society. The head of the family, Major Buchan, is almost absurdly set in his ways and utterly unable to imagine a world different from the one he knows. He has his own form of hubris. He reposes so much confidence in his inherited code of family virtue and honor and is so sure that he himself embodies them that he is blind to the issues that are pulling the country apart. He self-righteously repudiates his own son for enlisting in the Confederate army. It takes the wreck of his family and the destruction of Pleasant Hill by Union soldiers to bring him to a realization of his folly. The realization is too much: he hangs himself.

Major Buchan is not, then, the perfect foil for his son-in-law, answering each of George Posey's defects with an antithetical virtue. Good drama does not allow such neat polarities; nor does human history. As depicted in *The Fathers,* the Buchans are too much immersed in their own immediate and parochial customs and habits to "see" what they are, for one has to be aware of other modes of living to become fully conscious of one's own. But, of course, to learn that one's own values are not necessarily the only or even the best values may begin the process of finally disowning them.

Ransom had very pertinently said: "Give us Dualism or we'll give you no Art," and Tate would surely agree. The art appreciated by the Buchans, one judges, must have been a very unsophisticated kind of art, and so, historically, was that which appealed to the men and women of the Old South. Why this was so and why a great southern literature had to wait until the third decade of the twentieth century for its creation would, years later, become the subject matter of Tate's great definitive essay, "A Southern Mode of the Imagination." For southerners had to see the old virtues threatened with loss before they could come—in literature, at least—to realize fully what those virtues were. How can one know the dancer from the dance? It may be even more difficult for the dancer herself, caught up as she is in the dance, to "see" herself dancing.

Before leaving the subject of *The Fathers,* we ought to consider one other aspect of the author's judgment on the "modernity" of George Posey. Tate finds—a thoroughly "southern" thing to do—an analogy for Posey in the past, and specifically in ancient Greek legend. As the youngest of the Buchans, Lacy, the narrator of the novel, walks back to Pleasant Hill, grievously ill, pretty much out of his head, his dead grandfather appears to him and, in an attempt to help Lacy understand George Posey, tells Lacy the story of Jason, who with the other Argonauts sought the Golden Fleece.

The ghost of Lacy's grandfather begins by describing George as the typical alienated man of our own times. The grandfather, of course, does not use this newfangled term. What he actually says is: "My son, in my day we were never alone, as your brother-in-law is alone." To translate into our present-day terms, George Posey lacked the sense of community, of beliefs and values unquestioningly shared, that in an earlier day bound men together.

Like Jason, George had tried to master "certain rituals" that the King of Colchis (Major Buchan) had insisted Jason, now that he had come to Colchis, should learn. But Jason found it impossible to learn them. He fell in love with the king's daughter, Medea, "a high-spirited girl of a more primitive society than that from which the arrogant Jason came." (Tate, one notes, is willing to allow that the Buchans were more primitive than the Poseys. Elsewhere in the novel the Buchans are stated to be more civilized than the Poseys, though less refined. In the contexts in which the words are used here, *primitive* and *civilized* are compatible, for an arrogant sophistication is antithetical to both states of society.)

The grandfather goes on to say that it was Jason's misfortune to "care only for the Golden Fleece . . . while at the same time getting himself involved with the humanity of others, which it was not his intention but rather of his very nature to betray. . . . He was a noble fellow in whom the patriarchal and familial loyalties had become meaningless." What counts here is not the soundness of the grandfather's interpretation of the Greek legend about Jason, but that a spokesman for the old southern society would be likely to impose such an interpretation on the situation in question—that, and the significant fact that it was the habit of such southerners to discover in the myths and histories of the past analogies for their own manners and morals.

I have dwelt at this length on *The Fathers* because it is not only a fine and still undervalued novel, but because it dramatizes very forcefully theories about the culture of the South that appear in Tate's several essays on that culture. Even if those theories are not always shared by other southern writers, the interpretation of southern culture that is embodied in *The Fathers* will provide a useful model against which to measure divergent interpretations. The argument that I shall develop is that in the main there is agreement.

A dominant theme in Robert Penn Warren's fiction is the partial man's attempt to regain his wholeness. Characteristically, Warren's heroes suffer in their alienation and struggle toward the knowledge that will bring their powers back into harmony with each other and with the world in which they live.

In what is probably Warren's most widely read novel, *All the King's Men,* Willie Stark, the idealist turned into a power-hungry demagogue, and Adam Stanton, the idealistic young scientist and physician, are frankly described as men who were destined to destroy each other because "each was doomed to use the other and to yearn toward and try to become the other, because each was incomplete with the terrible division of their age."

It may be significant that the characters in Warren's fiction who are least afflicted by self-division are people like the old buffalo hunter in *Nightrider* or, in *Heaven's Gate,* Ashby Windham, the hillbilly who experienced conversion and found a Christian vocation. Both are men who come out of a more primitive culture. Modern civilization makes fragmentation almost inevitable, but Warren, of course, never countenances the attempt to relapse into an innocent arcadianism. His heroes must strive for a "new innocence," a mature reintegration of the self.

Warren has somewhere described the process by which this reintegration is achieved as "experience redeemed into knowledge." His poetry as well as his fiction makes it plain what kind of knowledge is involved: not an aggregation of facts or the refinements of scholarship, but a knowledge of reality that involves self-discipline. The old term for it, of course, is wisdom. The quest of all Warren's protagonists is the acquisition of wisdom.

Though his fiction and his poetry reflect the same basic interests and concerns, it is in his poetry that Warren's concern with what I have called the cultural crisis is revealed most nakedly. A rather late poem entitled "Stargazing" presents in almost ultimate purity the split that rends apart man's experience and alienates him from nature. The speaker begins by declaring that "The stars are only a backdrop for / The human condition." But as the poem develops, we learn that he once saw them otherwise. For in answer to his companion's remark that he does not look at the stars, he concedes the point and states why he no longer looks at them. He knows

That if I look at the stars, I

Will have to live over all that I have lived
In the years I looked at stars and
Cried out, "O reality!"

Now he knows better, for if reality encompasses the human condition, then the stars have no part in that reality. Nature and man's inner life seem to be separate realms of being. Though he has to think of nature as a nurturing force ("The stars / Love me"), and though nature is lovely to contemplate ("I love [the stars]"), the stars do not love God. Nonsense? Or if the statement does make sense, then what is that sense?

It is this: the world of purpose, meaning, piety, and aspiration lies outside the self-subsistent, self-authenticating system by which a star or a starfish lives and moves and has its being. In this context the Christian God is anthropomorphic indeed; not merely an idea shaped by man, but an image of man himself. The God of Genesis who created the universe has shrunk to an idea within the human skull. But if the reader concludes that the speaker is content with this situation, I think he has underestimated the poignance of the last lines of the poem: "I wish [the stars] / Loved God, too. I truly wish that." A poem of this sort is moving, but as an intellectual structure it is deeply searching, too. The dramatic situation on which it focuses is the fact of the Cartesian division.

A whole group of Warren's latest poems show his fascination with religion. "A Way to Love God," "Answer to Prayer," "Trying to Tell You Something," "Old Nigger on One-Mule Cart Encountered . . . in the Back Country"—these are only a few of Warren's poems of the 1970s that exhibit a search for absolute truth that is ultimately religious in its nature. It would be rash, however, to claim that these poems are Christian, even though in some important respects they may be compatible with Christianity. In any case, their relation to Christian orthodoxy is not the issue here. My point is simply that Warren takes seriously the tragicomic situation of man, that creature whose consciousness allows him to respond to the majestic or poignant or terrifying beauty of the universe about him, but yet who is barred from the blind and insensate life of the universe by his very ability to respond. The general theme, of course, is not new. It is essentially that of Keats's "Ode to a Nightingale." But Warren has used the context of contemporary civilization to bring the same theme home to us.

Can it be said that William Faulkner also is concerned with this split within man, this contest between heart and head? Yes, emphatically so; but in much of Faulkner's work the theme is so deeply embedded in the drama of the novel or story that a superficial reading may miss it altogether. Is it, for example, to be found in a novel such as *Sanctuary*? I would unhesitatingly answer yes. But since I have limited space here for illustrations from Faulkner, I shall refer only to some of the clearest instances in his work.

Perhaps the most obvious is "The Bear," which relates the story of the young Isaac McCaslin's initiation into the wilderness. Through his tutor, the old hunter Sam Fathers, Isaac comes to know the power and the beauty of nature and yearns toward its unwearied immortality, for throughout its myriad seasonal changes it remains itself. Isaac learns to respect the very creatures that as a hunter he kills, for Sam Fathers has taught him that he must not kill wantonly and that nature itself is to be loved and revered, not only as the necessary resource for man's very life, but as a model of the harmony and unselfconscious delight that man should seek in his own life.

Isaac is profoundly moved by his vision of nature as, for example, when he visits the graves of the great hunting dog Lion and Sam Fathers. Though all creatures must suffer death, in a larger sense there is no death. Nature takes her creatures back into herself and she herself cannot die. Yet Isaac McCaslin knows better than to try to make his own life the instinctive life of a natural creature. He cannot be an arcadian. He is not the unfallen Adam, innocent of fire. He is a fallen man who must assume the burden of consciousness, who is condemned to experience guilt, self-doubt, and responsibility.

"Natural" man, however, fascinated Faulkner from the very beginning of his literary career. There are to be found among his characters a number of faunlike men. Donald Mahon acts on impulse and lives a fresh, instinctive life; Benjy Compson and Ike Snopes, two of Faulkner's famous idiots, are so deeply merged in nature that they are just barely human. Faulkner uses these innocents as foils to point up the vicious inhumanity of the Jason Compsons and the Flem Snopeses of our human world, or else to point up the heavy burden necessarily assumed by men who aspire to be fully human. His fauns cannot serve as the heroes of his novels; that role can belong only to the person who possesses a heart in conflict with itself, the contest that Faulkner declared to be the only one worth writing about. Thus, in spite of the great celebrations of nature that we find in his novels and stories, it is history that is the domain of the human being, the domain in which that being's necessary and inevitable struggles, not only with others but with himself, take place.

Does the contemporary world offer an area in which human beings can demonstrate what they are? I suppose that Faulkner would have to admit that it does. Virtue is not confined to past ages; grace is not a matter of chronology. Yet it is plain that there were elements in the contemporary world that, in Faulkner's opinion, tended to limit man's possibilities for heroism and even for attaining a complete humanity. The increasing abstraction and complexity of political, social, and economic life in modern America tended to depersonalize one's relationship with his fellows, as did the mechanization of work and man's deeper involvement with the machine. The erosion of the community and of the family and the breakdown of traditional manners and morals were other aspects of the process. So also was the power of the mass media and the shameless exploitation of whatever was sensational. Faulkner's essay "On Privacy" makes quite plain his deeply held feelings about the invasion of his own privacy, but clearly more than personal pique was involved. The willingness to violate a person's private life simply to make money thereby was for Faulkner a betrayal of the Founding Fathers' proclamation of liberty for every citizen.

The best evidence of Faulkner's attitude toward the modern world, however, is to be found in his fiction. There is his acid description of life as lived by the rich in southern California ("Golden Land"), or his sardonic indictment of the motor age in *Pylon,* or his rage at the military bureaucracy in *A Fable,* or his various attacks on American respectability, of which *The Wild Palms* will provide a good example. True, the passages just referred to are spoken by characters who do not necessarily express Faulkner's own sentiments. Yet the evidence of Faulkner's distaste for, and active reprehension of, twentieth-century American life—including the peculiar faults of his native region—is overwhelming. This is clear whether the criticisms are implied in his fiction or are delivered to the public as from himself.

With reference to the heroic periods in American history and the nonheroic and too slavishly respectable present age, there is an interesting passage in a letter in which Faulkner is commenting on Warren's *All the King's Men,* to which a friend had called his attention. Faulkner had been much taken with the tale of Cass Mastern. Mastern had betrayed a friend and caused indirectly a slave girl to be sold down the river, probably to a New Orleans brothel-keeper. In remorse for what he had done, he accepts responsibility for his sin and attempts to expiate it, seeking his death as a private serving in the Confederate army, deliberately exposing himself but taking care not to fire a shot against the enemy. Young Jack Burden finds great difficulty in understanding Cass Mastern's story, though he does come to do so before the novel closes.

Faulkner wrote in the letter to his friend: "there has been little in this country since [1860–1870] good enough to make good literature. . . . since then we have gradually become a nation of bragging sentimental not too courageous liars. We seem to be losing all confidence not only in our national character but in man's integrity too. The fact that we blow so hard so much about both of them is to me the symptom."

I shall not urge the reader to take this judgment with absolute seriousness; I don't know myself precisely how much weight to give it. Yet taken in the context in which Faulkner made it, the remark can tell us a good deal about his scheme of values. The stress of a war within a nation—whether you call it a Civil War or a War Between the States—was one which indeed tried men's souls. It made the most severe demands upon one's sense of principle and courage, one's virtues and resources of character. Faulkner has certainly not been the only American who has regarded the mid-nineteenth century as America's truly heroic age.

The crisis in culture that I have been examining is of another order entirely: it has to do with a division not within a nation or a community, but within the individual soul, the fruits of which are listlessness and lack of purpose, or an indifference to principle that comes from the individual's basic confusion as to who he is. To illustrate from one of Faulkner's novels, *Flags in the Dust*, Miss Jenny Du Pre and Old Bayard Sartoris, both of whom had lived through the Civil War, know who they are and know what they believe. But neither Young Bayard, a fighter pilot in World War I, nor his fellow townsman, Horace Benbow, with his "sick nervous face," who had served as a YMCA secretary, knows. Now that they have come home, they have no clear conviction as to what they want to do. Both are deracinated—Horace, the would-be poet and ineffectual dreamer, quite as much as Bayard, the violent man of action, who can now find no meaningful action in which to fulfill himself.

With Faulkner, the division within modern man is of the first importance, but it never emerges as a preachment or even as an articulated abstract idea. So also with Warren, though in novels such as *All the King's Men*, or *Flood*, or *Band of Angels*, a specific theme does approach formulation in explicit terms. Of course both Faulkner and Warren deal with particular characters in a particular cultural climate, or else they would not be true artists at all.

The novelist Walker Percy tends to be more directly "philosophical" in his handling of the climate of ideas. He goes further in describing the peculiar malaise of characters like Binx Bolling or Will Barrett. That is to say, Percy concentrates on the symptoms of what he regards as the special sickness of the modern world. He provides a somewhat detailed diagnosis and, though he is properly cautious and undogmatic, he does suggest a remedy that may possibly cure it. Such a strategy risks turning the fiction in question into a novel of ideas, risks making it prescriptive rather than descriptive, and Percy's last two novels have been impugned for just such faults. I believe, however, that if *Love in the Ruins* and *Lancelot* are read perceptively, it will be seen that the author has provided more qualifications of the intellectual issues and more hedges against simplistic applications than most of the reviewers have succeeded in finding.

Be this as it may, my concern here is simply to draw attention to the fact that the crisis in culture achieves full magnification in this writer's work. Percy knows his Kierkegaard; as a convert to Roman Catholicism, he knows his Christian theology; and as a serious student of linguistics, hermeneutics, and symbolism, he is not under the rhetorical limitation of having to use an old-fashioned vocabulary.

To approach matters from a different angle, Walker Percy makes direct contact with the national and even international stream in his attempt to avoid writing the "southern novel." This maneuver has been quite conscious on his part, as some of his remarks in published interviews make plain. Yet I know of no present novelist who is more "southern" in every sort of way than is Walker Percy. Perhaps he would claim that his basic attitude is that of a modern Roman Catholic intellectual, and the claim is fully vindicated in his fiction. Yet as an observer of the southern scene, he can scarcely be bettered as he describes the sights, smells, and sounds of the French Quarter in New Orleans; or the chatter and posturing of a concourse of automobile sales in Birmingham; or the precise differences in manner and accent between a damsel from Winchester, Virginia, a girl from Fort Worth, and a big, strapping drum majorette from Alabama. Whether or not Percy fancies himself as a writer of the southern novel, his southern heritage has stood him in good stead as he deals with his chosen theme, the alienation within man's soul. One can say the same of Ransom, Tate, Warren, and Faulkner.

Here, one might ask: do other southern writers deal with the theme of the terrible division of the age; and if so, do they also benefit from their southern experience and heritage? In the cases of Flannery O'Conner, Caroline Gordon, and Andrew Lytle, the answer is clearly yes to both questions. With such writers as Eudora Welty, Katherine Anne Porter, and Marion Montgomery, all of whom draw on a southern background, the concern for man's psychic disorientation is demonstrably there, though it is less easily abstracted as an articulate theme.

What advantages does the southern writer have in dealing with what I have been calling the crisis in our culture? His first advantage is that the South is still the least "modern" part of the country in its values, habits, and associations. It has been less riven by the severing of ends from means, techniques from values. Whatever the sins and deficiencies of the South, there has been less abstraction and intellectual confusion. There is still some personal connection with the past, some sense of history, and the stabilizing effect of traditional moralities. Whether or not religion can be said to flourish in the South, it still remains a force. The sense of community has not been totally lost. There is still a folk culture in being.

Change has come—and of course is still coming—but the questioning of old attitudes and values is a powerful stimulant to observation, memory, and cogitation. If the loss of the old provokes in some no more than the irritation at being disturbed, it sends others back to an examination of their first principles. If the new constitutes a challenge to the old ways, in the philosopher and the poet the old may offer a counter challenge to the new.

4

Religion and Literature

$\sim$

*L*et me begin this discussion of literature and religion by citing Matthew Arnold's celebrated prophecy about the future of poetry. Nearly a century ago Arnold declared that the future of poetry was immense. Now that, in his opinion, science had disposed of religion, poetry had to assume the burden of providing civilization with its values, a burden that religion had formerly borne. The prophecy was brilliantly accurate. A generation later, Stephen Dedalus in Joyce's *Portrait of the Artist as a Young Man* was declaring himself to be a *priest* of the imagination. The last four decades of our century have given us an opportunity to observe some of the consequences of this priesthood. For example, the poet Wallace Stevens said, a few years ago, that "in an age of disbelief, it is for the poet to supply the satisfactions of belief, in his measure and in his style." Roy Harvey Pearce, in his *Continuity of American Poetry,* salutes Stevens's achievement in supplying such satisfactions. Pearce alludes to Ralph Waldo Emerson's "hope for a writer of the future who would take upon himself the duties of poet, philosopher, and priest," and then goes on to make the remarkable statement that though "Stevens' later writing [may not be] quite poetry, we must attend closely to it." Why? Because, Pearce asserts, it is perhaps "something beyond poetry. In any case, it is, for good and for bad, one of the most elaborate apologies for poetry conceived of in modern times. More important, it is as a consequence one of the most elaborate apologies for man." I am not sure that I entirely understand Pearce's statement, but the tone of this whole passage is that of a lyrical affirmation of literature's having become philosophy or religion.

But I must not imply that everyone applauds poetry's having become a kind of religion. René Wellek, one of the most esteemed critics of our day, though acknowledging the tendency of modern literature to assume the functions of religion, disapproves. Wellek writes that "recent criticism [at every point tends to slide] over into psychology, sociology, philosophy, and theology." Having abandoned its central concern—the art of literature— criticism now "looks constantly everywhere, wants to become sociology, politics, philosophy, theology, and even mystical illumination."

In the interest of clarity I should at once admit that my own sentiments are in accord with those of Wellek rather than Pearce. I think that we have to distinguish between the functions of literature and religion. Though I grant that there is a profound sense in which all experience is one and though I concede that every human activity relates to every other and that life is indeed a seamless garment, still, having made this concession, I would insist that it is in everybody's interest to maintain the distinctions between logic and ethics, science and religion, poetry and philosophy. If, for example, we believe that there is such a thing as literature, then it behooves us to try and define it and to indicate how literary discourse differs from other kinds. If there is no real difference, then in honesty we ought to say so and drop what has in that case become a redundant term.

In a day in which too few people study philosophy, in which the so-called normative sciences, logic, ethics, and aesthetics, are largely neglected, and in which the great majority of literary people have no religion, it is to be expected that the role of literature could become inflated and that there should be consequent confusion as to what its real function is.

The confusion, however, is of long standing and has a venerable history. Literature and religion do overlap at points and they do have much in common. In a more primitive and heroic age the artist and the scientist, the philosopher and the priest were often undifferentiated. Several of these functions might be united in one spiritual leader of the people. Even in later and more sophisticated times the lack of clear differentiation tended to persist. Like religion, literature is suffused with terms that appeal to the human heart. The interpretation may be merely implicit in the work, as when a lyric poet meditates on a flower, or it may be quite explicit and circumstantial, as when a novelist traces the history of a family or a society. But whether implicit or explicit, slightly or massively detailed, the literary artist brings together events and observations and moods into a pattern which has its coherence of attitude. The poem or novel or play gives us—if we want to use polysyllabic terms—a value-structured experience.

A religion makes some ultimate claim on our belief. It demands a commitment. A literary experience, on the other hand, does not. When we read George Herbert's poem "Love," we may believe, as Herbert evidently did, that there is indeed a spiritual presence in the universe whose name is love. But the reader of the poem is not compelled to believe in Herbert's God of love. For him the love mentioned in the poem may be simply a human attitude which the poet has momentarily mythologized. Or the reader may enter into the spirit of the poem briefly and tentatively and then, perhaps with melancholy or perhaps with indifference, dismiss the notion as a pleasant fancy which makes no real claim on his belief. We can, in order to describe this fleeting and merely provisional belief, employ Coleridge's well-known formulation and call it a willing suspension of disbelief.

In this matter of belief, however, the religious experience is, I take it, radically different. It *does* make some claim upon our belief. In saying this, I am not forgetting the difficulties of the wayfaring Christian. Even the saint may have to experience the dark night of the soul, and the most devout believer will at times have to pray the agonized prayer, "Lord, help thou my unbelief." But having recognized that the course of holy love does not always run smooth, any more than does that of romantic love, and that belief is not always steady and continuous, even so, religion, necessarily and on principle, asks something more than a temporary suspension of disbelief.

Yet even if I have given a true account of the difference between poetry and religion, one still must concede that religion and poetry have much in common and indeed that the same document may be viewed by one person as poetry and by another as religion. All of us are familiar with literary works that were once expressions of religious faith but which are now regarded as merely "poetry." In view of the evidence for this sort of thing, one might be forgiven for thinking that this is the normal state of affairs: for expecting, that is, for religious energy to subside and to pale out until we are left with simply a bit of poetry, just as one of the radioactive metals like uranium finally stops radiating and subsides into a stable and duller metal like lead—though the contemporary follower of

Matthew Arnold will prefer to think of the final product as a more precious metal—gold, say.

Yet it is possible to argue that religion does not simply dissipate itself and run down into poetry, and to deny that religion always comes to an end in this way. Indeed, I shall maintain a contrary position and argue that poetry needs religion, and that the relationship between religion and poetry is a polar relationship in something of the same sense in which we speak of the poles of an electric battery, one positive and the other negative, poles that mutually attract each other and thus generate a current of energy. Such indeed is the argument that I now want to urge.

Consider, for example, some of the ways in which religious terms and symbols figure in love poetry. It is amusing—and possibly significant—that the lyrics of Tin-Pan Alley constantly make use of religious terms. The beloved, though she is a creature of flesh and blood, a female mammal, is often described as a goddess. She is at least something out of the ordinary, perhaps like a dream walking. The moment of bliss which the lover has shared with her is heavenly. Moreover, it is a divine rapture; the proof of its being so is that for her he would, like a man on a religious pilgrimage, climb the highest mountain or cross the deepest sea. He pledges to her a devotion that is deathless and for all eternity, now and forever, amen.

This kind of extravagance cannot be explained as simply the result of the confusions incident to a cheap and decadent culture. Much of it is, goodness knows, cheap enough, but love poetry has for a long, long time been using religious terms in something of this fashion. One remembers John Donne's brilliant use of religious images in order to dramatize profane love. In his "Canonization," for example, the lovers cheerfully give up the world, become hermits, and are prepared to suffer martyrdom: "We can dye by it, if not live by love." These saints of love accomplish miracles, they will have their "legend" as might a medieval saint; they predict their own canonization and envisage the lovers of a future time invoking their prayers. Obviously the religious terms in this brilliantly witty poem are used metaphorically. The lovers are ready to renounce the world but not the flesh. They have not taken the anchorite's vow of chastity—for the hermitage to which each retreats is the other's body, and the miracles which they work consist in such things as rising from the bed of love, not listless or quarrelsome, but still devoted change-lessly to each other; or in their ability to drive the whole world's soul into the mirrors of each other's eyes, so that in giving up the world they actually possess the world in each other.

Donne does this sort of thing very often; but, of course, he sometimes reverses the process and uses, not religious terms in order to dramatize romantic love, but erotic imagery in order to describe the experience of divine love, as when he closes one of his "Holy Sonnets" by telling his God that

Except you enthral me, [I] never shall be free,
Nor ever chaste, except you ravish me.

One could illustrate similar points from other poets, including Shake-speare and Dante. For a very long time the poets of the Western tradition have found it necessary to discover in the religious experience analogies for the erotic experience. If the category of the divine were to become watered down or if it disappeared, plainly our love poetry would have suffered a loss. I can make this same general point in another way. Every-one has observed the fact that avowed atheists are often able to curse very heartily. But would they do so if nobody believed in God? If there were no slightest vestige of religion left? Surely there must be the possibility of blasphemy if a fervent curse is to carry any conviction. One cannot have blasphemy without at least some tiny trace of belief.

Donne, who was a believer—probably he was so, even as the wild Jack Donne long before he became the dean of St. Paul's—Donne knew the difference between religion and poetry since he so obviously makes use of a tension between the two in his profane love poetry and in his Holy Sonnets. Yet even a poet who is not orthodox in his beliefs or is not a believer at all may find it desirable—and perhaps may find it actually necessary—to fill his poetry with religious symbolism and with specific references to Christian rite and dogma. This is surely true of William Butler Yeats.

To put my case briefly: I shall argue that in spite of Yeats's own waver-ings from the faith and in spite of his occasional direct repudiations of it, the driving power of many of his poems comes from his use of religious symbols which were still vibrant in the community of which all his life he counted himself a member—symbols which therefore must have still carried some special resonance for him.

Let me cite three poems, in part or almost in entirety. They are all from his mature period, though none of them is one of his celebrated poems. That they are not is perhaps just as well, for a glittering showpiece might divert attention from the problem with which we are here concerned.

The first of these poems, entitled "The Mother of God," attempts to describe the feelings of the Virgin Mary as she contemplates the fact of the birth of her divine child.

> The threefold terror of love; a fallen flare
> Through the hollow of an ear;
> Wings beating about the room;
> The terror of all terrors that I bore
> The Heavens in my womb. . . .
>
> What is this flesh I purchased with my pains,
> This fallen star my milk sustains,
> This love that makes my heart's blood stop
> Or strikes a sudden chill into my bones
> And bids my hair stand up?

In a sense the poem is a neatly orchestrated set piece, a pattern of predictable contrasts: the young mother's human love for her baby set off sharply against her sense of terror and awe at what she knows to be the child's true nature. The poem is a study in the "terror of love," the terrible knowledge that she bore "the Heavens in [her] womb," the sense that the child represents something from the heavens, a "fallen star," and yet is something that her mother's milk sustains; in a shockingly contradictory sense its frail life depending upon her frail humanity.

One could argue that this poem is a kind of "exercise"—certainly no declaration of personal faith. But at the least the poet is exploiting emotions that arise from beliefs held by millions of his contemporaries.

With this poem, another of his poems entitled "Wisdom" stands in sharp contrast. "Wisdom" owes less to memories of Fra Angelico and the piety of the Middle Ages than to conjectures of a nineteenth-century German professor expounding the higher criticism.

The true faith discovered was
When painted panel, statuary,
Glass-mosaic, window-glass,
Amended what was told awry
By some peasant gospeller;
Swept the sawdust from the floor
Of that working-carpenter.
Miracle had its playtime where
In damask clothed and on a seat
Chryselephantine, cedar-boarded,
His majestic Mother sat
Stitching at a purple hoarded
That He might be nobly breeched
In starry towers of Babylon
Noah's freshest never reached.

Yeats here sees the "true faith" as something concocted by the poet and the artist. The account of someone like Saint Mark, a "peasant gospeller," is swept aside in favor of what the painter and the sculptor and the worker in mosaic could do to enhance and transform the gospeller's simple narrative. The poem exalts the artist as the priest of the eternal imagination and credits him with the discovery of the "true faith." Here Yeats is very close to Joyce's Stephen Dedalus.

Now let us set beside these two poems a third, "A Prayer for My Son." It opens with a statement of the father's anxiety for his infant son and his prayer that "a strong ghost" may stand "at the head / That my Michael may sleep sound." Indeed, the poem begins as a kind of rewriting of the child's poem "Angels standing by my bed, / Two at foot and two at head." And yet the poem is far more than a parody of that childhood prayer. This speaker apparently really does want the ghost to hold a "sword in fist." Moreover, the last two stanzas are tender, serious, and written, one supposes, with full conviction. The poet addresses his Maker.

Though You can fashion everything
From nothing every day, and teach
The morning stars to sing,
You have lacked articulate speech
To tell Your simplest want, and known,
Wailing upon a woman's knee,

All of that worst ignominy
Of flesh and bone;

And when through all the town there ran
The servants of Your enemy,
A woman and a man,
Unless the Holy Writings lie,
Hurried through the smooth and rough
And through the fertile and waste,
Protecting, till the danger past,
With human love.

These last stanzas put the great doctrine of the Incarnation in its most poignant terms. The Lord of creation, the sustainer of the universe, who taught "the morning stars to sing," condescended to take on infant's flesh and was thus inarticulate like any other mere human child, "wailing upon a woman's knee," unable to tell his simplest wants. By taking on Himself the vulnerability of human flesh, He made His own safety depend upon the strength of merely human love. The presentation of the issues is perfectly orthodox and could be regarded as thoroughly traditional. In the poem, of course, the doctrine is given a contemporary and even personal focus. The father who utters this prayer asks God to put Himself once more into the human situation, to take account of the dangers to which the poet's own child is exposed, and to add His divine strength to support the fragility of the parent's merely human love. The accent here is that of genuine prayer.

Have we any right, then, to infer from Yeats's ability to write this and other such poems that he was after all a believing Christian? Perhaps, though I would want to be very cautious here. The poetry that Yeats wrote in the course of a lifetime exhibits many postures. It would be difficult to say which of them represents the true man in his ultimate belief.

In any case I have presented this little sheaf of Yeats poems not in order to establish that Yeats really believed in Christianity but in the hope of demonstrating something else. Undoubtedly Yeats found in the history of Christianity and in its rites and dogmas a tremendous resource for his poetry, though not the only resource by any means. Yeats also knew a great deal about Rosicrucianism. He had attended the séances of Madame

Blavatsky. He had studied Buddhism. He was steeped in the myths of the Greeks. These exercises of the human spirit at various ages and in various cultures evidently were very important to him. Presumably such beliefs told him something important about the fundamental human situation. One might even venture to put the matter in this way: the evidence of the poems would suggest that Yeats felt that one could not represent humanity in its full dimension without appealing to man's vision of God.

I have remarked earlier that poetry, even that of profane love, needs a religious symbolism, one not watered down but at something like its full strength. Yeats's "Prayer for My Son" would seem to illustrate this point. Even the poem entitled "Wisdom," which is skeptical in tone, not in the least pious, and which probably did derive from Yeats's reading in the higher criticism of the scriptures—even this poem would seem to demonstrate some sense of religious beliefs actually held. The priesthood of the artist leans upon the fact of an earlier literal priesthood. Otherwise the metaphoric priesthood, the priesthood of the imagination, will seem trivial.

In "Prayer for My Son" there is an even greater need that the religious symbols should have some kind of authentic grounding. That "A Prayer for My Son" should make use of Christian symbols, rather than Greek or Buddhist symbolism, is significant. In any of Yeats's poems in which the note of prayer becomes dominant, Christian symbolism and the belief associated with that symbolism tend to come into the foreground. I think that it is clear that Christian symbolism retains a very special power for Yeats and that this power was bound up with the fact that the Christian culture was in some sense alive for him, perhaps because it was a living part of the cultural community with which he identified himself, intellectually and emotionally.

My general point amounts to this: even if the belief in question is one that is not held personally by the poet or is held by him only provisionally—momentarily held in a willing suspension of disbelief—these provisional acceptances are easier for the poet if they are held in a more ultimate sense by his own community and thus are beliefs that have nourished and shaped his own attitudes toward the world.

Poetry, then, we may say, needs religion; even nonreligious poetry needs it; even poetry subversive of religion needs it. For how can one be properly subversive if there is nothing to subvert? Poetry needs religion for the same reason that it needs other concrete expressions of human life, other human actions; for poetry is a dramatization of, and thus an indirect commentary upon, characteristic human action.

So much for religion as an ingredient, and usually an essential ingredient, in the poetry of the greatest range and depth and complexity. But poetry needs religion for another reason. It needs for religion to carry on certain functions with which poetry might otherwise be tempted to encumber itself.

When poetry tries to assume the functions of religion, it risks limiting itself and restricting its range of belief. The provisional beliefs of poetry harden into a fixed creed. Poetry loses a certain precious freedom, for its task becomes that of justifying a particular course of action—instead of contemplating imaginatively various courses of action.

The point that I am attempting to establish is comparable to one made by T. S. Eliot some years ago. At that time the so-called new humanists, under the leadership of Irving Babbitt and Paul Elmer More, were urging the claims of a revised humanism to undergird or perhaps even to supersede Christianity. Eliot denied the proposition that humanism could provide an adequate substitute for religion, but he admitted the value of humanism and assigned it an important role. Religion needed humanism, for humanism, as Eliot put it, "makes for breadth, tolerance, equilibrium, and sanity"—virtues that the world can scarcely get along without. The general role that Eliot assigned to humanism corresponds to that which I would here assign to poetry. For I am arguing that the function of poetry is "not to provide dogma"—to paraphrase Eliot on the function of humanism—but to act as "a mediating and corrective ingredient in a positive civilization founded on definite belief."

Does civilization need a "definite belief"? Cannot man live by imagination alone? From time to time men have indeed thought so, and have even made the attempt. Our own century has provided signal instances of a purely aesthetic religion—that is, aesthetics substituting for religion as when we find the artist or the philosopher trying to shape his own life into a work of art, or attempting to view history, including human suffering, loss, and catastrophe, as part of a great drama which has its beginning, its complicated middle, and its end.

To be able to view ugliness and horror and pain as an aesthetic spectacle, a spectacle to which even horror and pain make a necessary and positive contribution, and the final bitterness of which is mitigated once one sees that they are required for the complex harmony finally achieved— to do this is to take a very detached view of mankind indeed. A few of the philosophers and poets of earlier centuries occasionally attempted such a view. Error and defect, seen not in detachment from the mighty whole but placed in the full context of experience, turned out to be not evil at all, so the philosophers declared, but only partial good. Such reasoning seemed specious to that staunch eighteenth-century moralist Dr. Samuel Johnson, and he exposed it to some of his most withering sarcasm; yet Alexander Pope's belief that "whatever is is right" smacks of such reasoning.

In our own time a related notion is expressed in some of Yeats's poems. The twentieth-century poet is more daring than the poets of the English Enlightenment and in my opinion more nearly successful. In "The Gyres" Yeats could proclaim:

> . . . beauty dies of beauty, worth of worth,
> And ancient lineaments are blotted out.
> Irrational streams of blood are staining earth;
> Empedocles has thrown all things about;
> Hector is dead and there's a light in Troy;
> We that look on but laugh in tragic joy.

In another of Yeats's poems in this period, even tragedy is described as founded on gaiety:

> All perform their tragic play,
> There struts Hamlet, there is Lear,
> That's Ophelia, that Cordelia;
> Yet they, should the last scene be there,
> The great stage curtain about to drop,
> If worthy their prominent part in the play,
> Do not break up their lines to weep.
> They know that Hamlet and Lear are gay;
> Gaiety transfiguring all that dread.

Thus the poet is able to face with a certain equanimity the breakup of civilization and the destruction of all that he has loved. He can face it even with a kind of joy. But it is difficult to maintain such an attitude even in poetry. Only the great poet can prevent its degenerating into hollow bluster or fustian stoicism. It is even more difficult to make it yield a personal faith which will provide any comfort for grief or which will assign any meaning to human loss.

Detachment, aesthetic distance, impartiality, the sense of the rich and complicated whole in which even human suffering has its necessary part—these are the qualities that I have attributed to poetry, including some of our greatest and most robust poetry. Such qualities are precious; but human beings, I believe, also need ethical values and full commitment. In my opinion it would be a mistake to mix the modes and so confuse either of these two most important activities with the other. We need both of them.

Let me attempt then to sum up in this wise: literature celebrates the health of a culture; it reveals its depth and richness, including its inwardness. Where culture is not healthy, literature has a special utility in making a diagnosis of the situation. A sound diagnosis of our condition, though it is necessary to the finding of a proper remedy, is not the same thing as the remedy. Diagnosis is not prescriptive. Indeed, for a given situation there may be more than one kind of remedy. Or if this metaphor of diagnosis and remedy seems inadequate, then let me fall back upon more general language. Literature renders for us, concretely and dramatically, what it feels like to live in such and such a cultural situation—in that of Homer's Greece, or Dante's Italy, or in that of the America of the 1970s. A comprehension of literature requires of us an outreach of the imagination; it does not require final commitment. But every religion worthy of the name has always demanded final commitments and has enjoined specific actions.

Happy the man who possesses both: religion and poetry, faith and imagination, the one complementing the other, neither cramped and misshapen through being forced to substitute for something other than itself. I say happy the man who possesses both, but I say this in the full knowledge that a great many people, and many through no special fault of their own, are not so privileged.

It would be stupid and wrong to pretend that one had any simple solution to offer them. One can't put on a faith as if it were an overcoat—

adopt one because it renders us more comfortable or might help us to appreciate literature. In any case, I am not qualified to give a lecture in Christian apologetics. But one can ask that we all try to understand the present cultural situation, that we try to define our terms and use them responsibly, and that we be wary of conceptions that would turn literature into an ersatz religion or religion into a kind of fairy tale with ethical implications.

5

Frost and Nature

It is easy for most readers to think of Frost as a typical nature poet. He clearly knew nature intimately—that of his New England in particular—and in poem after poem he described it lovingly, with a keen eye for its detail and with an evident joy in its plangent beauty. I see before me poems such as "A Prayer in Spring," "Mowing," "After Apple Picking," "The Wood Pile," "Range Finding," "Nothing Gold Can Stay," "To Earthward," "Spring Pools," "Two Tramps in Mud Time," and dozens and dozens more. There can be no question as to Frost's knowledge of the natural scene, his love for it, and a yearning to find in nature a solace and comfort for human ills.

Though Robert Frost regarded Matthew Arnold as one of the finest poets, in some respects his favorite poet, he was to disagree sharply with what Arnold had said about man and nature in one of his sonnets, "In Harmony with Nature." The poem is addressed, as the subtitle indicates, "To a Preacher." Since the poem is not very well known and since it will serve as a good introduction to my topic, I shall quote it.

In harmony with Nature? Restless fool,
Who with such heart dost preach what were to thee,
When true, the last impossibility—
To be like Nature strong, like Nature cool!

Know, man hath all which Nature hath, but more,
And in that more lies all his hopes of good.
Nature is cruel, man is sick of blood;
Nature is stubborn, man would fain adore.

Nature is fickle, man hath need of rest;

Nature forgives no debt, and fears no grave;
Man would be mild, and with safe conscience blest.
Man must begin, know this, where Nature ends;
Nature and man can never be best friends,
Fool, if thou canst not pass her, rest her slave.

If it is necessary to spell out Arnold's message in bolder detail, we can prosify the last two lines thus: "You are a fool to think that you can strike up a close friendship with nature. Though as a man you are a natural creature, nevertheless, if you can't surpass Nature, then you are bound to remain enslaved to Nature."

In his poem "New Hampshire" Frost expatiates on the sonnet. A certain city man who thought the only decent tree was a tree reduced to lumber—"educated into boards"—attacks a whole grove of trees with an axe. But he doesn't have the courage to carry out his tree murder and soon drops his axe and runs away, quoting Arnold's line: "Nature is cruel, man is sick of blood."

Frost goes on to comment further on this fainthearted piece of urbanity by writing:

He knew too well for any earthly use
The line where man leaves off and nature starts,
And never overstepped it save in dreams.
He stood on the safe side of the line talking—
Which is sheer Matthew Arnoldism,
The cult of one who owns himself "a foiled,
Circuitous wanderer" and "took dejectedly
His seat upon the intellectual throne. . . ."

As we now know, it was to Goethe that Arnold is referring in those concluding lines, and not, as Frost evidently supposed, to himself. What prompted Frost's bitter reference to Arnold? Frost's biographer, Lawrance Thompson, suggests that it was Arnold's attacks on Puritanism, a subject on which Frost was sensitive and defensive since he claimed to be a Puritan himself. Thompson's suggestion does not satisfy me, and I remain puzzled, all the more so since I mean to argue in what follows that Frost, in poem after poem, shows that he knew very well where nature ended and humanity began, and that he himself recognized that the limit is all but an unbridgeable chasm. Maybe Frost simply didn't like Arnold's primness of tone or his didactic manner. Certainly Frost found his own, and to my mind, much more satisfying way to describe the man-nature relationship. But I don't apologize for beginning with the Arnold sonnet, for it has the virtue of putting bluntly—even flat-footedly—this matter of the relation of nature to human nature, one of Frost's most significant themes.

Frost's beautiful poem "Two Look at Two" may seem to present an exception to Frost's usual attitude toward nature. This poem relates how two lovers on an evening walk up the mountain slope stop at a ruinous stone wall. On the other side of the wall stands a doe. To their surprise and delight, she does not take alarm and bolt. She gazes at the human pair with what seems to them an almost friendly curiosity and finally moves on out of sight. The human pair feel, as the poem tells us,

> A great wave . . . going over them,
> As if the earth in one unlooked-for favor
> Had made them certain earth returned their love.

This poem, almost alone among Frost's poems, suggests that nature does give some sort of answering response to the pulsations of the human heart, and it is clear that our poet would happily embrace this Wordsworthian belief. But "Two Look at Two" is the only poem of Frost's that comes even close to such an affirmation. And even here the belief takes the form of an aspiration rather than an article of faith. It is significant that the incident occurs at dusk, the time of illusions, that the experience occurs to a pair of lovers, prone to project their own tenderness upon the event and disposed to believe that the bond of love that unites them answers to that which links the doe and the buck; and finally, and most important of all, the experience of union is prefaced by the words "As if the earth . . . returned their love."

If we look at Frost's poems taken as a whole, we find the poet's essential position is put in quite other terms. Instead of the fond belief that "nature never betrayed the heart that loved her," Frost's more realistic view is that nature is not aware that the human world exists at all: nature is deaf and dumb to all human aspirations.

A classic example of Frost's typical stance is presented in his delicately phrased poem "The Need of Being Versed in Country Things." Frost, or at least the *persona* who speaks this poem, has, in the course of a walk, come upon what is left of a burned-down New England farmhouse. Somehow the barn has escaped the fire, but the house has been destroyed and the site abandoned. In fact, the only sense of life about the barn is that created by the phoebes that go in and out of the broken windows to the nests they have built in the barn loft. Frost vividly pictures the scene: there is still standing the central chimney of the house. He compares the burned-out house to a dead flower in which the petals have fallen away, leaving the pistil standing.

The comparison seems to be quite apt. Many years ago in New England, my wife and I heard one morning that an eighteenth-century house a few miles away had burned during the night. We hurried up to see it, for we hoped to buy from the owners any hinges, door latches, or other early ironwork that could be retrieved from the ashes in order to use them in our own eighteenth-century house. We were not able to get any ironwork, but we did get the confirmation of the justness of Frost's simile.

But back to the scene that Frost has described. Other things that have survived the fire are the lilacs which have grown around what was once the ruined house; there is a "dry pump" that flings up "an awkward arm," and there are other relics of some family's disaster and the loss of their hopes. It is a scene of desolation, and the poet tells us that the murmur of the birds was "more like the sigh we sigh / From too much dwelling on what has been."

At this point in the poem, we stand where many a pre-Romantic of the middle and late eighteenth century stood. Such poets loved scenes of what they liked to call a "pleasing melancholy." Nature itself, through the voices of the phoebes, seems to make an appropriate response to the desolation of the scene and to express its sympathy for man's loss.

Then something quite remarkable happens in the poem. The pleasing melancholy of pre-Romantic vintage gives way to a very different attitude. The poet suddenly goes modern on us. He points out that there is no reason for the phoebes to be uttering anything like a human sigh for man's sorrow. Why should the scene seem in the least sad to them? After all, "for them the lilac renewed its leaf / And the aged elm, though touched with fire; / And the dry pump flung up an awkward arm; / And the fence posts carried a strand of wire." Since birds don't get their water from pumps, the fact that this one is out of order raises no problems, and since birds need only one strand of wire on which to perch, a fence with only one strand of wire is just as useful to them as a fence with three or four. Indeed, the poet goes on to say

> For them there was really nothing sad.
> But though they rejoiced in the nests they kept,
> One had to be versed in country things
> Not to believe the phoebes wept.

The poet is here really having it both ways. The scene does suggest to an observer that nature itself sympathizes with man's plight and mourns with him over the fragility of his existence. But the present observer is, after all, a hard-bitten modern. He is a man "versed in country things." He knows that the phoebes only sound mournful, and that they are sublimely indifferent to man's fate. For him, the notion that nature cares for man and speaks in sympathy to him is only an illusion.

Here is another example of the same theme: Frost's poem "Come In." The speaker begins his poem by telling us that at twilight, at the edge of a wood, he hears a thrush singing.

> Far in the pillared dark
> Thrush music went—
> Almost like a call to come in
> To the dark and lament.

Again, the observer is almost deluded into believing that nature is here speaking through the voice of the thrush, and that she is inviting man to join her in her lamentation. But this observer is also a hard-bitten modern. In the concluding stanza, he does a complete *volte face:*

> But no, I was out for stars;
> I would not come in.

His original plan was an evening walk to look at the stars, not to enter the darkened woods to listen to thrush music, and he refuses the invitation, almost too sharply—for he obviously catches himself, evidently remembering his manners. After all, it would be presumptuous to assume that nature had issued any invitation for him to join her in her melancholy mood, and so with a new shift of tone, the speaker adds:

> I meant not even if asked,
> And I hadn't been.

The punch line of the poem is, of course, the last. The speaker knows that it is only what seems to human ears a sweet sadness in the thrush's song that has momentarily deceived him into thinking that nature has any word for him. The thrush itself does not know that a man out for a walk is passing by the wood in which it sings. It does not know, and nature does not know that man even exists.

In Frost's poems on this theme—and "Come In" is typical—nature, though beautiful and sometimes heartbreakingly lovely, is quite indifferent to man. She commiserates with man no more than she commiserates with the dying elk or the lightning-stricken oak or the withered wildflower. Man, with his consciousness, is separated from the rest of nature by a barrier much more formidable than the wall across which the human pair looked at the mated buck and doe.

Frost, in short, is quite "unromantic" in his attitude toward nature, and if we are to understand his poetry and his art we must get this matter clearly in mind. Perhaps one of the best ways to enforce this point is to compare Frost to some of his modernist contemporaries. What I now shall proceed to do would not have been discouraged, I believe, by Frost himself. Frost, of course, liked his own way of putting things. He carefully cultivated his Yankee cranky conservatism, but he distinctly did not like to be considered an old fogy, inhabiting a backwater withdrawn from the mainstream of current poetry.

He had no desire to be regarded as a merely folksy, New England local colorist. The angriest I ever saw him was when some critic had remarked that his volumes were coffee-table stuff—the sort of thing that a couple who had made a little money and now lived in a fake New England saltbox

house like to display in the living room along with the North Carolina–
made cobbler's bench and a reproduction spinning wheel.

So the ghost of Robert Frost will not mind my placing him, on this
issue at least, in the ranks of the modernist poets, poets such as Auden
and Eliot. Consider, for instance, Auden's poem entitled "The Fall of
Rome." It is a poem written in crisp, almost staccato quatrains. The
reader quickly discerns that though the poem is ostensibly about the fall
of Rome, it is really about the fall of any civilization, including our own.
Take the lines:

> Caesar's double bed is warm
> As an unimportant clerk
> Writes *I do not like my work*
> On a pink official form.

The "pink official form" belongs to the world of modern letterheads,
memo pads, and business forms, and jars oddly—the poet, of course,
means it to do so—with the Roman Empire's civil service, which used the
stylus and wax tablet.

As the poem opens, nature is gaining on the world of humankind.

> The piers are pummelled by the waves;
> In a lonely field the rain
> Lashes an abandoned train;
> Outlaws fill the mountain caves.

But if technology is going to pieces and needs repair, the inner lives of the
citizens, including the upper classes, are a problem too.

> Private rites of magic send
> The temple prostitutes to sleep;
> And the literati keep
> An imaginary friend.

We don't have temple prostitutes—we have to make out with bunny clubs
and massage parlors—but practices very like "Private rites of magic"
abound. Every newspaper carries the daily astrological guide for the masses,

and as for the elite, plenty of them are narcissistic, hypercivilized, and afflicted with various kinds of neurotic tics.

What to do? The problem is difficult. The Catos of the time always ask for a return to the good old days and extol the "ancient disciplines." But even if this could really serve to recall the more sober citizens to their duty, trouble breaks out elsewhere: the "muscle-bound Marines / Mutiny for food and pay."

The poem ends, however, with two stanzas which take us away from a world of economic and technological breakdown, and a narcissistic, physically damaged, and probably corrupt citizenry. The closing stanzas read as follows:

> Unendowed with wealth or pity,
> Little birds with scarlet legs,
> Sitting on their speckled eggs,
> Eye each flu-infected city.
>
> Altogether elsewhere, vast
> Herds of reindeer move across
> Miles and miles of golden moss,
> Silently and very fast.

Why should the little birds be endowed with pity any more than with wealth? Nobody has ever taught them the uses of wampum or other currency, or pity either. Besides nature takes care of itself, can't help doing so—and is quite indifferent to what happens to men. Little birds will keep hatching out their young and the species will go on regardless of whether catastrophe overtakes Nineveh or Rome falls, or New York begins to totter.

With the last stanza we get even further from civilization: we are in Alaska now, or Siberia, and the reindeer, responding to their natural drives, set out on their annual trek in accordance with their seasonal timetables by simply following what nature has programmed into their nervous systems.

The world of nature is foolproof, by which I don't mean that human fools, by doing certain things to the environment, can't wipe out natural species. But left reasonably to themselves, and with a relatively undamaged environment, the creatures do pretty well take care of themselves. Natural laws cannot be broken. They can only be fulfilled. Yet the animals are at the mercy of their instinctual drives. Their power of choice is strictly limited. They also have very limited memories, and, one supposes, a very limited notion of the future. In fact, they live in a virtual present—like Keats's nightingale that was not "born for death"—was, that is, subject to no racking anxieties about the future, and could not imagine any other state than that which he now enjoyed. No wonder Keats called him an "immortal bird." The human being, of course, is not like that. He is a mortal creature, to be sure, obviously an animal like all the rest, with animal needs and desires. But man, with his self-consciousness, can feel forebodings and anxieties, memories of past failure and of guilt. But, of course, there is a positive side of the ledger. Man takes pride in his heritage and in past accomplishments, and he has his hopes and plans and purposes to be realized in the future.

As Auden would put it, mankind inhabits the realm of *history*, which is the peculiarly human realm, whereas all the rest of the creatures live only in the world of nature. Man's world is a three-dimensional world from which the rest of animal creation is barred. Man has language—man is a symbol-using and symbol-making animal—and that makes all the difference.

In his various essays, Auden spells this out in his prose. Though Frost does not spell out these matters in Auden's terms, nevertheless the distinction between nature and history and the peculiar nature of man are implicit in nearly every poem that Frost ever wrote.

A great many other modern poets would concur. W. B. Yeats would clearly concur. I have remarked that Keats's nightingale did not know that it was ever going to die. But Keats himself was haunted by the knowledge that he would die, and after he began to spit blood, he knew that he would die very soon. Frost's phoebes, whose cry resembles a human lament, are also immortal birds—they do not know that they are mortal or that they do not inhabit a timeless world.

Yeats wrote a brilliant little poem on just this theme. His poem concerns the assassination of Kevin O'Higgins, an Irish politician for whom he had great regard. O'Higgins knew that his life was threatened, and because he knew and yet defied his assassins, he showed that he rose superior to death. But here is the poem for your own inspection.

Nor dread nor hope attend
A dying animal;
A man awaits his end
Dreading and hoping all;
Many times he died,
Many times rose again.
A great man in his pride
Confronting murderous men
Casts derision upon
Supersession of breath;
He knows death to the bone—
Man has created death.

In the last line, Yeats may seem to claim far too much. How can he say that man has *created* death? But the statement is simply an exfoliation of what is implicit in the total context. The other creatures cannot conceive or imagine what it is to be dead. In a very real sense, then, man has created the notion of what it is to die and cease to be.

Man's consciousness—his sense of the past and of the future, and his consequent purposes and responsibilities—are indeed both man's glory and his bane. But—and this is the important matter—they involve his being more than simply a natural creature. Doing what comes naturally befits an animal; it is beneath the dignity of the truly human being.

Do I seem to have wandered far from the theme of nature's indifference to man? I do not think so. The indifference is bound up with the many ways in which the human being has to push beyond nature.

This is not, of course, to say that man should not love nature. Frost clearly did; so did Auden and Yeats. But though man may properly love nature, he must not assume that nature loves him. Frost, I believe, never does make this assumption.

Let me invoke one further modernist poet, T. S. Eliot. Frost, it seems plain, felt a certain rivalry with Eliot, and certainly some of Frost's friends saw Eliot's poetry as implying a denigration of Frost's own. Actually, when Eliot and Frost finally met, we were told that they got on with each other very well. But their very differences—real or fancied—make Eliot a good choice for my purposes here.

In T. S. Eliot's unfinished play, *Sweeney Agonistes,* one of the characters,

Sweeney, a rather raffish urban Irishman, is exchanging some banter with a girl by the name of Doris. They are at a party and he laughingly threatens to carry her to a "cannibal isle." He says to her:

```
Sweeney:  You'll be my little seven stone missionary!
          I'll gobble you up. I'll be the cannibal.
Doris:    You'll carry me off? To a cannibal isle?
Sweeney:  I'll be the cannibal.
Doris:                    I'll be the missionary.
          I'll convert you!
Sweeney:  I'll convert you!
          Into a stew.
          A nice little, white little, missionary stew.
```

Sweeney then proceeds to tell Doris what life is like on a "Crocodile isle." There are no telephones, motorcars, or any of the rest of the paraphernalia of civilization. On the island there is nothing to see "but the palms one way / And the sea the other way, / Nothing to hear but the sound of the surf." But the island really offers everything, for Sweeney declares that there are in fact only three things in life, and when Doris asks him what they are, Sweeney answers, "Birth, and copulation, and death, / That's all, that's all, that's all, that's all, / Birth, and copulation, and death." Then comes the following song:

Song by Wauchope and Horsfall

Snow as Tambo. Swarts as Bones.

Under the bamboo
Bamboo bamboo
Under the bamboo tree
Two live as one
One live as two
Two live as three
Under the bam
Under the boo
Under the bamboo tree

   Where the breadfruit fall
And the penguin call
And the sound is the sound of the sea

Under the bam
Under the boo
Under the bamboo tree.

Where the Gauguin maids
In the banyan shades
Wear palmleaf drapery
Under the bam
Under the boo
Under the bamboo tree

Tell me in what part of the wood
Do you want to flirt with me?
Under the breadfruit, banyan, palmleaf
Or under the bamboo tree?
Any old tree will do for me
Any old wood is just as good
Any old isle is just my style
Any fresh egg
Any fresh egg
And the sound of the coral sea.

Doris: I don't like eggs, I never liked eggs;
                And I don't like life on your crocodile isle.

Song by Klipstein and Krumpacker

Snow and Swarts as before

My little island girl
My little island girl
I'm going to stay with you
And we won't worry what to do
We won't worry what to do
We won't have to catch any trains
And we won't go home when it rains
We'll gather hibiscus flowers
For it won't be minutes but hours
For it won't be hours but years
And the morning
And the evening
And noontime
And night
Morning
Evening

> Noontime
> Night

> Doris: That's not life, that's no life
>   Why, I'd just as soon be dead.
> Sweeney: That what life is Just is
> Doris: What is?
>   What's that life is?
> Sweeney: Life is death.

This account of life on a South Sea island is a rather jumbled affair—and one supposes that the poet satirically meant it to be so. The people singing about the delights of this simple life have evidently never been in the South Sea islands themselves, and they have added to the clichés of the earthly paradise some details that don't quite fit. For example, there are in fact no penguins found on a South Sea island and probably no banyan trees. One element in this muddled, composite picture comes from the old-fashioned cartoon of lugubrious white missionaries sitting in great iron pots over a fire, with the cannibal chief, now turned chef, presiding over the affair. Sweeney's South Seas paradise is obviously fake.

What Eliot has done is to present modern alienated man's confrontation with a nature which modernity has de-animated and neutralized. Even if the boredom incident to the meaningless routine of urban life may make nature seem for a moment an escape from the meaningless, a retreat into a healthful, rich, and organic world, the escape is illusory.

Man receives from nature finally only what he brings to it. Nature will prove just as boring as the world from which modern man seeks to escape. Man's attempt to shed his humanity by becoming simply a natural creature like a fruit-bat or a penguin won't work. For this maneuver to succeed he would have to give up the very consciousness that provides nature with its mystery and its beauty.

As Frost's poems make plain, he has no delusions that a mere relapse into nature can save us. Again, as we have seen, as a good modern, Frost is reconciled to the fact that nature is indifferent to man. But this acceptance does not leave him in despair. Man's life is not meaningless.

Perhaps this is as far as I ought to go. But I think that it is as far as I need to go to set forth Frost's essential relation to nature. I shall leave it to others to speculate about Frost's ultimate metaphysical concerns. In any case, it is high time to return to Frost's own poems and to his own characteristic treatment of man's amphibious nature, a creature immersed in the world of nature and yet able, if not to step out of it, at least to hold his head above it.

Frost's poem "A Leaf Treader" is apt to my purpose here. The poem describes an autumn day in New England. All day the speaker has tramped back and forth in his woodlot. The brightly colored autumn leaves are falling all about him, and he has trodden many a leaf into the mire underfoot. In line 4 he explains—rather oddly, as it would at first seem— "I have safely trodden underfoot the leaves of another year." Why "safely"? Why this note of apprehension and fear? What has been worrying him comes out very clearly in the next stanza, though the tone of that stanza is whimsical and laced with a good deal of self-irony. The gist of the stanza is this: every autumn the speaker has come to speculate on whether he will end up on top of the autumn leaves or the autumn leaves will end up on top of him. Thus he observes:

> All summer long they were overhead, more lifted up than I.
> To come to their final place in earth they had to pass me by.
> All summer long I thought I heard them threatening under their breath
> And when they came it seemed with a will to carry me with them
>   to death.

The leaves have been, then, threatening him throughout the summer months, but their power has resided in more than threat. As he tells us in the first lines of the last stanza:

> They spoke to the fugitive in my heart as if it were leaf to leaf.
> They tapped at my eyelids and touched my lips with an invitation
>   to grief.

Thus there is something in man himself that responds to the pull of the seasons, something that yearns to give up the world of toil and anxiety and might even welcome a subsidence into the peace of death. The second line of this stanza has a realistic reference: the leaves blowing through the autumn wind do, some of them, tap at his eyelids or touch his lips, as if they were urging him to weep or to express his grief in words. At this point in the poem we are very close to the thrush's invitation in the fourth stanza of "Come In." The leaves' invitation cannot be dismissed in cavalier fashion. Man, like the leaves or the grass, is here today and gone tomorrow. Frost's speaker acknowledges that he is deeply involved in the processes of nature and is momentarily tempted to respond. But he pulls himself together and with a remarkable shift in tone concludes the stanza and the poem:

> But it was no reason I had to go because they had to go.
> Now up, my knee, to keep on top of another year of snow.

The special quality of tone of the third line is very important. It always reminds me of my own childhood when if the children next door were called in by their mother but I hadn't yet been summoned, I was tempted to express my good fortune by saying, "Well, I'm not going in. Just because you have to go in is no sign I have to." That some such tone is involved here is all to the good. This particular poem must not, at this point, take itself too seriously. And the poet proceeds to give the poem one further twist. With the last line, he remembers that his triumph over the autumn leaves may be short-lived. Man's effort never stops; soon the snowflakes will be coming down and the next pressing problem will be to stay on top of the snow rather than to allow the snow to provide a winter blanket for him.

There is another short poem of Frost's, however, that puts more precisely the relationship of man to the brute creation, but also pays its respects to those men who pride themselves on their ability to calculate and reason. The poem to which I refer is the celebrated "Stopping by Woods on a Snowy Evening."

When the man in the sleigh pulls over to the side of the road to look at the snow falling in the woods, he indicates that he believes he knows the owner of the woods. He remarks rather pointedly:

> He will not see me stopping here
> To watch his woods fill up with snow.

Why does the speaker go to the trouble of saying this? It is hardly a criminal offense to stop and look at another man's property. Yet the speaker does hint that the owners of those woods might be suspicious. After all, why should anyone stop to look at woods on a snowy evening? Because he has some kind of land deal on his mind? Or because he is a little touched in the head? A man who stops just to look is scarcely acting like a rational man.

Now if the owner of the woods would find it queer that the man in the sleigh should stop to gaze at this property in a snowstorm, certainly the horse that pulls the sleigh thinks so:

> My little horse must think it queer
> To stop without a farmhouse near
> Between the woods and frozen lake
> The darkest evening of the year.

> He gives his harness bells a shake
> To ask if there is some mistake.
> The only other sound's the sweep
> Of easy wind and downy flake.

Actually, what the speaker surmises his little horse must "think" and what he surmises that the owner of the woods would think define the observer's own position. He is poised somewhere between the two. Neither pure practical calculation nor pure instinctive response can find a place for aesthetic appreciation. Neither horses, polar bears, nor nightingales are, so far as we can tell, aesthetic creatures. This is not to say that animals do not have their own sense of well-being and happiness, but that is different from detached contemplation indulged in for its own sake. The horse is clearly *not* enjoying the sight of the woods filling up with snow. But neither would the practical-minded property owner enjoy the sight of his woods, or any other man's, filling up with snow.

I do not want to weight this charming little poem too heavily with moral and intellectual import. But, then, it is much more than a single-minded vignette of the New England landscape. I submit that it at least implies a definition of man. Man is the aesthetic animal, able to contemplate nature without reference to practical considerations. He is also the ethical animal. Yes, the poem touches on these considerations too. For the man in the sleigh, much as he would like to linger over the scene—perhaps he even feels an impulse to give up the human effort and simply sink back into nature, for the woods are indeed "lovely, dark, and deep"—nevertheless drives on. Why? Because, as he tells us, he has promises to keep.

We are not told what these promises are. They may be weighty or trivial. But he feels a responsibility to fulfill them, to put matters in Auden's terms: the person who is truly human transcends the realm of nature and inherits the realm of history, for only there can he truly fulfill himself.

To sum up: Frost neither worships nature nor fears her. In a very real sense he belongs to her and is one of her children. He finds her infinitely interesting and lovely, but he knows how little he can ask of her. Nature is quite unconscious of his very existence. Man's gift of consciousness actually separates him from her and from his fellow creatures. But Frost is not tempted thereby to get above his raising. He doesn't let his own power of consciousness go to his head. Thus, he doesn't proclaim with Blake the supremacy of the imagination over nature, nor with Emerson declare that he "esteem[s] nature [to be a mere] accident and an effect [of spirit]." For Frost, man is indeed a peculiar being. But if I were forced to find a just analogue for Frost's definition of man, I think that I could do no better than to go back to Psalm 8, with its wonderful lines: "What is man, that thou art mindful of him? and the son of man, that thou visiteth him? For thou hast made him a little lower than the angels. . . ." But rather than quote the rest of the Psalm, let me simply conclude with the note supplied by the editors of the Jerusalem Bible. Their summary of the account of man given in Psalm 8 will very nearly fit the account implied in Frost's poems: "Man, frail yet made in the likeness of God, on the border between the spiritual and material worlds, rules the natural creation. . . ."

6

The New Criticism

$\mathcal{T}$o undertake a discussion of the New Critics is very much like embarking on the hunting of the Snark. The New Critic, like the Snark, is a very elusive beast. Everybody talks about him: there is now rather general agreement as to his bestial character; but few could give an accurate anatomical description of him. Even when one believes that the Snark has actually been netted, he usually turns out to be not a Snark at all but a Boojum.

Who, after all, are the New Critics? John Crowe Ransom, who almost accidentally supplied them with a name? R. P. Blackmur? I. A. Richards? T. S. Eliot? People like these do not fit the stereotype neatly. Richards, for example, contradicts the current stereotype by his heavy stress on the reader, not the work. Allen Tate breaks out of the stereotype by showing from the beginning a keen interest in history. Two of his earliest books are biographies and many of his later essays are concerned with cultural history.

One could name other critics who fail to fit the pattern. In fact, after some preliminary sorting and sifting, I am usually the person chosen to flesh out the agreed-upon stereotypical diagram. In short, if a genuine Snark can't be found, then a Boojum will have to do. I'm not, of course, very happy with this state of affairs. I am well aware that no compliment is intended when I am so often pointed out as "the typical New Critic" or when a fashionable young critic sneers at what he calls "Well-Wrought-Urn-ism."

In view of this situation, I think it just as well to make this essay on the New Criticism a personal one. I shall prefer to talk about my own position rather than defend the occasional lapses, deficiencies, or biases of the so-called New Criticism. So much for the negative side. On the positive side, if I am to be forced to accept the term after all, then I want to define it so that it will actually reflect my own values and beliefs, not those of others, least of all those of a strawman.

Let me begin by repeating a bit of ancient history. When in the early 1930s Robert Penn Warren and I found ourselves teaching "literary types and genres" at a large state university, we discovered that our students, many of whom had good minds, some imagination, and a good deal of lived experience, had very little knowledge of how to read a story or a play, and even less knowledge of how to read a poem. Some had not been taught how to do so at all; many had been thoroughly mistaught. Some actually approached Keats's "Ode to a Nightingale" in the same spirit and with the same expectations with which they approached an editorial in the local county newspaper or an advertisement in the current Sears, Roebuck catalog.

In this matter the textbooks that had been put in their hands were almost useless. The authors had something to say about the poet's life and the circumstances of his composition of the poem under study. Mention was made of Keats's having listened to the song of a nightingale one evening as he sat in the garden of his residence in Hampstead. But the typical commentary did not provide an induction to this poem—or into poetry generally. The dollop of impressionistic criticism with which the commentary usually concluded certainly did not supply the need. The editor's final remarks on the poem were vague, flowery, and emotive. The only person who could make much sense of these remarks had to be a person who was already able to read the poem and who had become reasonably well acquainted with it.

Faced with this practical problem, we set about to produce a textbook of our own—two, in fact: *An Approach to Literature* and *Understanding Poetry.* Neither book was long on biographical and historical background— nor on the editors' warm pulsing feelings about the poem or story. These calculated omissions were noted almost at once and put down as proof of the fact that we had no use for biography and history, and that we were cold-blooded analysts who found no pleasure—certainly no joy—in literature.

Yet in a small, cheaply manufactured book—*Understanding Poetry* in 1938 sold for $1.40 a copy—how much commentary do you have space for? We were trying to apply the grease to the wheel that squeaked the loudest. Besides, the typical instructor, product as he was of the graduate schools of that day, had been thoroughly trained in literary history, or so we assumed. (Clearly he had not been taught much else.) We believed that he could be counted on to supply historical and biographical material. We were concerned to provide help of another sort.

Warren and I were not out to corrupt innocent youth with heretical views. Our aims were limited, practical, and even grubby. We had nothing highfalutin or esoteric in mind. We were not a pair of young art-for-art's-sake aesthetes, just back from Oxford and out of touch with American reality.

Our personal interest in biography and history was never taken into account. Warren's first published book was a biography and his first volume of fiction, a historical novel. As for myself, my thesis at Oxford had been an edition of an eighteenth-century correspondence—brass-bound research indeed, with many pages showing a fairly thin layer of text resting solidly on two columns of footnotes in finer print. My first published book concerned the derivation of pronunciation in the southern states from English county dialects such as those of Devonshire, Dorset, and Sussex. No precious aestheticism here either.

Yet the notion that we dismissed the importance of history clung to us. My publication of *The Well Wrought Urn* (1947) probably served to confirm the indictment. The experimental character of that book was, I assumed, quite plain. It was devised frankly to test an idea—namely that authentic poems from various centuries possessed certain common elements. In stressing the common elements in all literature, I was consciously cutting across the grain of English studies as then established. Yet the very plan of the book should have made the experimental character unmistakable. In any case I had not left it to mere inference: it was spelled out on several pages. In the preface, for example, the charge that I had neglected history or discounted its importance was predicted and dealt with: "I have been anxious to see what residuum, if any, is left when we have finished subtracting from [a poem] its references and relations to the culture out of which it came."

In my chapter on Wordsworth's Intimations Ode I observed that it might "be interesting to see what happens when one considers the 'Ode' [not primarily as a document in Wordsworth's spiritual autobiography, but] as an independent poetic structure, even to the point of forfeiting the light which his letters, his notes, and [his] other poems throw on difficult points." I went on to add, however, that this "forfeiture . . . need not, of course, be permanent." Looking back at this passage, I still do not think the proposal I made there unreasonable or excessively doctrinaire. The cautious reader is given sufficient notice of what kind of commentary to expect on Wordsworth's ode, and, by implication, on the other nine poems discussed in the book.

But the title! An urn is something static, shaped, rigid. Surely a poem is fluid, dynamic, a transaction between poet and reader. Yet what has happened to the reader's metaphoric sense if an obviously figurative title, borrowed from one of the poems discussed in the book, has to be frozen into a literal application? I thought that, for a book which sought to find a structure common to all genuine poetry, Donne's praise of a well-made object, however small, was apt. After all, what he sets up as its opposite is the vulgarly ostentatious "half-acre tomb." Donne was not the only poet who compares a poem to a static object. A very different kind of poet, Wordsworth, compares the body of his poetry to a gothic cathedral, with its "ante-chapel," and "the little cells, oratories, and sepulchral recesses, ordinarily included in these edifices." Readers have allowed Wordsworth his analogy without imputing to him the notion that poems are "static."

When Hugh Kenner came to write his essay "The Pedagogue as Critic," he obviously had very much on his mind the detailed treatment of individual poems such as one finds in *The Well Wrought Urn* and in *Understanding Poetry*. In fact he reduces the New Criticism to a classroom strategy. The aims, limitations, and possible achievements of *Understanding Poetry* constitute, as he sees it, the boundaries of the New Criticism. This maneuver provides him with a handy means for dismissing the New Criticism—at least under that name—as having any real substance. Thus he is able to ignore such questions as whether T. S. Eliot or Yvor Winters or Allen Tate is, or is not, a New Critic. This, as I have already suggested, may be to the good. But his essay amounts to a clever caricature, with the bold exaggerations and oversimplifications that an effective caricature demands. He depicts the pedagogue chalking up his key words and his diagrams on the blackboard for the enlightenment of his students. For

Kenner's pedagogue conceives of a poem as a verbal machine. Thus he devotes himself to explaining the workings of its gears, pistons, and ignition system. He remains oblivious to the fact that the poems are meant to be intoned rather than merely perceived as characters on a printed page.

Kenner does point out extenuating circumstances. He concedes that the American cultural scene in the 1940s and 1950s needed something of the kind. In fact Kenner remarks that in making up his "catalogue of omissions and distortions" of which he asserts the critic-pedagogue was guilty, his purpose is "not to denigrate the critic-pedagogue, but to define his characteristic limits of activity, by way of defining what he can do superlatively well, and why, in the 1940s and 1950s, it mattered so much." (Question 1: Have today's students become so adept at reading that they no longer need what the New Critic could do "so superlatively well"? The literacy rate continues to fall nationwide. Question 2: How can Kenner believe that his New Critics ever did this job superlatively well when he accuses them of regarding a poem as merely a verbal machine, a kind of mechanism?)

Kenner's bill of particulars against the New Critic–pedagogue is powerfully urged, and the implication clearly is that we need now something different and something that goes beyond the New Critic's "characteristic limits of activity." Presumably critics like Kenner will provide it. To this point I shall return, but for now I quote Kenner's summation: "The curious thing is how a classroom strategy could come to mistake itself for a critical discipline."

Is this sentence a politely figurative way of avoiding saying that the New Critic–pedagogues, including the authors of *Understanding Poetry,* mistook their proffered teaching methods for a true critical discipline? Or does Mr. Kenner mean that the college teachers who bought the book—or books like it (Kenner got into the game by once writing such a book himself)—mistook a teaching method for a critical discipline? Perhaps it doesn't matter. In any case there is a more important question to be asked. Doesn't any teaching strategy have some relation to a critical discipline? I think it does. Though none of the so-called New Critics—least of all I—ever set up as a system-builder, a definition of literature and a conception of its function are clearly implicit even in my own critical writings.

It would seem that Kenner's principal objection to the New Critic's classroom strategy (critical discipline?) consists in what Kenner takes to be the New Critic's misguided dismissal of the cultural background of a work. With this we return, not surprisingly, to an old and still prevalent indictment that I shall presently consider. But first I must point out that Hugh Kenner offers a strong hint that he himself can show the proper way to manage literary criticism.

Kenner tells us: "Not to distract students with peripheral information, that is one thing; to pretend to oneself, as some New Critics did, that the information has no status whatever, is something else." But what is peripheral information and what is central? Kenner does not say directly, but he remarks that "Shakespeare's 'golden lads' . . . has exerted power over countless imaginations despite the virtual loss of the information that what he wrote down was a Warwickshire idiom for dandelions."

A footnote directs us to his *The Pound Era* (a truly rich and interesting work), in which Kenner discusses this bit of information more fully. After quoting the first stanza of the song at Fidele's grave (*Cymbeline* 4.3), which concludes "Golden lads and girls all must / As chimney-sweepers, come to dust," Kenner runs the changes on the meaning of "golden": "'golden,' because once precious when they lived; 'golden,' touched with the nobility and permanence of gold . . . ; 'golden,' in contrast to 'dust': a contrast of color, a contrast of substantiality, a contrast of two immemorial symbols, at once Christian and pagan: the dust to which all sons of Adam return, the gold by which human vitality braves time; dust, moreover, the environment of chimney-sweepers, against whose lot is set the promise of shining youth, *la jeunesse dorée,* who may expect to make more of life than a chimney-sweeper does, but whom death at last claims equally. 'Golden,' magical word, irradiates the stanza so that we barely think to ask how Shakespeare may have found it."

Kenner's account of "golden," I should say, is standard stuff, the sort of thing that an old-fashioned New Critic might have written; though Kenner speaks in a more exalted strain than mere pedagogues are wont to reach. The phrase *golden lads* has indeed "exerted power over countless imaginations," whether or not we ask how Shakespeare came by the words. This is why some of us think that this kind of information (i.e., the meaning and associations of the words as used in the poem) is *central* information, not peripheral.

Nevertheless it would be highly interesting to learn how Shakespeare came by the words—if we can indeed ever gain such information. Kenner tells us how he did, and in doing so, he presumably advances beyond what he takes to be the narrow frontiers of the New Criticism. A "visitor to Shakespeare's Warwickshire"—Kenner does not name him but I too have met him—told Kenner that he once "met a countryman [in Warwickshire] blowing the grey head off a dandelion" and remarking, "We call these golden boys chimney-sweepers when they go to seed." This circumstance allows Kenner to imagine that "perhaps on the afternoon of the first performance [of *Cymbeline*] if there were no Warwickshire ears in the Globe to hear that Warwickshire idiom, the dandelions and their structure of meaning simply dropped out. Yet for 350 years no one has reported a chasm." True enough, but perhaps they have failed to do so because there was no chasm to report.

Let us see how Kenner explains the dandelion simile for us. Speaking like a good pedagogue himself, he asks his reader: "And all is clear?" But he takes nothing for granted. The dandelions that have gone to seed "are shaped like a chimney-sweeper's broom." But are the terms of Shakespeare's comparison the golden lads (and let us not forget that he mentions golden girls too) and the blackened little urchins who cleaned the chimneys, or is the second term of his comparison the special brush used to clean the chimneys? It is the long-handled brush with bristles at the end of it that resembles the gone-to-seed dandelion with its long stem and fuzzy top.

The *Oxford English Dictionary* indicates that *chimney-sweeper* can refer to either the boy or the brush. The *OED*'s first meaning refers to the boy who climbed the chimney; the second reads: "A stiff radiating brush fixed on a long jointed rod, used for cleaning chimneys." But if the *OED* is correct, to the ears of Shakespeare's Warwickshire neighbors watching a performance of *Cymbeline* in the Globe the word *chimney-sweeper* could not have meant anything other than the boy who cleaned the chimney, for the special brush that resembles the gone-to-seed dandelion was not introduced until 1805. Dandelions may have been referred to as golden boys in Elizabethan Warwickshire. Who knows? But the second meaning simply wasn't available in the early 1600s. Mr. Kenner seems here to have supplied us with information that is not even peripheral information; but instead with some highly ingenious speculation, charming enough in its way, yet without factual support, biographical or historical.

I do not mean to imply—let me repeat—that the study of how particular literary works came about, detailed accounts of authors' lives, the history of taste, and the development of literary conventions and ideas are not obviously worthy of pursuit. That is not the issue here, though it is true that a number of the so-called New Critics have preferred to address themselves primarily to the writing rather than to the writer; and a few of us to regard as the specific task of literary criticism the interpretation and evaluation of the literary text. To borrow a term from Austin Warren and René Wellek's *Theory of Literature,* such an *intrinsic* criticism is to be distinguished from *extrinsic* criticism and general literary scholarship.

If some of the New Critics have preferred to stress the writing rather than the writer, so have they given less stress to the reader—to the reader's response to the work. Yet no one in his right mind could forget the reader. He is essential for "realizing" any poem or novel. Moreover readers obviously vary extremely in their sensitivity, intelligence, and experience. They vary also from one cultural period to another: the eighteenth century apparently tended to find in Shakespeare something rather different from what the nineteenth century found or the twentieth century now finds. Reader response is certainly worth studying. This direction is being taken by many of our more advanced critics today. Yet to put the meaning and valuation of a literary work at the mercy of any and every individual would reduce the study of literature to reader psychology and to the history of taste. On the other hand to argue that there is no convincing proof that one reader's reaction is any more correct than another's is indeed a counsel of despair.

Let me summarize by using the most homely analogy that I can think of. The real proof of the literary pudding is in the eating thereof. It is perfectly proper to look at the recipe the cook says she followed, to take into account the ingredients she used, to examine her intentions to make a certain kind of pudding, and her care in preparing it—or her carelessness. But the prime fact for judging will still be the pudding itself. The tasting, the eating, the experience is what finally counts.

It is time to drop such analogies and to turn to more detailed and systematic discussions. "The Intentional Fallacy," when W. K. Wimsatt and Monroe Beardsley published it in 1946, was thoroughly misunderstood. Most readers have concluded that the authors dismissed the poet's intentions as unimportant, or that they believed that the poet had no intentions and that his work issued from a kind of mindless "trance" as described in Plato's *Ion,* or that they forgot that literary works were produced by warm-blooded human beings whose heads were filled with ideas, beliefs, prejudices, and who were themselves the products of a particular cultural environment.

"The Intentional Fallacy" as an essay has its difficulties, but a careful reading of it today would rectify the worst of those misconceptions. In any case the discussion of intentionalism in Beardsley's *Aesthetics* (1958) or the whole subject as reviewed and reassessed in Wimsatt's "Genesis: An Argument Resumed" (1968) would do so. In his 1968 essay Wimsatt considers and appraises a host of objections and rejoinders, and disposes of them in masterly fashion.

One or two brief examples will have to suffice. For example, Wimsatt affirms that it is perfectly reasonable to use a literary work to throw light on its author.

> From the work to the author (when one wishes to be biographical) is not the same as from the author (outside the work) to the work. These directions remain opposites no matter how numerous and complicated a set of deflectors and baffles we set up between the two termini.
>
> The fact is that we can, if we wish, learn with relative certainty from biographical evidence that some personae are close to or identical with the author and some are much different from him. . . . Almost everybody rushes to confuse the persona of Gray's *Elegy in a Country Churchyard* with Gray himself. In fact it can be shown on quite convincing biographical evidence that the melancholy poet who is the anonymous speaker of that poem is very close to the melancholy poet Thomas Gray. . . . Nevertheless, the *Elegy* is not *about* the historic person Gray. The self-contemplative speaker remains anonymous. The poem itself, if it were anonymous, would be intact.

Surely this passage cannot be quoted to the disparagement of literary biography or literary history; nor does it make any unreasonable separation of the author and his work. For example, if we want to read Byron's *Childe Harold* primarily for the light it throws on Byron, why not? *Childe*

Harold, particularly cantos 1 and 2, is not very impressive as poetry; perhaps it is most useful as a kind of register of the moods of that world-weary young man. Human nature being what it is, a good many people, if the truth were known, would much rather read a life of Byron than *any* of his poetry. Gossip is more interesting than fiction—even to many of the literati.

Another passage from "Genesis" constitutes as good a brief summary of the issue as I can find.

> The closest one [can] ever get to the artist's intending or meaning mind, outside his work, would still be short of his *effective* intention or *operative* mind as it appears in the work itself and can be read from the work. Such is the concrete and fully answerable character of words as aesthetic medium. The intention outside the poem is always subject to the corroboration of the poem itself. No better evidence in the nature of things can be adduced than the poem itself.

To use a metaphor drawn from the law courts, "evidence outside the poem" is always secondhand (or even hearsay) evidence as compared with the evidence presented by the text itself. Such a position seems to me not in the least unreasonable. It does not deny the suggestive value of evidence from outside the poem; moreover it leaves literary biography and literary history intact, for it does nothing to inhibit our human interest in or systematic study of writers and the whole process of literary creation. Nor does it forbid the study of reader response. Finally it does not conveniently overlook the fact that every critic is himself a reader who needs to be continually conscious of his own prejudices, possible blind sides, and imperfect responses to the work he is reading. Clearly he must try to become the ideal reader.

In her interesting *On the Margins of Discourse* Barbara Herrnstein Smith heaps a bit of polite scorn on the concept of the ideal reader as providing a way out of our problems in the interpretation of literary texts. But no one claims that the ideal reader actually exists in flesh and blood. The ideal reader is a platonic idea, an ideal terminus never actually attainable. Nevertheless common sense and an appeal to the dictionary and to the text in question would indicate that some of us read more sensitively and intelligently than others. If "better" is a demonstrable fact, then "best" is at least a useful ideal, something we must try to approximate as nearly as possible, even if it is never fully attainable. To say that there is no way to prove that one reader's interpretation is better than another's means the end of any responsible study of literature.

Besides a preference for emphasizing the text rather than the writer's motives and the reader's reaction, does there exist any other possible common ground occupied by the so-called New Critics? If so, it is probably "close reading." But it might be more accurate to substitute "adequate reading." "Adequate" is, to be sure, a relative term; but so is "close." (How close is close enough?) The substitution of "adequate" might help relieve the New Critic of the jeweler's eyepiece with which he is equipped as he is commonly pictured when engaged in a microscopic study of a text. Some documents do require a more careful reading than others; that again seems a reasonable surmise. "Twinkle, twinkle, little star" requires less careful reading than Wordsworth's "The Solitary Reaper." (I'm not forgetting, of course, that some modern theorists could turn even "Twinkle, twinkle" or "Mary had a little lamb" into a verbal labyrinth, "and [find] no end, in wandering mazes lost." Consider, for example, the number of meanings of "lamb" and the number of analogues for "Mary." To a richly stored literary mind these two words offer almost infinite possibilities. In fact only weariness of the flesh or the adoption of an arbitrary terminus need bring such a free-ranging process to an end.)

In January 1979 Hillis Miller published (in the *Bulletin of the American Academy of Arts and Sciences*) an account of Wordsworth's "A Slumber Did My Spirit Seal." It is a truly remarkable example of how much one can read out of a poem (if he first allows himself to read almost anything he likes into it). Miller begins with an account of the poem that, in spite of some elaboration, resembles very closely that of the so-called New Criticism. (I published, for example, such an account in 1948.) But Miller's first several paragraphs serve only as a runway for the takeoff into what amounts to an intercontinental—possibly interplanetary—flight.

One of the several contrasts in the poem has to do with the terms in which the girl is described in the first stanza and in the second. In the first she is called a "thing" that "could not feel / The touch of earthly years." In the second she becomes a "thing" like a rock or stone. Miller properly points out that as described in the first stanza Lucy had "seemed an invulnerable young 'thing': now she is truly a *thing*, closed in on herself like a stone." His next several paragraphs elaborate this point. We are told that Wordsworth's play on the word *thing* exists also in German. Miller then quotes two passages from Martin Heidegger. In the second of these passages Heidegger refers to the story in Plato's *Theaetetus* about the "whimsical maid from Thrace" who laughs at the philosopher Thales because he, failing to see "the things in front of his very nose," fell down a well. Heidegger observes that the philosophical question "What is a thing?" will always cause housemaids to laugh. Such a question, Miller opines, would also provoke laughter in Wordsworth's Lucy.

As items in a process of almost free association, all of this is interesting— the more so perhaps because one is allowed to nod to Heidegger and to Plato. But Miller has taken us all around Robin Hood's barn—even though a pleasant excursion—in order to make a rather obvious contrast between two senses of "thing." The old folk song about Billy Boy's pro-spective bride, a song that Wordsworth may well have known, as he could not have known the writings of the yet unborn Heidegger, would have provided him with the meaning of "thing" that Miller would like to invoke for the term as used in the first stanza.

"Can she bake a cherry pie, Billy Boy, Billy Boy?
Can she bake a cherry pie, charming Billy?"
"She can bake a cherry pie quick as a cat can blink its eye,
But she's a young thing, and cannot leave her mother."

Though poets do not necessarily go by the dictionary, consider the *OED*. Meaning 10: "Applied to a person, now only in contempt, reproach, pity or affection (especially to a woman or child)." But if one reads still further, one notices that all the *OED* examples of *thing* as expressing pity or affection have a qualifying adjective such as "sweet thing," "noble thing," "poor thing." As used without a qualifier (10b) *thing* seems always contemptuous or reproachful—senses that would be inapplicable to Lucy. If one takes this circumstance seriously, noting that "thing" in the first stanza of the Wordsworth poem has no qualifying adjective, one might feel constrained to look further to find just what Wordsworth meant by "thing" in his first stanza.

OED's meaning 7 ("An entity of any kind") can be applied to human beings, and this meaning would sufficiently justify "thing" as Wordsworth uses it in the first stanza. The girl once seemed an immortal being, an entity impervious to time. Keats uses "thing" in this sense in his "Eve of St. Agnes." In stanza 25, to Porphyro, Madeline seems more than mortal: she wears "a glory, like a saint"; she seems "a splendid angel" as she kneels, "so pure a thing, so free from mortal taint." "Thing" as applied to a young woman is used here not in affection or pity but rather in awed wonder—as I suggest it is in the first stanza of "A Slumber." Later, in stanza 37, Madeline uses "thing" when she refers to herself as "a deceivèd thing;— / A dove forlorn and lost." But here we have the qualifying adjective.

In Wordsworth's second stanza Lucy has clearly become a "thing" in a sharply contrasted sense, that designated by *OED* meaning 8b: "A being without life or consciousness; an inanimate object, as distinguished from a person or living creature." This contrast between meaning 7 (an entity, a being, which may be a human being) and meaning 8 (an inanimate object) is surely the basic contrast in Wordsworth's poem. That contrast is actually indicated in one of the *OED*'s illustrative quotations: "He that getteth a wife getteth a good thing; that is, if his wife be more than a *thing*."

Yet any forced implication made in Miller's interpretation of "thing" seems negligible in the light of some of his further extrapolations. Thus Miller tells us that among the oppositions to be found in this eight-line poem are: "mother as against daughter or sister, or perhaps any female family member as against some woman from outside the family; that is, mother, sister, or daughter as against mistress or wife, in short incestuous desires against legitimate sexual feelings." (Shades of the late F. W. Bateson!) Miller later says that it perhaps does not matter "whether the reader thinks of Lucy as a daughter or as a mistress or as an embodiment of his feelings for his sister Dorothy. What matters is the way in which her imagined death is a re-enactment of the death of [Wordsworth's] mother as described in *The Prelude*."

Though I of all people have to feel abashed at quibbling over other people's discovery of paradoxes, I confess that I find absurd some that tumble forth in Miller's exegesis. For example: "To be touched by earthly years is a way to be sexually penetrated while still remaining virgin"; or "the poet has himself somehow caused Lucy's death by thinking about it."

Miller remarks that this poem "in the context of the other Lucy poems and of all Wordsworth's work enacts one version of a constantly repeated Occidental drama of the lost sun. Lucy's name of course means light. To possess her would be a means of rejoining the lost source of light, the father-sun as *logos*." The woman in this poem, of course, is not actually named. Miller calls her "Lucy" because "A Slumber" belongs to a grouping of poems which Wordsworth's editors have themselves made and decided to call the "Lucy poems." Yet if we are to be free-ranging, what about Wordsworth's poem "Lucy Gray"? Here the girl is specifically named Lucy, and the poem is again about the death of a girl. Would "Gray" hinder our considering this Lucy as also a daughter of the sun? (Should Wordsworth have named her Lucy Bright or Lucy Ray instead of Lucy Gray?) Or is the contradiction between "light" and "grayness" intended and somehow meaningful? Wordsworth's editors have not assigned "Lucy Gray" to the Lucy group. If they had, I have no doubt that some ingenious explanation, paradoxical or otherwise, would be discovered to clear up the difficulty. But enough of excerpts. The reader will need to peruse the whole of Mr. Miller's essay to be able to do justice to his argument and to my reactions to it.

I have to confess that there is a certain mad plausibility in this and such other ventures in interpretation. Granted an agile mind and a rich stock of examples from the world's literature, granted modern theories about the doubleness of the human mind and the ways in which secret meanings can underlie surface meanings (and one can sometimes "mean" one thing by uttering its opposite), it is possible to construct readings that make a kind of glittering sense. The real trouble is that the game is almost too easy to play. With so lax a set of rules to govern the play, one might be able to do something with even "Humpty Dumpty sat on a wall" or "Hey diddle diddle, the cat and the fiddle."

In ambitious interpretations of this sort it helps, of course, to deal with an author about whose life we have a great deal of information. A writer such as Shakespeare would be more difficult, but even here the game is not impossible. By reading back from the work into a hypothetical life, one could doubtless construct a base from which to find further meanings in the texts themselves.

How typical of the new movements in criticism is this essay of Hillis Miller's? It would be hard to say, and I shall simply note that Miller's subtitle reads, "The Crossways of Contemporary Criticism," and that he prefaces his account of "A Slumber" with a general review of the recent history of critical theory and practice. Apparently he means for his reader to assume that in this essay he is exploring some of these newest paths.

René Wellek has written that "surely one of the most urgent problems of literary study today" is that of putting some kind of "theoretical limits on [literary] interpretation," now that "total willfulness has been running riot." Wellek's essay was written well before Miller's essay appeared, and I do not suggest that Wellek had this essay or any other by Miller in mind. Yet Miller's extraordinary construction does illustrate what can happen when there is a lack of theoretical restraints. Literary interpretation becomes a game of tennis played without a net and on a court with no backlines.

In *Literature against Itself* Gerald Graff vehemently denounces all such license, but he does not stop at that. Almost everything that has happened in literary criticism since the heyday of Henry Seidel Canby and George Lyman Kittredge gets roundly swinged—the Structuralists, the Deconstructionists, the proponents of an affective criticism, the Northrop Fryes and the Hillis Millers, the Jacques Derridas and the Frank Kermodes, and many another. They make up a strange assortment of bedfellows. A more apposite figure here might be a motley group of wrongdoers hustled before the bar.

In his attack Graff lays about him so indiscriminately that he sometimes slashes innocent bystanders and even potential allies. I, for example, agree with, and even applaud, some of his indictments. But I cannot accept his contention that the New Critics are themselves responsible for all or most that has gone awry since the 1950s. Specifically I beg to be excused from being cast as the Pandora who, though not meaning any harm, nevertheless foolishly opened the fateful box and loosed all the present evils upon the literary world. Graff's scolding of the New Critics signally fails to take into account recent powerful movements in philosophy and in western society generally. The kind of debacle that Graff describes would have occurred had not a single New Critic ever been born. More unjust still is the fact that Graff's censure derives from a misunderstanding and an essentially false assessment of what most of these critics were saying. Let me say that my reference to Graff here is not gratuitous. One of his eight chapters is entitled "What Was New Criticism?" and he rings the changes on the New Criticism throughout the whole book.

Graff believes that the basic sin of the New Critics was their repudiation of the referentiality of literary language. True, their purpose was merely "to expunge from the mind of the educated middle class . . . the genteel schoolmarm theory of literature, which had defined literature as a kind of prettified didacticism." Though Graff says he finds it difficult to mourn the disappearance of the schoolmarm theory of literature, what the New Critics succeeded in doing, he insists, was to cut literature loose from any connection with reality.

I dispute his conclusion. Allen Tate, for instance, asserts that a true poem provides "knowledge of a whole object, its complete knowledge, the full body of experience [the object] offers us"; and in an early work I wrote that a genuine poem offers us "a simulacrum of experience." It may be said to imitate experience by "*being* an experience rather than any mere statement about experience." But I want to raise a prior question that Graff never answers: What kind of didacticism would be substituted for the schoolmarm didacticism? A Ph.D.'s didacticism? Would that necessarily be any better? What didacticism would be a proper and wholesome kind of didacticism? And if all literature is didactic, how would Graff distinguish between a poem and a sermon or a poem and an essay? I think that sermons and moral essays are valuable and have an important place in the human economy, but I don't want to confuse them with poetry or fiction. Poems and novels have their own character and function and their own characteristic relation to reality. On this whole matter Graff remains distressingly vague.

He does relieve his general censure of the New Critics by making a few concessions. He admits that "to repudiate art's representational function is not necessarily to leave no link between art and reality." I'm not sure that the New Critics repudiated anything more than literal copying and the necessity for a one-to-one correspondence with reality. Yet, though this qualification makes his concession seem generous, Graff insists that such a repudiation "is to reduce reality to a trivial role in the partnership." It doubtless could, but I see no signs of that in, say, Eliot or Auden or Tate, or in many others that Graff would call New Critics. They all are very much in earnest about the importance of reality—if *that* is the issue.

The strength of *Literature against Itself* is almost wholly negative: Graff's sharp condemnation of certain excesses in critical theory and practice. But he is very vague in setting forth positive solutions. He seems reluctant to face crucial problems. He sometimes writes as if some of the problems have not been with us from almost the beginning. For example, he deplores "an implicitly defeatist acceptance of art's disinheritance from its philosophical and social authority." But how far back in history do we have to go to find art in undisputed possession of philosophical authority? At least back to pre-Socratic times; for Plato explicitly denied it such authority. The issue here is not whether Plato was correct, but the age-old character of the issue.

In general Graff lays too heavy a burden on literature. He implies that unless one can find philosophical authority in it, we have nowhere else to find such authority. Unless we can claim an easy and obvious referentiality in a poem, then we have lost our hold on reality itself. It is as if philosophy, religion, and even common sense were not available to us. These may not be available to some of the people that Graff is attacking. But if I must be birched, I want my punishment to have some relation to my own sins of omission and commission.

Years ago T. S. Eliot remarked that we were still living in the age of Matthew Arnold, who believed that literature could and should take over the burdens once performed by a now exploded religion. I believe with Eliot that it cannot, for literature has its own and indispensable function, which does not duplicate that of religion or of philosophy, or certainly that of science. In a special sense, then, Graff's enemies are Arnoldians; but Graff may be the noblest Arnoldian of them all in that he too would apparently lay upon literature the whole burden of acquainting us with reality. Certainly he wants a stable and responsible philosophy. So do I. But I do not ask that literature provide the ultimate truth about reality. Graff sometimes writes as if he thinks it does.

For a more detailed and carefully objective answer to Graff (and others)

I refer the interested reader to two articles by René Wellek in *Critical Inquiry:* "The New Criticism: Pro and Contra" (summer 1978) and his rejoinder to Graff's "New Criticism Once More" (spring 1979). In his 1978 essay Wellek agrees with my view that those persons commonly designated as the New Critics were "far from unified." He even considers the wisdom of abandoning the "concept [of a New Criticism] and [the] term." But he decides that, after all, there is "some sense in grouping these critics together" and proceeds to make what I consider the best case that can be made for seeing them as a group.

His description and assessment of the New Critics is summed up in the final paragraph:

> I will not conceal my own conviction that the New Criticism has stated or reaffirmed many basic truths to which future ages will have to return: the specific nature of the aesthetic transaction, the normative presence of a work of art which forms a structure, a unity, coherence, a whole, which cannot be simply battered about and is comparatively independent of its origins and effects. The New Critics have also persuasively described the function of literature in not yielding abstract knowledge or information, message or stated ideology, and they have devised a technique of inter-pretation which often succeeded in illuminating not so much the form of a poem as the implied attitudes of the author, the resolved or unresolved tensions and contradictions; a technique that yields a standard of judgment that cannot be easily dismissed in favor of the currently popular, sentimen-tal, and simple; The charge of "elitism" cannot get around the New Critics' assertion of quality and value. A decision between good and bad art re-mains the unavoidable duty of criticism. The humanities would abdicate their function in society if they surrendered to a neutral scientism and indifferent relativism or if they succumbed to the imposition of alien norms required by political indoctrination. Particularly on these two fronts the New Critics have waged a valiant fight which, I am afraid, must be fought over again in the future.

Speaking for myself, at least, the preceding paragraph is the best con-cise summary that I know of what some of us thought we were doing. As for our accomplishments, I am happy that Wellek believes that we waged "a valiant fight" for those ideals. In any case, as I contemplate the present literary scene, I agree with him that the war is not over. The same issues will have to be fought over again and again in the years ahead.

7

The Waste Land

A Prophetic Document

One who interprets *The Waste Land,* as I do, not only as a unified poem but as a trenchant commentary on the culture of the twentieth century, must take into account Eliot's statement to Theodore Spencer that *The Waste Land* "was only the relief of a personal and wholly insignificant grouse against life: it is just a piece of rhythmical grumbling." Yet how different it is from the not-so-rhythmical grumblings of Allen Ginsberg's "Howl" and many another "confessional" poem that poured forth from personal grievances a half century later. Eliot's grouse against life took some very strange and arresting forms—even very learned forms, with allusions to literature, history, and religion—that did not fall on altogether deaf ears. One might say that whereas the mountain labored only to produce a ridiculous mouse, Eliot's insignificant grouse grumbled rhythmically and produced a monumental poem.

Some commentators hooted at Eliot's addition of the notes, calling them an encumbrance, mere filler to pad out a slim book, at best a distraction. Yet if Eliot had not added them, his readers quickly would have; indeed, they have been adding to them ever since.

I would like to know more about the context in which Eliot made his celebrated remark to Theodore Spencer, and the tone of voice in which he uttered it. No matter what the context or the tone of voice, however, it is possible to accept quite literally Eliot's statement of what the composition of *The Waste Land* meant to him at the time, and also to give full credence to what it has come to mean to its readers and what it came to mean to Eliot himself.

For Eliot was also capable of giving quite a different account of his feelings at the time he was putting his great poem together. Valerie Eliot cites this passage from her husband's essay on Pascal (1931) and reports that Eliot said he was describing his experience of composing "What the Thunder Said":

> . . . it is a commonplace that some forms of illness are extremely favourable, not only to religious illumination, but to artistic and literary composition. A piece of writing meditated, for months or years, apparently without progress [as we now know *The Waste Land* was], may suddenly take shape and word; and in this state long passages may be produced which require little or no retouch. . . . You may call it communication with the divine, or you may call it a temporary crystallization of the mind.

In Eliot's celebrated comment on Joyce's *Ulysses*—a comment, it is important to remember, that he published in 1923, just one year after the publication of *The Waste Land*—he stressed Joyce's discovery of the "mythical method," which, he said, other writers in our day must adopt. He indicated that it might be the only feasible way of "controlling, of ordering, of giving shape and significance to the intense panorama of futility and anarchy which is contemporary history." It is not my purpose to discuss the mythic method here. What I want to stress is Eliot's characterization of modern history as a "panorama of futility and anarchy." He is speaking here not merely about the modern world portrayed in *Ulysses* but of the actual condition of the world that any future writer will have to face.

I have my own morsel of evidence to add. Over fifty years ago I wrote a commentary on *The Waste Land* which I sent to Eliot, with something like fear and trembling, for the author to pass judgment on if he would. He did reply and, among other things, wrote: "It seems to me on the whole excellent." This sentence was pleasing to read, of course, but I want to dwell on something else in that letter, which I believe is especially pertinent to the problem I have been discussing. "I think that this kind of analysis is perfectly justified so long as it does not profess to be a reconstruction of the author's method of writing," he said. "Reading your essay made me feel, for instance, that I had been much more ingenious than I had been aware of, because the conscious problems with which one is concerned in the actual writing are more those of a quasi musical nature, the arrangement of metric and pattern, than of a conscious exposition of ideas."

Fortunately, my essay did not require revision on those matters, since I had not touched them; I had tried to make it a straightforward treatment of symbol and theme. Besides, I had already learned that writers compose not off the tops of their heads but out of the depths of their beings—that conscious design, though it can be important, is never the whole story. Eliot was to say all this much more acutely in some of his own later criticism.

At any rate, I decided not to quote the Eliot letter when I published the essay in the *Southern Review* in 1937 and, later, in *Modern Poetry and the Tradition,* since it seemed a not altogether legitimate or dignified way to promote my point of view about the poem. In addition, if a reader raised the question as to whether the poet is necessarily the best reader of his own work, I could not answer with a categorical yes. I decided to content myself with the private knowledge that the poet himself had approved of what I had done.

The foregoing may be seen as a lengthy introduction meant to suggest that whatever emotional relief the composition of *The Waste Land* gave Eliot, it is nevertheless a poem about the past and the present of our culture—one that raises searching questions about our world but does not necessarily provide answers.

One of Tennyson's characters speaks of being "the heir of all the ages, in the foremost files of time," and so, in a sense, was Eliot—but he did not savor that circumstance with the exuberance of Tennyson's Victorian optimist. Instead, he shared with certain others a sense of the culture's failure and breakdown. At the end of World War I, many of the brightest minds saw that what had occurred had dealt not only a fatal blow to the European cultural unity but perhaps a devastating blow to the meaning of culture itself. Technology, the opening up of the "dark" continent of Africa, and the westernizing of Asia had given promise of a peaceful and progressive world. Then the war that could not happen, happened. The traumatic shock was greater than that caused by the Second World War; indeed, many believed that the First World War made a second one inevitable.

Ezra Pound reacted in his own way and developed his own theories, and proposed, to the horror of some of his friends, his own remedies. Yeats was to say later that he had not foreseen the "growing murderousness of the world," but in 1919, standing by his daughter's cradle as he listened to a storm howling in off the Atlantic, he imagined "That the future years had come, / Dancing to a frenzied drum, / Out of the murderous innocence of the sea." (Events have proved him generally correct about the character of those future years: a second global war, the cold war, and many active local wars.) When Joyce acted as a carefully distanced observer and a devotee of a cyclical view of history, he found his own way to accommodate himself to one more general collapse of a culture; but when he turned his eye to his native Ireland, he portrayed its decadence with an almost loving exactitude of detail.

American writers generally reacted to these events by moving to the political left, cautiously, and sometimes enthusiastically, accepting some version of communism. In the southern states a few intellectuals questioned the doctrine of progress and its economic expression in industrialism. They were concerned about the weakening of traditional values, the erosion of family ties, and the breakdown of the community—changes certain to happen with the shifting of populations, especially from rural areas to the larger cities. Such fears were scoffed at as being of no real importance or as antiquated notions that must not be allowed to get in the way of America's march forward. The buzzword in those days was what it is today: progress.

I mention these various reactions if only to show that Eliot was not alone in his concern for the past and what, for good or ill, the break with traditional value systems entailed. Should they be simply discarded as obsolete? If so, what should replace them? These issues were on Eliot's mind early in his poetic career, at least as early as the composition of "The Love Song of J. Alfred Prufrock," for that poem provides a glimpse of an effete, if not decadent, society and introduces a principal character who is committed to nothing and aware that he does not dare make even the most trivial commitment.

As for *The Waste Land,* I will confine my discussion to only two aspects of this wonderfully rich poem: first, the two kinds of life it depicts, dream life and waking life; and second, the fragmentation of the older culture and its consequences. There is much more to discuss, but I shall find these two matters quite enough for the time I have at hand.

At this point I want to introduce the name of Eric Voegelin, a man of whom Eliot had possibly never heard. I have not come across his name in any of Eliot's writings, though I have made no thorough search for it. He taught in this country in the 1930s, having come here as a refugee from Austria after Hitler's seizure of that country. Voegelin was not a Jew, but he had won a place on the list of the proscribed because he had repeatedly denounced both Communists and Nazis alike. Either group would have shot him, but the Nazis got there first: they were pounding on Voegelin's apartment door in Vienna just as he was crossing the Swiss border.

Voegelin was a remarkable scholar. He had a full command of the classical languages, plus Hebrew; he was completely at home in German, French, and English; he had apparently read everything, and read it all with a Germanic thoroughness. Though a historian and political scientist, he was very much interested in literature. When the poems that eventually would form *Four Quartets* began to appear, I was surprised to find that this Austrian refugee was doing carefully detailed commentaries on them at a time when most of the English department was unaware of their very existence. I asked him why he was so concerned with Eliot's poetry, and he replied that he was interested in what one of the most profound minds of our generation was thinking. He wanted to follow precisely Eliot's ideas, especially those on history and religion.

Voegelin died some years ago, before finishing his masterpiece, *Order and History,* a monumental work that fills some four and a half volumes, but he left a number of shorter volumes on the same subject. One of these is entitled *From Enlightenment to Revolution,* which Voegelin regarded as a sort of spinoff from *Order and History* and did not mean to publish. But in 1975 Professor John Hallowell of Duke University persuaded Voegelin to let him publish it and wrote for it a very interesting introduction. I would like to quote a brief section of that introduction because it provides a condensed account of the general lineaments of Voegelin's theory of history, one which seems to me to throw a good deal of light on Eliot's work, including *The Waste Land* itself.

[Voegelin's] remarkable intellectual achievement, which may well become a landmark of twentieth-century scholarship, invites by its broad scope and profound insights comparison with the work of such men as Hegel, Spengler, and Toynbee. While it shares with these works an attempt to elucidate a philosophy of history, it respects the ultimate mystery of human existence and claims to have found but one constant in history, "the constancy of a process that leaves a trail of equivalent symbols in time and space."

We actually find such a trail of symbols in *The Waste Land.* Moreover, these various symbols tend to possess the tensional quality which Voegelin says is characteristic of the language human beings have always been forced to use—forced, that is, because they are creatures who are so obviously animals and yet also aspire to godlike powers and attributes— whenever they speak seriously of the meaning of their own existence. The following paragraph from an unpublished essay by Voegelin, which Hallowell quotes in his preface to *From Enlightenment to Revolution,* may help explain what Voegelin means by symbols that involve tension and make use of "a language of tension":

Existence has the structure of the In-Between, of the Platonic *metaxy,* and if anything is constant in the history of mankind it is the language of tension between life and death, immortality and mortality, perfection and imperfection, time and timelessness, between order and disorder, truth and untruth, sense and senselessness of existence; between *amor Dei* and *amor sui, l'âme ouverte* and *l'âme close;* between the virtues of openness toward the ground of being such as faith, hope and love and the vices of infolding closure such as hybris and revolt; between the moods of joy and despair; and between alienation in its double meaning of alienation from the world and alienation from God. If we split these pairs of symbols, and hypostasize the poles of the tension as independent entities, we destroy the reality of existence as it has been experienced by the creators of the tensional symbolisms; we lose [thereby] consciousness and intellect; we deform our humanity and reduce ourselves to a state of quiet despair or activist conformity to the "age," of drug addiction or television watching, of hedonistic stupor or murderous possession of truth, of suffering from the absurdity of existence or indulgence in any divertissement (in Pascal's sense) that promises to substitute as a "value" for reality lost. In the language of Heraclitus and Plato: Dream life usurps the place of [waking] life.

It is no wonder that a man whose general theory of history can be described in this fashion would be intensely interested in reading "East Coker" when it first appeared.

What are some of these tensional symbols in *The Waste Land?* Some are fairly obvious: life experienced at such an intensity that it resembles death; dry bones which are to live again as parts of flesh-and-bone organisms; the absurdity of dying gods (as if immortal beings could ever die); a search for truth of life which is to end in a ruined chapel surrounded by graves.

Some of the consequences of our destroying the tensional language in which Voegelin says man's experience of existence has to be described are evident in the world of Eliot's poetry. For example, Prufrock perceives that the men and women of the special world he inhabits are not really alive but live in a kind of dream world or death-in-life. Gerontion says that he has been driven into a sleepy corner, a sort of Sargasso Sea where no winds blow and nothing really happens. But he has not completely lost his perceptions, any more than Prufrock has lost his, and he clearly makes out the characteristics of the situation—his own and that of his culture: quiet despair; hedonistic stupor; history known only as, say, Henry Adams knew it; art treated as a kind of religion, and religion conceived of merely as art. Gerontion has known all these evasions and knows that they are evasions. He has made no commitments, for he has not been willing to limit the complete freedom that he demands for himself; he keeps all options open until death puts an end to options.

Just as the only vital image to be found in "Prufrock" is the vision of the mermaids "combing the white hair of the waves blown back," so the only truly vital image in "Gerontion" is that of the "Gull against the wind, in the windy straits / of Belle Isle, or running on the Horn." Life in such latitudes is exhilarating, demanding commitment and effort, and is therefore a proper symbol of reality and the waking life. The relaxed, uncommitted dream life is not real life at all.

The Waste Land, of course, begins with people who are living, or at least trying to live, only partially. They are evidently content to feed "a little life with dried tubers" and to be covered "in forgetful snow." They don't want to be waked up: they prefer not to become truly alive. I remind you of Voegelin's definition of real life, which, he asserts, is always lived in tension with a knowledge and acceptance of the fact of death; but I ask you to recall also Voegelin's list of some of contemporary society's ways to avoid facing reality lived so strenuously: the relapse into "quiet despair or activist conformity to the 'age,'" "drug addiction or television watching," "hedonistic stupor," and so on. This reads uncomfortably like a description of our contemporary world, as if Eliot's great poem had turned out to be actually prophetic. I mean to postpone the issue of prophecy, however, for a while.

One of the most striking things about *The Waste Land* is its fragmentary character. That was the aspect of the poem that at once impressed its readers. Conrad Aiken, in a friendly review, praised the poem but regarded it as a "brilliant and kaleidoscopic confusion."

The protagonist—the consciousness that moves through the poem—is thoroughly aware that the fragments among which he moves *are* fragments, for he knows of what totality they were once a part and what meaning each contributed to and derived from the whole. Yet he also knows that many people do not regard them as fragments of anything. They have now been reduced to mere decorative details: "The change of Philomel, by the barbarous king / So rudely forced," for example, is simply part of the rich detail of the room described; seen from another perspective, it is reduced yet more drastically to simply another of the "withered stumps of time." Even Shakespeare's reference to a miracle of transformation that counterbalances the change of Philomel—"Those are pearls that were his eyes"—is trivialized when put to ragtime. In short, the protagonist does not see these fragments as meaningless, as a wandering Bedouin might regard the ruins of a Hellenistic city somewhere in the desert: to him the fragments speak a comprehensible language, they still contain a live meaning. In the end, therefore, he does not discard them; he shores them against his own ruins. His personal problem is simply an aspect of the general problem. (It is interesting to note that Eliot first wrote not "shored against my ruins" but "spelt into my ruins." Did he mean something like "spelled out their meaning into the meaning of my own fragmented self"? If so, he was perhaps wise to adopt a less involved statement.)

The protagonist has resolved to buttress himself with these fragments of the past. After all, he is not the first to be confronted by spiritual drought. Ezekiel and the author of Ecclesiastes had gone through a like experience. So had those in the Middle Ages who told the story of the wounded Fisher King whose personal curse was also his dominion's curse. So had ancient Thebes, whose affliction was also occasioned by the misdeeds of its ruler. The past is important to the protagonist. It may even contain wisdom, though rarely of the sort that would occur to a social engineer or to the typical politician. But the actions that wisdom may propose are at once too simple and too inward to be attractive to modern man. Besides, the past is generally out of fashion today. An increasingly secular society is dedicated to progress, a doctrine not subject to question and reinforced by a technology that has indeed achieved spectacular results. Such a society has little use for the past. The result is that the fragments which appear in *The Waste Land* have by our time been broken into smaller and smaller fragments, and whereas the protagonist of *The Waste Land* knows what they were broken off from, many of those living in the United States today see them as meaningless bits and pieces, mere detritus.

The most ominous development of all is that the schools, far from vigorously combating this loss of the past, have complacently allowed it to disappear. There is plenty of evidence to this effect. Most of us are familiar with the statistics: for instance, there are 23 million adults in this country who are functionally illiterate. But some of you may not have heard of a study done by the Library of Congress to try to find out how many of our younger people read books. The definition of a book adopted for the purposes of the survey was minimal, for any printed matter bound in either soft or hard covers was to be regarded as a book. Any person who in one year read at least two of these assemblages of printed copy was declared to be a book reader. Even with such loose definitions as these, of the young people between the ages of eighteen and twenty-five, only 4 or 5 percent could qualify as book readers. Here, of course, we are talking about little more than sheer literacy. Nothing is said about the quality of the books read. The novelist Walker Percy has recently estimated that there are perhaps one hundred thousand readers of serious books in our population of about 240 million. Percy made no survey, but he is a shrewd observer of contemporary American society; because he is a novelist, I suspect that he has access to detailed information about the sales figures for contemporary fiction.

When people stop reading, the past begins to glimmer away. But we don't have to depend upon literacy figures to sustain a dismal view of what is happening to our general knowledge of the past. There is plenty of direct evidence. E. D. Hirsch's recent book *Cultural Illiteracy* is full of supporting details. Some of you may know Hirsch's story about the teacher who declared that he had never met a single college or high school student in Los Angeles who could tell him the years when World War II was fought. The same teacher goes on to say, "Nor have I found one who could tell me the years when World War I was fought. Nor have I found one who knew when the American Civil War was fought." Granted, dates are not the most important thing that we learn. Yet a completely dateless history, one with a scrambled chronology or no chronology at all, is almost meaningless.

Hirsch's book has come under attack for its "elitism," and its list of terms that literate Americans ought to know has been challenged. While almost any of us could propose worthy deletions and additions to Hirsch's list, I think that his general case is thoroughly proven. Anybody who has had very much experience in teaching college undergraduates knows how thin is their knowledge of American history, and their grasp upon the history of Europe or any other part of the world is weaker still.

Hirsch believes, and convincingly demonstrates, that this has come about by deliberate changes in educational theory. But the study of history is also under attack from another quarter. In an article in the *Southern Review* Judith Weissman argues that deconstructionist theorists are the enemies of history, since they feel that not only does history have no intrinsic value but that, with its rules, precepts, and prejudices, it does the free spirit of today a great deal of harm. She feels that the deconstructionists would cheerfully abolish history altogether. Whatever our reasons for dismissing history—whether because of poor educational theory in our schools or what may be truly called the treason of the clerks themselves—the damage done is serous. We are condemned to live in a comparatively narrow segment of time, that of our own generation. This means that our experience is far less rich than was normal in earlier times. It means that we have a more meager background against which to make our choices and decisions. The larger human community to which we might belong shrinks or disappears entirely, and the individual, thrown back on his own impulses, may become alienated or else vulnerable to the tyranny of state bureaucracies.

Furthermore, with the loss of history and consciousness of the past, we obviously lose the "complex symbols" through which Eric Voegelin holds that societies in the past have always expressed themselves: Ezekiel's valley of dry bones; the myth of the dying god; the knight on a quest to discover the secret of life. I have named some of those referred to in *The Waste Land,* but obviously there are many others that have fallen out of public consciousness. This fact was brought sharply home to me a few years ago when I was teaching in the South, in what was reputed to be the heart of the Bible Belt. In a class of about thirty college juniors and seniors, I found exactly one student who could identify a rather familiar quotation from the New Testament. Had I gone back into some of the coves in the mountains, I might have done better. But the students who had made it to the state university represented a different intellectual world—one in which what used to be called the Holy Scriptures obviously had little place.

In the intellectual world of today, the climate of Eliot's *Waste Land* has not moderated. The drought has intensified with the passage of years, and the qualities spelled out by Voegelin and dramatized in Eliot's poem are all here, too—but in magnified form: the quiet despair (and nowadays it is not always so quiet), activist conformity to the age, hedonistic stupor, television watching. The Smyrna Merchant or his equivalent is on many a corner in our cities, and his pockets are now full of something other than currants. Madame Sosostris has emigrated to these shores. She has laid aside her "wicked pack of cards" but she is still adept at working up a horoscope, perhaps with the aid of a computer. She is justly proud of her clientele—it comes from the highest ranks of society. Those who have to put up with humbler fare can find it in the astrological columns of a thousand daily newspapers. For the hunger to know the future is still powerful.

The fact that we have put men on the moon doesn't seem to have affected the popular belief that it has mysterious powers over men's fate. Similarly, modern science has not defined the ultimate goals of life, and it can never hope to do so, since the scientist deals with means, not ends and purposes. The responsibility of defining the good life seems to be left more and more to our thriving advertising industry.

Is Eliot alone in what most Americans would describe as an overly pessimistic estimate of our society? Not quite. Yeats, at some points, would join him. I'm thinking, for example, of the following lines from "The Seven Sages":

> Whether they knew or not,
> Goldsmith and Burke, Swift and the Bishop of Cloyne
> All hated Whiggery; but what is Whiggery?
> A levelling, rancorous, rational sort of mind
> That never looked out of the eye of a saint
> Or out of a drunkard's eye.
>   All's Whiggery now.

Faulkner is also sometimes close to Eliot. No, I have not forgotten his Nobel Prize speech and his belief that man was a tough critter, practically unkillable. But in an essay like "The American Dream, What Happened to It?" he complains of moral disasters that had happened in America— disasters that are probably irreversible.

Strangely enough, the social critic Christopher Lasch, in his book entitled *The Culture of Narcissism,* scores our present society for very much the same ills that appear in *The Waste Land.* He deplores the modern dismissal of the past, which he sees as a treasury from which we may draw "the reserves . . . that we need to cope with the future." Lasch is also worried by the "atrophy of older traditions of self-help" and distrusts the individual's dependence "on the state, the corporation, and other bureaucracies." He also points out that "a society that has reduced reason to mere calculation can impose no limits on the . . . immediate gratification of every desire, no matter how perverse, insane, criminal, or merely immoral."

Like many other modern thinkers, Lasch considers religion an illusion. Nevertheless, he mourns its loss, for nothing has been found to take its place. He says elsewhere that our society provides "no logical place" not only for religion but also for "compassion, or contemplative reason"— which is to be expected from a "culture of narcissism," in which every person is fixated upon himself. No one could be more different from Christopher Lasch than the unpleasant Mr. Eliot,

With his features of clerical cut
And his brow so grim
And his mouth so prim,

but both notice the spiritual aridity of modern society. The contrast between the two men only reinforces the significance of their agreement.

Yet does this mean that I believe I have convinced the reader that Eliot was a true prophet, that the infection he sensed in Western culture early in the century has gone on apace for more than sixty years, that today even more of the population flees from reality (means of escape are many and various), that more of us live in a dream state than in a waking world? I doubt that I could have convinced anyone who was not already convinced. In fact, how would one go about convincing members of a thoroughly secularized society—and nowhere is it more thoroughly secularized than in its universities—that the way our world may well end is with a whimper rather than with a bang? The bang we can well believe in. We can accept Eliot's early vision of

De Bailhache, Fresca, Mrs. Cammel, whirled
Beyond the circuit of the shuddering Bear
In fractured atoms.

Never mind what the young Eliot meant by that. We know what it could mean, for we know something about splitting atoms. But how could our world possibly expire with a whimper?

The artist who insists on speaking of how or when the world will end faces a dilemma. It is that of the famed playwright-actor who rushed onto the stage before a packed first-night house, shouting "The theater is on fire! Rush for the exits!" and was wildly applauded. What an opening! the audience thought. What a play! What an actor! He almost makes you think that the theater is really burning! Indeed, the more frantically he pleaded with the audience to leave, the more lustily they clapped their hands. Art had triumphed over fact, appearance over reality. Something similar happens when we read *The Waste Land:* the nightmarish vision of a civilization breaking up is done so well that we almost believe the breakup is real. But, of course, we know that it isn't.

I had best leave the matter at that, and make no attempt to settle such questions as whether the culture will end with a bang or a whimper and whether it will end at all. I shall be content simply to put *The Waste Land* into what I hope is a new perspective, that of prophecy. Hence my invoking the names of Eric Voegelin, Christopher Lasch, and even Walker Percy to indicate that in Eliot's criticism of our culture—criticism implied or explicit—we have more to deal with than the genteel fastidiousness of a clerically minded intellectual.

On the other hand, I must be careful not to overstate the extent of Eliot's overt claims to a prophetic role. Prufrock, though he has seen his head, like that of the prophet John the Baptist, brought in on a platter, refuses the title: "I am no prophet—and here's no great matter." But later, in *The Waste Land*—in one of the notes, to be sure, not in the text—Eliot does tell us that "Tiresias, although . . . not indeed a 'character,' is the most important personage in the poem. . . . What Tiresias *sees,* in fact, is the substance of the poem." Now Tiresias is a properly certified prophet. Odysseus seeks him out when he visits the land of the dead in order to learn what the future holds for him. When Tiresias appears in *The Waste Land* itself, he says that not only does he know in advance what will occur, but that he also has "foresuffered all."

Tiresias also appears, although his name is not mentioned, in the epigraph that Eliot affixed to *After Strange Gods;* the two and a half lines of Greek verse quoted there are taken from Sophocles' *Oedipus Rex.* They come at the end of a speech made by Tiresias to Oedipus in which Tiresias tells the king, though in somewhat riddling terms, the hideous truth about himself. Tiresias has done so reluctantly and is quite doubtful that he will be believed. Bernard Knox translates the concluding sentence (which Eliot used as his epigraph) thus: "Go think this out, and if you find that I am wrong, then say that I have no skill in prophecy." Though the man who speaks is confident that he tells the truth, he is well aware of how unpalatable that truth will be. I think that this choice of such an epigram is pure Eliot: his old standby Tiresias is brought in again but not named; there is a reference to the play from which the quotation is taken, but the Greek verse is left untranslated. It is a claim to prophecy so modest as to be unnoticeable. Pound didn't call his friend "Old Possum" for nothing.

Yet there is still another way—a more accurate one, I think—of talking about Eliot's prophetic stance. Eliot did not shrink from controversy, and in his essays he was always willing to take a controversial stand. But his poetry was another matter. One remembers his statement to the effect that in prose we express our ideals, but poetry must concern itself with truth. In literature, if points are to be argued they must be discussed by the characters or must take the form of a debate within the heart and soul of one of them: the author must not argue with—or, worse still, make pronouncements at—the reader. The work must be essentially dramatic, not discursive.

With all this in mind, can we fairly say that whatever Eliot's conscious intention, *The Waste Land* is a prophetic poem? I think we can, particularly if we remember what the word originally meant: an utterance of a deep and important truth, often thought of as divinely inspired. The sense of prediction came somewhat later. It is easy to see how important truths about present things often do have predictive merit. In Eliot's poetry there are insights into problems of the age that indeed foreshadow events to come. The poet doesn't set up to be a fortune-teller, but he often records psychic disturbances and changes in the cultural climate that may become serious problems later on.

But in this matter of whether *The Waste Land* is a prophetic document, I shall simply invoke again Eliot's own chosen spokesman, Tiresias: "Go think this out. And if you find that I am wrong, then say that I have no skill in prophecy."

8

Faulkner's Criticism
of Modern America

∾

*F*aulkner did not at all mind speaking out about the world in which he lived. At one time or another he complained of many features of our American lifestyle: of our haste, of our activism—though we all said that we approved of culture, we couldn't find the time to read a book or listen to music or look at a picture—of our commercialism, of business so often pursued merely for the sake of business, of our tendency to reduce nearly all human relations to the cash nexus, of our huckstering salesmanship, and of the value we placed on respectability. One of the characters in *The Wild Palms,* Harry Wilbourne, makes a notable comment on the subject of respectability. He tells a friend that it is idleness that breeds all of America's real virtues, virtues such as "contemplation, equableness, laziness, letting other people alone," whereas it is such prime virtues as thrift and independence that breed all the special modern vices, which are "fanaticism, smugness, meddling, fear, and worst of all, respectability."

Closely allied to this fear of what your neighbors may think of you is something that sounds like its direct opposite: your own nagging desire to know the worst about your neighbor—the wish to find out all about his private life—and a willingness, if necessary, to violate his privacy.

The vices I have named are precisely those that any artist might be expected to reprehend. Artists tend to be unconventional, even bohemian. Naturally, they decry the moral furniture of a typical bourgeois household: a commercial ethic, an urge to keep up with the Joneses, an undue regard for respectability, an itch to pry into our neighbor's private

113

life, and a concern to sell oneself to the public, to have a good "image," rather than to be oneself.

The modern vice that most outraged Faulkner, however, was the violation of one's private life. Its enormity had been brought home to him by attempted violations of his own privacy. These attempts came to a head in 1953 with the publication in *Life* magazine of "The Private World of William Faulkner." Though Faulkner had begged the editors of *Life* to desist, they could not be persuaded to leave him alone. Faulkner took the matter sufficiently to heart to devote to it one of his rare full-dress essays. It bears the title "On Privacy." It constitutes his most elaborate and considered attack on the value system of contemporary America.

In the essay, however, Faulkner undertakes to rise above his personal problem and take a large, overall view. What had happened to him, he tells the reader, was what had also happened on a level of much graver seriousness to more important figures such as, for instance, Charles Lindbergh and J. Robert Oppenheimer. Though the nation had rejoiced in Lindbergh's great achievement, it had not been able to protect his child, and when the child was kidnapped, it had not shielded his grief but had exploited it. Good manners and decency had been engulfed by the urge to make money by pandering to the public's greediness for the sensational.

It is worth noting that Faulkner chose as a subtitle for his essay on privacy "The American Dream: What Happened to It." Our republic had been born out of a dream. It had been founded to guarantee to every citizen freedom from oppression by the arbitrary power of princes, whether of church or state; yet though the nation had been born out of a revolt against one kind of enslavement, it had capitulated to another—the individual's enslavement by a mindless and venal mob. Pushy newspaper men, yellow-press journalism (even when printed on slick paper in a prestigious weekly magazine), political witch-hunting—these, in Faulkner's view, were no mere pimples on the body politic; rather, they evidenced a deep and malignant growth.

With the defeat of the South in 1865, the older regime did not abruptly cease to exist. Attitudes, ways of living, customs, and values survived—some good, some bad. Hence, in Faulkner's novels about southern life in the first third of our century, many of the qualities of the old South are still alive. Miss Jenny Du Pre, who had experienced the Civil War, did not die until 1930, and thus remained to counsel and sometimes judge the twentieth-century members of her clan. Bayard Sartoris, who saw the War as a boy and lived through the difficult Reconstruction period, did not die until 1919. So much for representatives of the old planter stock who lived on into the new time.

As for the poor whites of settlements such as Frenchman's Bend, their lives remained substantially unaltered until after the First World War. They owned no slaves to be freed, and if their economic lot did not suffer drastically because of the outcome of the Civil War, it certainly did not improve. They were small farmers and sawmill hands, and though they would have resented being called peasants, they hardly attained even to the state of a strong yeomanry.

For the blacks and for the poorer whites, the American Dream had remained a largely unfulfilled promise. Southerners in general, even those in better economic circumstances, had intellectual reservations about the American Dream. As C. Vann Woodward has well said: "In that most optimistic of centuries in the most optimistic part of the world, the South remained basically pessimistic in its social outlook and its moral philosophy."

Though the Founding Fathers had looked forward to a radiant future—"Long may our land be bright / With freedom's holy light"—for the South it hadn't quite worked out that way. For Faulkner in 1955, the American dream seemed to risk becoming the American nightmare. Salient features of this worsening condition as reflected in his novels are the loss of the wilderness and man's close contact with nature, the loosening of the bonds of community, the weakening of the old heroic virtues, whether those of the old planter stock or of the yeomanry, and the rise of a nakedly commercial ethic.

In "Delta Autumn," Faulkner's emphasis is on the violation of nature, the reduction of its beauty and mystery to a fixed cash value. In *The Hamlet*, this theme had been developed even further through the activities of the anti-hero of the book, the unspeakable Flem Snopes, chief of that predatory clan whose family name has now entered the language as a common noun meaning an underbred rapacious rascal. Flem Snopes is the poor but dishonest boy who made good in a spectacular rise from rags to riches. No business venture is beneath his notice if it promises to yield a profit. Since he possesses not even a vestigial sense of pity to embarrass him, not even widows and orphans can escape his rapacity. Honor, of course, is irrelevant to Flem, and on him even the ties of blood and kinship exert no restraint. Furthermore, he is a man without appetites or temptations. He lacks such vices as might distract him from moneymaking. He is impotent; he doesn't drink or smoke. His only vice is the love of money. It is a vice, not a passion, for Flem is not a warm-blooded animal. Nothing warmer than plain ice water flows through his veins.

Flem is one of Faulkner's most wonderful creations: an inhuman, human calculating machine—the very embodiment of the commercial spirit. Yet it would be a mistake to conclude that Faulkner as a man scorned money, or that he assumed as a matter of course that all businessmen were rogues. Faulkner has placed, in the same novel with Flem, V. K. Ratliff, the itinerant sewing-machine agent, who loves to bargain, is successful enough as a trader, and takes a heartfelt delight in meeting a foeman worthy of his steel. Ratliff is a man of the plain people, keenly intelligent, for all his lack of formal education. He is an excellent judge of character, has a fine vein of humor, and is a wonderful raconteur. One of the best of his yarns is his hilarious account of how Ab Snopes, Flem's father, was bested in a horse trade by that legendary trader, Pat Stamper of West Tennessee. More important for our purposes here, Ratliff is a man of honor, who would scorn to take advantage of the foolish, the poor, or the helpless. In *The Hamlet* Ratliff becomes something like the conscience of the county.

If Faulkner does not sourly dismiss all businessmen as base and contemptible, neither does he associate a huckstering commercialism with the poorer whites. In fact, Faulkner's most truly evil character, a man so eaten up with the love of money that he will steal from his seventeen-year-old niece, comes of plantation stock. Jason Compson has ancestors who were governors and generals, but he is mean-spirited. He actually enjoys inflicting pain.

The commentators on Faulkner who are in the habit of praising those Faulknerian characters who are willing to repudiate the heritage of the Old South ought to take note of Jason Compson and draw in their horns a bit. For if any character in Faulkner makes a root-and-branch disavowal of his personal and sectional heritage, it is Jason Compson. What, he asks, have his honored ancestors done for him? He is all for a realistic approach to a world in which he has come to believe that only the dollar counts. For Jason, even romantic love is reduced to the cash nexus. He confides that what he really likes is a good, clean, honest whore. With that kind of woman you know where you stand.

About all that Jason retains from his southern heritage is a fine flow of rhetoric, which, hardened and made acrid by his cynicism and urged on by his rapacious vitality, is something to hear. When his employer balks at using some sharp business practices, Jason sneers: "I'm glad I haven't got the sort of conscience I've got to nurse like a sick puppy all the time." Jason knows whereof he speaks: his conscience can digest almost anything.

Faulkner regarded as ominous the rise of the predatory Snopeses who had begun, with the help of such eager recruits to Snopesism as Jason Compson, to prey upon the old order. Faulkner once remarked to Malcolm Cowley that the question for the South was whether the Snopeses would take over the country. Later, he told the students at the University of Virginia that he was "terrified" of the Snopeses. Flem Snopes's lust for money obliterated all claims of family, clan, friendship, honor, and affections of every kind. But ties of this sort may also, of course, be frayed and weakened by other forces, and the loss of these ties—whatever the cause— was to Faulkner the important matter. For with the disappearance of such ties, there is a loss of community, and where community is lost, the individual becomes alienated. In the worst cases, the individual finds himself confronting not other human beings but a great impersonal machine, a faceless and anonymous force.

A few sentences above I have used the term *community*, but what is a community? W. H. Auden has provided us with a helpful definition. It is more than a crowd—a crowd is a group of individuals who come together purely at random. An accident occurs and a crowd gathers, completely heterogeneous human beings, brought together merely by propinquity and curiosity. A community is also more than a society. A society is a group of individuals related by function: so many butchers, so many bakers, so many tailors and candle-stick makers. The individual members in a society find it mutually profitable to live in a relation of symbiosis. But a community is something more than a society: it is a group of people held together by common likes and dislikes, loves and hates held in common, shared values. Where there is a loss of shared values, communities may break down into mere societies or even be reduced to mobs. The loss *is* ominous, for when men cease to love the same things, the culture itself is disintegrating.

The dissolution of community, the loss of the sense of participation in shared beliefs, is a matter of record in this country—and in Western Europe too. Many of the great works of the last fifty years—in fiction and in poetry—have to do with the breakup of an older order and the individual's attempt to deal with a fragmented world. Much of the work of Pound, Joyce, and Eliot, for example, reflects this cultural situation. Robert Penn Warren furnishes a useful summary. He describes the modern world as one of "moral confusion." It suffers "from a lack of discipline, of sanction, of community of values, or a sense of mission. . . . It is a world in which the individual has lost his relation to society, the world of the power state in which man is the victim of abstraction and mechanism, or at least at moments feels himself to be."

Faulkner was quite aware of how some of the great twentieth-century masters had handled the theme of alienation, and he shows his debt to them in such early novels as *Soldiers' Pay* and *Mosquitoes*. But whereas in writers such as Joyce and Eliot the alienated hero usually suffers his frustration in some great world city, Faulkner had, already in his third novel, silhouetted his despairing hero against a background of stability—against a traditional society in a small town in Mississippi—a society that was also an organic community, close-knit, provincial, even parochial. The very fact of its status as a community made its own ironic commentary on the hero's experience of meaninglessness.

One of Faulkner's masterpieces, *Light in August,* will furnish perhaps the clearest illustration of Faulkner's method for treating the alien, the exile, the rootless individual. Joe Christmas begins his conscious life in an orphanage, acquires as foster parents a stern Calvinistic evangelical and his beaten-down and submissive wife, and finally bursts out of this dour household, to try to find out who he is and to what he really belongs.

His various experiences have warped him away from nature, away from womankind, away from any kind of community—even from humanity itself. For example, because of the circumstances of his early childhood, he does not know whether he is white or partially black. He easily passes for white, and there is in fact no decisive evidence in the novel that he has any blood that is not white. But though he has tried to live at one time as a white man and at another time as a black man, he cannot accommodate to either role. In the end, he rejects both. In rejecting both communities, however, he rejects the possibility of ever becoming fully human.

What does Joe Christmas really want? More than once in the closing weeks of his life he remarks that all that he wants "dont seem like a whole lot to ask." Sometimes the desired thing seems to be peace, just to be let be; just not having "to carry my life like it was a basket of eggs." Yet the novel as a whole suggests that what Joe really wanted was something more special and complicated: he wanted to find himself, to be himself, to live his own life without external pressures and restraint.

Yet if complete liberty to be himself is what Joe meant when he re- marked "That dont seem like a whole lot to ask," he had deluded himself. For in our present culture it has proved to be more and more difficult to discover who one is and to fulfill that self in complete freedom. Even men far less handicapped than Christmas have found it so.

A very concise and lucid account of the precise nature of this difficulty is to be found in a long essay by Richard N. Goodwin, entitled "Reflec- tions: The American Condition." Though Mr. Goodwin's "reflections" range over a great number of topics, I shall cite only that portion of his essay that is most pertinent to Faulkner's criticism of the modern world: that is, that in which Goodwin discusses the individual in relation to his community—the individual's freedom considered as an absolute end in itself and freedom as an aspect of the individual's fulfillment of himself.

Goodwin points out that more than one thinker of the nineteenth century saw that "only within a community" could the individual find a social environment in which he could live a fulfilled life. The assertion may strike the ears of some of us as startling, for we all are thoroughly imbued with an ideology which "equates liberty with the absence of all bonds, all commitments, all restraints upon individual action." This ideology, Goodwin says, manifests itself quite clearly in the present-day "dissolution of the human connections traditionally sustained by social institutions such as family, community, common social purpose, and accepted moral authority."

Yet these frequently disparaged institutions of family and community, so Goodwin argues, constitute in fact the very "means by which individuals in society can join to create order and rule themselves." The phrase "rule themselves" is highly important. Lacking a common purpose and shared values, men cannot rule themselves; for when men really have no purposes in common, order is lost and true self-rule is rendered impossible. Individuals freed from *all* ties with their fellows have in common only wants, needs, and appetites. They thus become vulnerable to the pressures of the demagogue, the political manipulator, or the impersonal bureaucracies that today so effectually organize our activities.

In order to illuminate this crucial issue, I want to quote a little further from Goodwin. He insists that the purposes of the true individual are not mere individual preferences and opinions, but purposes which are "consistent with [those] of his fellows. [The true individual] seeks to satisfy his own wants and to cultivate his own faculties in a manner that is consonant with the well-being of others." Goodwin reminds us that Plato, in *The Republic,* asserts that the greatest good is the "bond of unity" in which "there is community of pleasures and pains"—in which "all the citizens are glad or grieved on the same occasions of joy and sorrow."

Goodwin adds his own comment: "Within such a 'bond of unity' the apparent contradiction in our description of freedom is resolved. If one exists as part of an organic community, its wants and necessities are not external [to one's self]. . . . The will of the individual [belonging to such a community] contains the social will, which is, then, an instrument of personal fulfillment rather than of external coercion." In short, true freedom is to be found only in the fulfillment of purposes common to, and shared by, other human beings.

Faulkner's story of Joe Christmas can thus be read as an account of a thoroughly alienated individual, a modern Ishmael who lives in chronic revolt against every kind of community, a man who feels that communal ties are simply shackles on his cherished independence, which is the only thing that gives meaning to his life. Joe's misconceived defense of his freedom turns out to be destructive—most of all to himself. But, of course, Faulkner's *Light in August* is not a political tract, but a study of a human being, in this case a man much more sinned against than sinning; who, if he is sick, has been mortally infected, and through no special fault of his own, with the disease of our times.

Mr. Goodwin's essay not only throws light on the connection of true freedom to the community. He offers a plausible explanation for the problem posed by Faulkner in his essay "On Privacy." There, as I have observed earlier, Faulkner remarks on the irony of the fact that, though the American nation had been created out of a desire to guarantee to every citizen freedom from the encroachments of arbitrary power, that very liberty had, in the course of two centuries, somehow led to the destruction of the inner core of man's liberty. "The American air," Faulkner there wrote, "which was once the living breath of liberty," has "now become one vast down-crowding pressure to abolish [freedom], by destroying man's individuality. . . ."

Faulkner's point is uncannily close to Goodwin's. Here is Goodwin: ". . . the ideology of individualism is [today] so powerful that we still look on bonds as restraints; on values as opinions or prejudices; on customs as impositions. The remaining structures of shared experience—the ties that make it possible for people to live with and through, and not merely alongside, one another—are assaulted as unjust obstacles in the way of liberty, as impediments to the free assertions of the self." Thus, Goodwin concludes, the "new consciousness" associated with the revolt against the old tyrannies of church and state "now inevitably becomes the enemy of human freedom." To sum up: the individual's attempt to throw off every kind of restraint has developed through a logic of its own from a liberating to a destructive force which, by dissolving the community, has left the individual alienated and robbed of his humanity.

Were Faulkner alive, he might very well have accepted Goodwin's essay as a detailed explanation of the question asked by the subtitle of his own essay "On Privacy." The subtitle, one remembers, reads "The American Dream: What Happened to It?"

Conversely, Mr. Goodwin might have very appropriately used Faulkner's subtitle as the subtitle of his own essay, for, like Faulkner's, his essay is an attempt to explain what went wrong with the American dream. Goodwin traces the rise of individualism not merely, as Faulkner does, back to the days of America's Founding Fathers in the late eighteenth century, but to the late Middle Ages. Thus, Goodwin's analysis will throw additional light on Faulkner's account of what happened to the American dream. In the Middle Ages, as Goodwin points out, the cash nexus scarcely existed. Medieval society was essentially a barter society. Men paid in kind or in service what they owed to their superiors. Cash settlements came later, only toward the breakup of the Middle Ages, and along with the rise of a middle class. The expansion of trade and the use of money payments brought to medieval society a welcome liberation, and with the development of better techniques in agriculture and manufactures, brought also a higher standard of living. But one has to set down on the debit side of the ledger facts such as these: there was a shift away from personal and concrete obligations to more abstract relations, those typically represented by money settlements. In the twentieth-century world, this development has gone so far that the individual frequently feels that he no longer has any personal relation to his employer nor any communication with him except through the computer. The loss of concrete and personal relationships, whatever the compensations gained elsewhere, is a genuine loss. As Goodwin sums up: "We citizens of the advanced-industrial, space-age West . . . live under the domination of an individualism whose conquest has been so thorough that it has torn the thread of individual life from the fabric of humanity. . . . The new consciousness through which the Renaissance attacked the injustices, the stagnation, and the material misery of the Middle Ages now, inevitably, suffocates human freedom."

The culture of the old South stands in sharp contrast to this new consciousness. Though the Old South was not medieval, it was a society based on the land; it was paternalistic, and if not a society at the barter level, certainly one that lagged far behind the economic development of Western Europe and of the northeastern states of America. Life on the southern frontier—and nearly everywhere else in the South after its defeat in the Civil War—was poor, provincial, pinched, and harsh. Yet it fostered highly concrete and personal relationships. If, for instance, you injured someone, it was hard to conceal from yourself the fact that you had done so. If you exploited a person, the fact of exploitation was quite naked. A slave was actually called a slave. A man's de facto wage-slavery was not, as so frequently in Victorian England and nineteenth-century New England, denied under the pretense that the person exploited was a free citizen who had the right to change his job and might do so if he found that he was unhappy with the bargain he had made.

It is small wonder, then, that Faulkner, writing out of this land-based, paternalistic, backward-looking, highly conservative society, should have possessed a special sensitivity to such matters as the dissolution of the old personal and concrete relationships, the shift to the cash nexus, the pressure of purely economic considerations, and the increasing stress on selling yourself to your boss or to the public, rather than simply being yourself. Eugene Genovese's *The World the Slaveholders Made* and *The Political Economy of Slavery* provide a massive documentation of the strength and pervasive character of paternalism in the Old South.

The abstract quality of space-age America goes back, however, to the very beginnings of the republic. Goodwin points out that our Founding Fathers took the "models" for their idea of the new nation from "centuries past"—such as the Republic of Rome or from the ideological constructions of eighteenth-century thinkers, particularly those of France and England. "To be French or British," Goodwin says, "or Chinese or Egyptian is to be part of a cluster of events and beliefs transmitted across centuries. The American idea [on the other hand] could not be formed from such continuity. . . . [We Americans] could form a stabilizing association only with an idea derived from national character and direction. . . . [Our] national idea differed from that of other nations in a crucial quality: It had to be constantly renewed, always made contemporary." It had to be constantly renewed because it was not the product of history and lived experience, but the reflex of an abstract idea that one must prove over and over if it is to be kept viable and relevant.

The American national idea so described differs markedly from the southerner's idea of the South. For the southern idea of itself is—or at least was yesterday—firmly anchored in history. It had grown out of experiences endured by the region as a whole, and it reflects memories of guilt, loss, and defeat, and not merely bright promises for the future. It has the emotional force of lived experience as distinguished from an abstract ideal to which one simply aspires. Not surprisingly, the world reflected in Faulkner's novels is drenched in history; it is knit together by a sense of community, and almost instinctively moves to resist whatever it regards as pressure from the world outside itself.

This is not at all to say that Faulkner judges his southern world to be perfect. As a man and as an artist, Faulkner has been very sharp on his region's faults. My argument is simply that his native region has provided him with a point of vantage from which to assess the characteristic failures of modernity.

Goodwin's essential confirmation of Faulkner's criticism of the modern world is highly pertinent to the matter of Faulkner's credibility. For Goodwin's indictment can hardly be dismissed as the peevish grumbling of a mere novelist, or the prejudices of a north Mississippi squire, whose ancestors were slaveholders. Goodwin is a Bostonian, a summa cum laude graduate of the Harvard law school, and an adviser and speechwriter for the late President Kennedy.

Some might feel that Goodwin's essay is powerful to Faulkner's hurt. For, set beside his masterful discussion, Faulkner's most considered essay on the subject is likely to appear awkward and fumbling. "On Privacy" is highly personal and almost turgidly concrete. But to put Faulkner's essay into competition with Goodwin's "Reflections" would be to miss the point entirely. Lucid exposition is Goodwin's métier. Faulkner's true métier is fiction.

Every great novelist has his wisdom, but he imparts it in his own mode. He doesn't make statements and offer arguments. He dramatizes fictional characters. His judgments are normally implicit, not explicit. But they engage human interest in a way in which the abstract statements of the political scientist never can. They make their appeal to the imagination. They carry dramatic force.

The work of the great literary artist, as a matter of fact, has never been more necessary than now. In a world which increasingly resembles the innards of a vast IBM machine, a world in which the human integers are likely to feel themselves dehumanized and left at the mercy of forces which, even when benign, are impersonal, we need the rich particularity and the imaginative reach of the literary artist. What he gives us is not life itself, but perhaps the next best thing to life itself: a simulacrum of life that helps us to come to terms with ourselves, to understand our history, and to get a firmer grasp on reality and truth.

I use the word *truth* advisedly, for by truth Faulkner did not mean statistical averages or graphs showing the growth of the gross national product. One of his characters in "The Bear" says to his younger kinsman: "Truth is one. It doesn't change. It covers all things which touch the heart—honor and pride and pity and justice and courage and love. . . . They all touch the heart and what the heart holds to becomes the truth, as far as we know truth."

This is the passage that Faulkner, years later, was to echo in his Nobel Prize acceptance speech, but one remembers that Wordsworth and Keats also speak of truth in almost the same terms.

Yet note that Faulkner writes: "What the heart holds to becomes truth, *as far as we know truth.*" That last proviso is all important. The truth that the artist is concerned with is always truth accommodated to the human heart, truth, not about mathematical equations or the stellar galaxies, but about the human being, his limitations and his capacities. It is for such truth that we go to the great artist, and at his best, Faulkner is a very great artist indeed.

9

Episode and Anecdote in
the Poetry of Robert Penn Warren

∽

*T*he central theme of Robert Penn Warren's poetry can better be designated as a fascicle of closely related themes: time, history, and human
identity. To elaborate a bit: Time is continuity but is also change. History,
written or remembered, is a record of the stream of time running
through humanity. Identity is consciousness, not merely of time and
change and history, but the consciousness of one's own history and of
one's self. The self is, of course, the very seat of consciousness.

From the beginning, this bundle of themes has been present in Warren's poems. It is very clearly apparent in "Speleology," the second poem
of his volume *Being Here*. We would do the poem and the poet wrong by
saying that this cluster of themes was "stated" there, for Warren rarely, if
ever, flattens the theme of a poem into a mere statement; on the contrary,
his habit is to render it or dramatize, or, if I am to describe the process in
more detail, to say what he wants to say through concrete images.

"Speleology" represents with beautiful concision Warren's whole cluster of themes. Like so many of his poems, this one developed, I suppose,
from an incident in Warren's own boyhood. At six, the boy discovers the
mouth of a cave. Having become more daring when he reaches the age of
twelve, he ventures into the cave. Besides, he now has a flashlight. Having
got far into the cave, he turns off his flashlight in order to experience
what it feels like to be enveloped in absolute darkness. In that darkness he
listens to the music of an underground river that flows below the ledge on
which he rests.

I shall quote the final stanzas of the poem:

Lulled as by song in a dream, knowing
I dared not move in a darkness so absolute.
I thought: *This is me.* Thought: *Me—who am I?* Felt
Heart beating as though to a pulse of darkness and earth, and thought
How would it be to be here forever, my heart,

In its beat, part of all. Part of all—
But I woke with a scream. The flashlight,
It slipped, but I grabbed it. Had light—
And once more looked down the deep slicing and sluicing
Of limestone where water winked, bubbles like fish-eyes, a song like terror.

Years later, past dreams, I have lain
In darkness and heard the depth of that unending song.
And hand laid to heart, have once again thought: *This is me.*
And thought: *Who am I?* And hand on heart, wondered
What would it be like to be, in the end, part of all.

And in darkness have even asked: *Is this all? What is all?*

The absolute dark, by enveloping and isolating the boy, gives him the feeling that he is the only living thing in this world of darkness, and so forces upon him the problem of his identity as a separate being. "Who am I," he asks himself, and by voicing this question, raises the further question of his relation to the world about him, for his steadily beating heart seems to be all that is alive—all that even has existence. The rest is void and emptiness.

Then comes the near loss of his flashlight and the moment of terror followed by the recovery of the light and his peering at the underground stream that runs below him—"where water winked, bubbles like fish-eyes, a song like terror."

Immemorially, time has been conceived as a flowing stream. One remembers, among others, the underground stream in Wordsworth's poem "Yew Trees" and, in Coleridge's "Kubla Khan," the river that runs "Through caverns measureless to man / Down to a sunless sea." The song sung by Warren's underground stream has at first lulled the boy into a kind of slumbrous reverie, but then, between the loss of his flashlight and his retrieval of it, what the stream sings changes to "a song like terror."

Why? Because the human being who can regard time as a river knows also that his life is actually a part of that river and that like one of the winking bubbles on its surface, his identity as a separate thing lasts only for a moment, since, bubble that he is, he too will quickly disappear as a separable thing and will simply lose himself in the general stream. The awful possibility may be that all human history is a rushing stream out of which individual human beings seem to arise but back into which they quickly disappear. "What would it be like to be, in the end, [simply] part of all?" In darkness he has "even asked: *Is this all? What is all?*"

In Warren's poetry, this theme of the human heart confronting time and history is dealt with in a great variety of ways. One way takes the form of meditative verse, and Warren has written, particularly in the last decade or so, a great deal of very fine poetry of this kind. But he has always had another favorite mode of presentation: presentation through an anecdote, an incident, a little story. Indeed, Warren has several times used the words "a short story" as a subtitle for a poem.

I do not want to imply that these meditative and anecdotal modes are sharply separate. They are not. The lyric "Speleology" that I have just discussed really combines the two modes—thus, the memory of a boyhood incident provokes in the grown man, long afterward, a meditation on the meaning of life.

Since, however, in any discussion of reasonable length one cannot treat the whole rich body of this poet's work, one has to make a selection. Because I have always been taken by the poems that provide an anecdote or tell a story, I have chosen, in this instance, to write about them. Most of these poems crackle with such intensity that we believe in them and this belief gives point to the poet's comments, observations, and the questions that seem to arise out of the incident he relates.

One of my own favorites has a truly sesquipedalian title, which reads "Old Nigger on One-Mule Cart Encountered Late at Night When Driving Home from Party in the Back Country."

If you have read the title slowly enough to take it in, then you already have a summary of the narrative that the poem embodies. But of course, any summary leaves out the vivid detail that gives conviction to the episode. For instance, the description of an unpaved country road in Louisiana on a hot July night:

Night is. No moon, but stars whitely outrageous in
Blackness of velvet, the long lane ahead

Whiter than snow, wheels soundless in deep dust, dust
Pluming whitely behind, and ahead all
The laneside hedges and weed-growth
Long since powdered whiter than star-dust, or frost, but air
Hot.

The man who speaks this poem was, at the time of the incident he recounts, more than a little drunk, and he was driving much too fast. Moreover, the old black man on the cart whom he encounters was clearly on the wrong side of the road. What the automobile headlights suddenly reveal just ahead is the mule's head, which seems to thrust at the car, a head with eyes that seem to "blaze from the incandescent magma / Of mule brain." Then the driver sees also the old black man's eyes,

Man-eyes, not blazing, white-bulging
In black face, in black night, and man-mouth
Wide open, the shape of an *O*, for the scream
That does not come.

By wrenching his car to the left, taking the ditch, which is luckily, or providentially, shallow, the driver swerves around the junk-laden cart, recovers the road, gets home safely, and eventually to bed. But later that night he wakes and attempts a sonnet on his near brush with death. It must have been a Shakespearean sonnet, for it ended in a couplet, and this couplet is all that the driver can now remember. The couplet refers to the old black man on the mule cart as

One of those who gather junk and wire to use
For purposes that we cannot peruse.

Clearly, on this night the driver has proved much more adept with the steering wheel than with the pen. He knows it, and abandons the would-be poem.

Abandon the sonnet he can, but the memory of the incident does not abandon him. For, years later, in a cold climate and in a higher latitude— forty years later in Connecticut, I would say—that night of near calamity comes back to him, and this time he has a vision of the old man's return to his shack of a home.

> . . . I see,
> By a bare field that yearns pale in starlight, the askew
> Shack. He arrives there. Unhitches the mule.
> Stakes it out. Between cart and shack,
> Pauses to make water, and while
> The soft plopping sound in deep dust continues, his face
> Is lifted into starlight, calm as prayer. He enters
> The dark shack, and I see
> A match spurt, then burn down, die.

Is what the speaker sees here in his mind's eye what really happened on that night long ago? Or is it merely what he wants to believe happened— or is he somehow compelled to believe that such occurred: that when the old man got home he quietly resumed the routine of his shabby and constricted life and then prepared to go to bed just as he would have on any other night, not shaking with terror or stunned and numbed. Whether or not he actually uttered a prayer, the poet imagines that his act of lifting his face to the stars was as "calm as prayer."

Has the poet meant to suggest that the old black man is a stoic, inured to hardship and difficulty, and so not to be unduly shaken by even a brush with death? Or does he in his imagination see him as a devout Christian who is steadied by his trust that he is in the hand of God? The two conjectures that I have offered may (though they may not) help account for the lines in which the driver who nearly killed the old man now addresses him:

> And so I say:
> Brother, Rebuker, my Philosopher past all
> Casuistry, will you be with me when

I come to the end of my journey? The speaker does not specify where the end of his journey will occur. He simply asks

> . . . will you be with me when
> I arrive and leave my own cart of junk
> Unfended from the storm of starlight and
> The howl, like wind, of the world's monstrous blessedness,
> To enter, by a bare field, a shack unlit?

Entering into that darkness to fumble
My way to a place to lie down. . . .

We English professors, always looking for literary analogies—after all,
we make our livings that way—may see a likeness between Warren's old
man on the junk cart and the old leech gatherer of Wordsworth's poem
"Resolution and Independence." Both old men are homespun philosophers who have won to a truth to which the poet would like to attain.
Both serve in their resolute calm to quiet the anxieties of the two very
different poets who write about them. Maybe there is an analogy. But if
so, I must say, at the risk of irreverence, that I think I prefer Warren's
image to Wordsworth's.

At any rate, Warren's poem ends with an expression of hope that when
the man who speaks this poem at last enters his own dark shack, which I
have suggested may be his grave, he will go into it clutching in his hand,
as the poet puts it,

A hard-won something that may, while Time
Backward unblooms out of time toward peace, utter
Its small, sober, and inestimable
Glow, trophy of truth.

Can I see Arcturus from where I stand?

The final line may be puzzling. What is the relation of this last question
to the rest of the poem? Well, let's look back at the poem as a whole. It is
suffused with starlight. Early in the poem, the poet described the July
night in Louisiana as a night of no moon but of "stars whitely outrageous
in / Blackness of velvet." The accident that so nearly occurs is "under the
high stars." He imagines the old man, after he has unhitched his mule,
lifting his face "into starlight." And toward the end of the poem, the poet
imagines himself at his final arriving place as vulnerable to the stars—
"Unfended from the storm of starlight."

In Warren's poetry the stars often typify a universe that is, if not
actually hostile to man, at all events utterly indifferent to him. The stars
look down upon us from some more than Olympian height, and, as
Tennyson once described the gods of ancient Greece, sitting together on
their sacred mountain, "Careless of mankind."

The stars have a further significance: as the great constellations wheel around the earth through the course of the year, the twelve that make up the Zodiac amount to a celestial clock that measures off the months of each successive year. The stars carry with them the threat of time—though they themselves seem eternal and impervious to time.

What is this truth to which the poet implies the old junkman philosopher has won? A sense that all of us, even the humblest, live in God's all-seeing eye? And under His Providence? A consciousness that he has been saved from sudden death by that "amazing grace" vouchsafed even to the wretched—the grace of which he has doubtless often sung in church, the grace that "saved a wretch like me"? Or is his truth a stoic acceptance of a fate that sometimes destroys us almost haphazardly and yet sometimes unaccountably snatches us from destruction? Or is the old black man's truth a renewed sense of the joy of just finding himself still alive, a joy that the poet has called a few lines earlier the "world's monstrous blessedness"?

The poet doesn't say what the junkman's hard-won truth is. He leaves it up to the reader to imagine what such a truth might be. In any case, what will his own truth be, that truth that he hopes to possess at life's end? Again, we aren't told. But the poem as a whole suggests that it might well be a glimpse into life's meaning—a partial glimpse into the rich depths of human experience. If so, perhaps the beautiful last line, "Can I see Arcturus from where I stand?" might seem to underscore the point. The stars, as we have seen, dominate the poem, but this is the first time the poet has singled out one star, referring to it by name. The line might seem to ask: Can I, a mortal man, immersed in the human condition with the stringent limits that condition imposes on all human creatures—can I recognize from my poor vantage point and call by name even one particular star of the remote host that look down on us and seem to partake of the permanence of final reality?

Frankly, I have little confidence in this interpretation. Warren's final line sounds right. I'm sure of that. But I am not at all sure that I have grasped fully what it means.

Upon an earlier reading I was quite confident that I did know precisely what it meant. I took Arcturus to be the polestar. That seemed to me to make a lot of sense. The starry constellations in their apparent revolutions about the earth number man's days. Of all stars, only one, the polestar, is fixed. For the poet to ask whether he could see it would be a way of asking: Can I, condemned to the glittering flux and flotsam of mortality, ever be vouchsafed even a glimpse of that true symbol of eternity—that star around which all others move in celestial dance?

But the polestar, of course, is not Arcturus, but Polaris. Arcturus, though one of the brightest beacons of the northern skies, itself revolves around the polestar. I had been confused. Had Warren too confused the stars? If so, what a neat solution that would provide for my problem!

All of which reminds me of Richard Bentley, the great classical scholar of the eighteenth century at Cambridge University. Among other works, he produced a famous, or rather, an infamous, edition of Milton's *Paradise Lost,* in which he corrected Milton's fancied mistakes, right and left. Bentley didn't hesitate to substitute a word of his own devising for Milton's. After all, he argued, Milton was blind and couldn't oversee the proofreading of his great poem. He seems to have harbored no doubt that his own imagination was as good as Milton's and that his judgment was probably better.

I shall not follow Bentley's example by striking out Arcturus and writing Polaris in its place. Mr. Peter Davison has pointed out to me that the reference to Arcturus probably goes back to the Book of Job. In chapter 9, verse 9, we read "[The Lord] Which maketh Arcturus, Orion, and Pleiades and the chambers of the south." In chapter 38, verses 31–32, God, speaking out of the whirlwind, asks Job,

> Canst thou bind the sweet influences of Pleiades or loose the bands of Orion?
> Canst thou bring forth Mazzaroth in his season? Or canst thou guide Arcturus with his sons?

The general sense of these magnificent passages is clear enough, but it may be impossible to determine the exact meaning of Mazzaroth or Arcturus. One opinion is that Mazzaroth may be the constellation of Corona Borealis but just possibly the whole band of the twelve constellations that make up the Zodiac. There seems to be quite as much doubt about Arcturus. It is unlikely that the author of Job was referring to the modern identification, which is the brightest star of the constellation Boötes.

The scholars think it is more likely that the Arcturus of Job is the constellation of Ursa Major, the Great Bear. In contrast to the King James version quoted above, the Revised Version reads ". . . guide the Bear with his train." But other scholars argue that the star Aldebaran is meant. (Its "sons" or "train" would be the nearby smaller stars that make up the constellation of Hyades.)

The important matter here is not, I believe, a specific constellation or single star, but the Job echo in itself. For the plight of modern man as he tries to discover some human meaning in a universe that is at once beautiful, terrifying, almost infinitely remote, and awesomely majestic is not unlike Job's. The man who drove the speeding car and the old man on the junk cart are not only brothers of each other but brothers also of the great poet who wrote the Book of Job. Whatever the star, then, "Can I see Arcturus from where I stand?" provides a fine concluding line, and I am well content with this splendid poem as I find it printed.

The next poem that I shall take up is entitled "Ballad: Between the Boxcars." With this poem, by the way, I have much more confidence in my sense of what the poem means. A ballad has been aptly described as a song that tells a story. That's what this ballad does, and it is another of Warren's poems based on an anecdote or incident.

The first section of the poem is entitled "I Can't Even Remember the Name." The person whose name the poet can't remember is a fifteen-year-old boy who has been killed while trying to hop a ride on a freight train as it hurries through a little Kentucky town. In this first section we get an almost technical account of how to hop a fast freight: what to do and what not to do. The emphatic rhythm, the insistent rhyming on one monosyllable, and the steady repetition of *boxcars*—all these give the poem the very special character it has: a masterpiece of a roaring, stomping ballad. Space, however, will allow me to quote only the last two stanzas of the first section.

> He was fifteen and old enough to know perfectly well
> You go for the grip at the front, not the back, of the boxcars,

But he was the kind of smart aleck you always can tell
Will end flat on his ass, on the cinders, between the boxcars.

Suppose I remembered his name, then what the hell
Good would it do him now between the boxcars?
But it might mean something to me if I could tell
You the name of the one who fell between the boxcars.

In sum, this poem is about an event that might seem devoid of any significance—just the story of a senseless, meaningless death.

In the second section of the poem, which is entitled "He Was Formidable," the poet imagines some of the things which the boy might have become, had he lived. Since he was apparently formidable as a baseball player, even at fifteen, the poet imagines him as a hard-hitting player on a major league team:

So we dreamed of an afternoon to come,
In the Series, the ninth-inning hush, in the Yankee Stadium,
Sun low, score tied, bases full, two out, and he'd waltz to the plate
    with his grin—
But no, oh no, not now, not ever! for in
That umpireless rhubarb and steel-heeled hugger-mugger,
    He got spiked sliding home, got spiked between the boxcars.

Then the poet's fantasy of the might-have-beens takes a much more sober turn. The boy might have become manager of

        . . . the best supermarket in town,
Bright with banners and chrome, where housewives push carts up
    and down . . .

He might thus have inherited all the trappings of a solid, though modest, middle-class success, walking

. . . the street with his credit A-rated and blood pressure right,
His boy a dentist in Nashville, his girl at State Normal . . .

And the poet's fancy goes on to explore still other possibilities. The boy might have become—these things do happen—a celebrated scientist or a famous soldier: as scientist, a man

> . . . flushed with *Time*-cover renown
> For vaccine, or bomb, or smog removal . . .

The soldier,

> . . . a hero with phiz like hewn cedar, though young for the
> stars of a general . . .
> But no, never now!—battle cunning, the test tube, retailing,
> All, all, in a helter-skeltering mishmash thrown
> To that clobber and grind, too soon, between the boxcars.

Yet, the voice of the poet asks, suppose the boy had grown up and won fame. What, after all, is fame?

> . . . what is success, or failure, at the last?
> The newspaper whirled down the track when the through freight
> has passed
> Will sink from that gust
> To be of such value as it intrinsically must . . .

And what is that value? The value of any other dirty scrap of paper set afloat for a moment by the rush of air as the fast-freight of history hurtles past. The scrap of paper floats in the air for a moment and then sinks from sight.

The image presented here is a kind of masterstroke. Even now in our television age, fame is still associated with the printed word—one's picture on the cover of *Time* magazine, or one's profile printed less garishly in *The New Yorker,* or even the headline on the front page of a big-city daily. Moreover, history can plausibly be likened to the locomotive with its train of cars rushing out of the past into the future. How heedless it sometimes seems; how ruthless as it speeds along; how rapidly it moves. If a foolhardy youth tries to play with it as did the one whose name the poet cannot remember, it crunches him to bits without even pausing.

When I lived in a little west-Tennessee town as a boy I remember well how the fast trains roared through our town—only locals stopped at our tiny station—and I also remember the swirl of dust and blown papers that hovered for a moment in the wake of the fleeting caboose of the freight or of the observation car of the Pullman. I have no doubt that Warren is here remembering comparable scenes from his early days in Guthrie, Kentucky, and may indeed be remembering an actual death of the sort that his poem narrates.

The poem ends, not with a moral or even an observation, but with a question about the meaning of man's life in view of the apparently meaningless deaths all about us. Here are the last eight lines of the poem:

> And why should we grieve for the name that boy might have made
> To be printed on newsprint like that, for that blast
> To whirl with the wheels' fanfaronade,
> When we cannot even remember his name, nor humbly have prayed
> That when that blunt grossness, slam-banging, bang-slamming,
>   blots black the last blue flash of sky,
> And our own lips utter the crazed organism's cry,
> We may know the poor self not alone, but with all who are cast
>   To that clobber, and slobber, and scream, between the boxcars?

One should call attention to the brilliant play on the word *name*. Why should one grieve for "the name" that the boy might have won had he lived—that is, a "name" on the lips of the public—when the name that his parents, in their hope, once gave him is already forgotten? The dead boy is indeed one of the "nameless" ones—the anonymous little people of the world. Yet, whether we know his name or not, the poet indicates, we can grieve for him, for the good reason that we can see ourselves in him—we ourselves share in his cockiness and his follies just as he shares in our own humiliations and stunning defeats. The boxcars between which we fall may not be the literal ones that crushed him—nevertheless, we ought to be able to sympathize when that "blunt grossness," whatever its specific character, comes slam-banging, bang-slamming, to blot out for ourselves "the last blue flash of sky, / And our own lips utter the crazed organism's cry." In that moment, the poet asks, may we "know the poor self not alone, but with all who are cast / To that clobber, and slobber, and scream, between the boxcars."

In "Old Nigger on One-Mule Cart," Warren has his speaker finally address the aged man who came so close to being killed as "Brother," "Rebuker," and finally as "Philosopher." The last two terms could hardly be applied to the fifteen-year-old who met his death between the boxcars, but as we have just seen, the term *brother* is clearly implied. Truly, the brotherhood of mortals who come to grief is large: it takes in most of us. The poet may not be able to remember this victim's name, but nevertheless he acknowledges his spiritual kinship.

If "Old Nigger on One-Mule Cart" suggests that in the "lyrical logic and nightmare" of events, one may, after all, make out some pattern—not be forced to see what happens to human beings as unintelligible and without meaning—the "Ballad" goes no further than to raise the question of *Why*. No answer is suggested.

Such is the nature of a great deal of Warren's poetry. His little histories and anecdotes are never merely cautionary—warning us not to hop freight trains—nor are his little histories flattened into moralizations or generalizations; most frequently they simply put the question. Yet how forcefully they put it, and how important and how rich in their implications are such questions as Warren presents them. The difficulty in finding an answer to them becomes the very stuff of the poem, and the fact that each of us has to ask them of himself lights up the nature of human consciousness. By being compelled to confront these questions, we learn what we are.

One of Warren's finest poems on the quest for truth is an anecdotal poem entitled "Dragon Country." It is a remarkable yarn about a dragon that has taken up residence in, of all places, the state of Kentucky. Of course, everybody knows that dragons don't really exist, and so the inhabitants stoutly deny—in spite of evidence—that a dragon is making his raids on man and beast. Such an evil is too awful to exist. Every instinct demands that one say that it just couldn't be.

Warren as a poet faces this problem on another level—the technical level of making the impossible seem plausible. How can he make the presence of this dragon credible to the skeptical twentieth-century reader? Warren solves this problem brilliantly, for he is able to make the fabulous monster become convincingly alive. I'll give some examples.

When Jack Simms reported "What something had done to his hogpen /
They called him a God-damn liar." But then, having taken a look, they
opined that it was a bear, though no bear had been seen in the county for
fifty years. In any case, the scene at the hogpen, "With fence rails, like
matchwood, splintered, and earth a bloody mire," would indicate that it
had to be a truly enormous bear—a Kodiak grizzly, at the least. Later, a
wagon driver and his team fall victim to some horrible encounter. The
"wagon turned on its side" is found in the woods

> Mules torn from trace chains, and you saw how the harness had burst.
> Spectators averted the face from the spot where the teamster had died.

Descriptions of this sort almost make you a believer. The poem reminds
me of what Samuel Taylor Coleridge said about his share in the celebrated
volume, the *Lyrical Ballads*, written by himself and Wordsworth. Wordsworth's task was essentially that of making the ordinary and commonplace seem fresh and new, whereas Coleridge was to attempt just the
opposite: he was to take the marvelous and even supernatural, and endow
it with circumstantiality and a sense of reality. It is Coleridge's task that
Warren performs so convincingly in this poem.

Since Kentucky has a live hunting tradition, the citizens of Todd County
form big hunting parties and courageously set out to find the monster
and kill it. But what could they do when, after following the trail of
ruined fence and broken brush, they would always come to a place

> With weed unbent and leaf calm—[where] nothing, nothing was there.
> So what, in God's name, could men think when they couldn't bring to bay
> That belly-dragging earth-evil, but found that it took to air?

This dragon was evidently of the orthodox medieval kind, with great
leathern wings that allowed it to take off like a helicopter.

In time, things became desperate. The governor was asked to call out
the National Guard.

> We were promised troops, the Guard, but the Governor's skin got thin
> When up in New York the papers called him Saint George of Kentucky.

Yes, even the Louisville reporters who came to Todd County would grin.
Reporters, though rarely, still come. No one talks. They think it unlucky.

Finally, people sink into an apathetic despair. They refuse to talk about the depredations. If a man disappears, people simply say that he has taken a job out of the state. When Jebb Johnson's boot was found with part of his leg still inside it, Jebb's own mother denied that the boot was his. This is the state of affairs as the poem concludes, and the man who tells the story ends his account as follows:

Yes, other sections have problems somewhat different from ours.
Their crops may fail, bank rates rise, loans at rumor of war be called,
But we feel removed from maneuvers of Russia, or other great powers,
And from much ordinary hope we are now disenthralled.

The Catholics have sent in a mission. Baptists report new attendance.
But all that's off the point! We are human, and the human heart
Demands language for reality that has not the slightest dependence
On desire, or need—and in church fools pray only that the Beast depart.

But if the Beast were withdrawn now, life might dwindle again
To the ennui, the pleasure, and the night sweat, known in the
    time before
Necessity of truth had trodden the land, and our hearts, to pain,
And left, in darkness, the fearful glimmer of joy, like a spoor.

The next-to-last stanza may give some trouble. One thing that the poet (and his mouthpiece, the narrator of the poem) wants to be careful to disown is the cliché that there are no atheists in foxholes. Maybe there are not, but his point goes wider and deeper than that. What the poem is saying is that the human heart finally entertains a disinterested desire to know the truth about reality. Man doesn't want to accept a view of life simply because he is scared into it or because he feels that his needs demand that he hold it. Most of us, at our best, at least, entertain a disinterested wish to know the truth simply because it is the truth.

Why does the narrator of the poem go on to say that "in church fools pray only that the Beast depart"? It's not that he is blaming them because they, quite humanly, want evil to depart. Wouldn't we in 1981 like to see the Russian threat, inflation, and coronary thrombosis all simply depart? But if men pray only for a removal of the danger, they have missed the point. If dragons do exist, if the possibility of evil is part of our humanity, it's not enough just to want it somehow to go away. We'd better pray for a deeper knowledge of reality and of ourselves so that we may better stand up to evil like men and deal with it out of that knowledge.

The last stanza may be the most difficult of all: I interpret it to say that if the possibility of falling into evil is a condition of our humanity—of our freedom to choose between good and evil (which will depend, of course, upon our ability to make a true distinction between them)—then to acknowledge that the dragon of evil exists may be useful to us if we value truth and seriously dedicate ourselves to finding it. If evil does exist, to deny that it does is not going to be helpful to anybody.

Please allow me to try to restate this matter once more—in fairness to myself, but even more important, in fairness to the poet. The poet is not saying how lucky for these plucky Kentuckians to live in the dragon's country because the threat makes for a morally bracing atmosphere. Warren is no Manichaean who accepts with complacency evil as a necessary part of life. What he is saying is his own version of the Scriptural admonition urging us to know the truth because knowledge of the truth can set us free. So, let me attempt a paraphrase of the poem's concluding lines. The fact that the necessity of truth has trodden the land constitutes a good, for if our hearts have been trodden to pain, there has also been left in them, darkened though they be, "the fearful glimmer of joy." The implication is that truth is so precious that without knowledge of it— even of a fearful truth—we cannot hope to attain authentic joy.

Remember the lines from the poem "Old Nigger on One-Mule Cart," where the poet hopes that by the time he comes to his final resting place he may possess

A hard-won something that may . . .
                          . . . utter
Its small, sober, and inestimable
Glow, trophy of truth.

That "glow of truth" has been lighted from the same fire as the "fearful glimmer of joy" to which the poet refers in the last line of "Dragon Country." Yet, perhaps Warren has put his point most clearly of all in a fine phrase that I take from one of his longer poems—"experience redeemed into knowledge." Knowledge, for Warren, is redemptive, and it is the necessary condition of the attainment of any meaningful joy.

10

John Crowe Ransom

As I Remember Him

$\mathcal{E}$very poet to some degree reveals himself in his poetry, from the most frantic "confessional" poet who makes it a point of honor to tell all, on to the most reserved of our classical poets who prefer to keep their personal affairs to themselves. John Crowe Ransom was not interested in providing confessions, but three of his poems in particular served to make revelations of his personal life. "Tom, Tom the Piper's Son" is a good example. (I quote here the original title and text, which I prefer to the new title and revised text that he printed in his *Selected Poems* in 1974.)

> Grim in my little black coat as the sleazy beetle,
> And gone of hue,
> Lonely, a man reputed for softening little,
> Loving few—
>
> Mournfully going where men assemble, unfriended, pushing
> With laborious wares,
> And glaring with little grey eyes at whom I am brushing,
> Who would with theirs—
>
> Full of my thoughts as I trudge here and trundle yonder,
> Eyes on the ground
> Tricked by white birds or tall women into no wonder,
> And no sound—

Even here the "confession" is that he has gained the reputation of keeping his own counsel. As the poem develops we find that this grim little man who seems almost conscientiously nondescript is actually ambitious, proud, and passionate, and the poem thus quickly develops into a fresh and sharply featured descant on the irony of outward appearance masking inner reality, and so applies to many of us. But I am interested here in the way in which the poet in a mood of ironic self-deprecation sets forth the way in which he feels he must appear to the world around him: the little glaring grey eyes, the sense of being the withdrawn and reticent man, the born loner, inattentive of others, a man whose emotions are bottled up inside him, a little scuttling beetle of a man.

The poem is a caricature of the small, stocky (though not pudgy), trim gentleman that Ransom was, but caricatures in their overstatement do convey some positive truths.

Another poem, this time more directly revelatory of his poetry, is the charming *"Agitato ma non troppo,"* which prefaces the volume *Chills and Fever* (1924). Again, I prefer the more compact original version.

The poet acknowledges

> I have a grief . . .

But the poem has none of the august majesty of a great mature poet nor the poignance of a passionate young poet. It is not

> *like Dante's fury*
> *When Beatrice was given him to bury;*

nor does it resemble the note sounded

> *When the young heart was hit, you know*
> *How Percy Shelley's reed sang tremolo. . . .*

Ransom develops the theme a little further and then concludes the poem:

> *I will be brief,*
> *Assuredly I have a grief,*
> *And I am shaken; but not as a leaf.*

This poem provides an accurate account of the tonality and range of Ransom's poetry—the emotion is there, very real, completely genuine, credible, but the poet is never overmastered by it: the poet, one feels, is always in control of himself. If the label "a great minor poet" be not a contradiction in terms, and I think that it is not, it fits Ransom perfectly.

The validation of this description, if challenged, could be supported by the citation of poem after poem. I think that the case at this date requires no argument, though I mean later in this essay to provide some illustrations of the way in which the irony or pathos or simple quiet happiness of a human situation is convincingly rendered.

At this point, however, I want to mention a third poem in which Ransom confesses to a special and, by many an unsuspected, trait: his tendency to criticize the conventional wisdom, to question the dominant orthodoxy. Ten lines will illustrate. The poet imagines others saying:

"He crieth on our dogmas, Counterfeit!
And no man's bubble 'scapeth his sharp thorn.

"Nor he respecteth duly our tall steeple,
But solitary poring on his book,
Heareth our noise and hardly offereth look,
Nor liveth neighbourly with these the people."

With reason, friends, I am complained upon,
Who am a headstrong man, sentenced from birth
To love unusual gods beyond all earth,
And the easy gospels bruited hither and yon.

This may come as an unexpected revelation to those who think of Ransom as the mannerly, indeed quite courtly, southern gentleman who became the stout defender of what many Americans thought a hopelessly provincial culture.

Yet his sharp differences in ideas and attitudes from the southern culture he sought to defend and on occasion from the notions of his closest friends ought to be noted. I shall have special occasion to refer to these differences later in this essay. His independence of familial and tribal beliefs, even when he felt strongly the filial and tribal bond, seems to me one of his salient traits. He would in effect later repudiate the religion of his father, a Methodist clergyman, and yet at the same time revere his father and his father's office, and he would further the intellectual careers of his young protégés, like myself, while at the same time pointing out the limitations of their intellectual positions and their disagreements with his. Such was a triumph of good nature and loving concern over what must have been often an intellectual exasperation, but it never involved a softening of the rigor of his own position.

Such personal traits as these poems reveal to me now were not evident to me when I first encountered Ransom on the campus of Vanderbilt University. As for his personal appearance and manner, yes: the little gray eyes, the trim figure of a man just below early middle age and the sense of a person reserved and even rather remote—all of these thoroughly applied to him. But I had no sense of the inner man with his tremendous intellectual energy and his great gifts of the imagination.

This first conception or rather misconception remained even after he had become one of my teachers at Vanderbilt and remained through much of my college career. In due time I did indeed come to admire Ransom's poetry, and today I regard him as one of the finest minor poets writing in the English language of our century. Yet I never felt that I understood him—or even knew with anything like full comprehension the inner man.

I believe if Mr. Ransom had known this, it might have surprised him. For he was later to say that he and I were as much alike as peas in a pod: we were both the sons of Methodist preachers. We had both grown up in Tennessee. Both had got early a solid training in Latin, Greek, and mathematics—all in the tradition of the Old South, which resembled that of the English public schools.

We had both attended and received our B.A.s from Vanderbilt University and had both gone on to Oxford as Rhodes Scholars. We had both ended up in English departments in universities in the South that did not in those days set any excessive valuation on instructors who taught a subject as commonplace and to their eyes as unimportant as "English."

So much for our likeness in nurture and cultural background. Here Ransom's homely metaphor, "peas in a pod," makes entire sense. As I reread *Gentleman in a Dust Coat*, Daniel Young's biography of Ransom, I pick up other details of Ransom's early life that match easily with those of my own.

Thus, we had shared a life of genteel poverty in a Methodist parsonage in those days; the necessary counting of pennies; the worry when mid-autumn arrived and the pastoral appointments were read out and our family found out that we would stay on at least one more year in the town in which we were then living and would not have to move a hundred miles away, with new friends to make and a new school to attend. We also acquired a fierce family loyalty and a concern for, and a participation in, the problems that our mother and father had to face.

In reading Young's biography I even found mention of actual people whom I knew who had also touched John Ransom's life. For instance, at Oxford, Ransom, as Young tells us, took to lunch one day a "Miss Ann Hefley, daughter of a Methodist minister from Memphis." Her father was one of my father's good friends, and as a six-year-old child I remember "Miss Hefley." It was indeed a small world, pretty much their own, that the sons and daughters of southern Methodist parsons inhabited.

So in spite of what Ransom and I later grew up to be and in spite of the vast differences of talent and achievement between us, I ought to have been able to understand him rather well. But I did not and I do not now. I still have to say what Donald Davidson said to Allen Tate, both friends of Ransom: "I have never been able to understand that man. . . ." Davidson, after all, as Ransom's associate and colleague for years, had had a better opportunity to observe him than I had had.

Yet Ransom, whether I now understand him or not, made an enormous impression on my life and in a variety of ways, although he was not always aware of it. In the classroom, however, he influenced me hardly at all. I signed up for one of his classes in my second year at Vanderbilt, but within a week I dropped the course, for it was plain that I was not up to it and besides it did not interest me. Later I did take a course in writing with him, and I must have learned something, but except for various remarks that I remember having heard him make, only a few of which had anything to do with the writing process, I am not conscious now of having carried anything away from his instruction.

My experience was thus very different from Robert Penn Warren's experience in which there was apparently an almost instant meeting of minds between the precocious young freshman and the poet just approaching his great productive years. Warren has frequently spoken of that most fruitful association and the ease with which it came about.

I have no one to blame but myself, for the difficulty obviously lay in me. Perhaps "blame" is not the accurate term. Again, let me say, I was simply not up to it—too raw, still too confused about my aims and purposes. But again, other students shared my difficulty. Ransom set no great store by formal lectures, and he made no pretensions to being an inspiring teacher. His comments on the literary work being discussed were deliberately kept in low key. He was at his best in talking to the individual when some sort of personal relation had been established. It was not a matter of Ransom's indifference and certainly contained no element of intellectual arrogance. He simply knew that one could not force the horses to drink even if the waters to which the typically wild, young colt had been led were those issuing from the true Pierian spring. The process of teaching had to be in some real sense a participation, a shared slaking of a real thirst. I was not to discover all this until some years later in 1931 when I had my first real conversations with him while I was at Oxford and he and his family were spending a year in England.

Nevertheless, his very presence on the Vanderbilt campus in the 1920s was a powerful influence on my plans for the future. For in my last year at prep school, I had begun to discover poetry, and now to find at Vanderbilt that real live people were writing and publishing poetry settled matters for me. I wanted to be connected in some way with this marvelous romantic enterprise. John Crowe Ransom was a practicing poet. Never mind that he didn't look in the least like the pictures of Byron or Shelley. Never mind either that I could not for the life of me make anything of his poetry. (My training and personal impulses prepared me for only the romantics.)

There were, of course, other incitements than Ransom. There was Donald Davidson, who was also a poet and whose brother for one year was my roommate. Davidson was clearly some kind of romantic. Most important of all there was Robert Penn Warren, whom I was fortunate enough to have met in my freshman year. Warren was, as a student, actually publishing poetry and, out of pure kindness, had taken some notice of me. Our relationship at Vanderbilt was brief. He was off to graduate school at the end of my freshman year. But for me it was important, and indeed it was to bear quite unexpected fruit many years later.

In my own senior year, I at last began to grow up. I had found among my classmates other students who had literary interests. We set to work to collect and edit and get printed a little volume of student verse. We confided what we were doing to Ransom and Davidson, the principal Fugitives still on the Vanderbilt faculty, and got their blessing, but the relation scarcely amounted to anything like intimacy. We knew it did not and did not presume upon it. Ransom, for example, had shown us a kindly interest, but to me he was still a rather remote presence.

I did come to some understanding of his poetry, however. It happened easily and suddenly. I was in a friend's dormitory room one evening, rather idly chatting, when I opened a volume of Ransom's poetry lying there on the table before me and started reading—really reading, for I had gone over the poems many times before. Suddenly, the scales fell from my eyes. The code was broken, the poems became "readable." I do not mean that they became magically transparent. I continue to find fresh meanings in them and depths I had not noticed before. But a serious blockage had suddenly disappeared. I was now a true convert.

Two years later in 1929 when at Oxford I met up with Warren again, we had much talk about Ransom, and I learned for the first time of the plans to publish the collection of essays that appeared in 1930 with the title *I'll Take My Stand.* Warren was at that time working on his own contribution to it.

I already knew or later came to know all but one of the contributors. I read the book over and over. I found some of the essays more congenial and some more difficult than others. But I tried my best to assimilate the whole position, philosophical and political. I learned a great deal from my intensive study.

I doubted that the book had any future as a political instrument. I was well aware of the incredulous jeers it would provoke. One of the most important things that the reception of the book taught me was the commitment of the American public, north and south, east and west, to progress as a sacred dogma, the truth of which simply could not be questioned. It was one of those truths so plainly self-evident that it could not be rationally discussed. The person who could not wholeheartedly assent to it was either teasing or else touched in the head, or perhaps, if he still persisted, a real subversive.

Ransom's essay was one of the most philosophical expositions in the collection, and, to my mind, one of the most able as a well-constructed argument. It represented him at his very best as a thinker and as a stylist. He was also the principal author, as I was later to learn, of the "Introduction: A Statement of Principles." This short account manifests the same virtues as his essay: clarity and force. Here is Ransom on industrialism and its labor-saving devices.

> But a fresh labor-saving device introduced into an industry does not emancipate the laborers in that industry so much as it evicts them.

Such has proved to be a sound observation. One of the most obvious results has been in agriculture. Some fifty years ago about 40 percent of our population worked on farms; now, the farm workers are under 10 percent. In general, more of our people are now at work in distributing and marketing products than in actually producing them. The shift has been praised for eliminating much heavy manual work, much that is sheer drudgery. But desk work can be a form of drudgery, too, and much of it is.

Two more of Ransom's statements touch on this problem.

> It is an inevitable consequence of industrial progress that production greatly outruns the rate of natural consumption. To overcome the disparity, the producers, disguised as the pure idealists of progress, must coerce and wheedle the public into being loyal and steady consumers, in order to keep the machines running. So the rise of modern advertising—along with its twin, personal salesmanship—is the most significant development of our industrialism.
>
> The regular act of applied science is to introduce into labor a labor-saving device or a machine. Whether this is a benefit depends on how far it is advisable to save labor.

Again, the elimination of drudgery seems generally a gain; but the value of time saved from labor will depend very much on how the saved time is spent. If the worker is left only with time to kill, or with a life that is boring, or with only shallow and superficial amusements to pass the time, he is really little better off. If his work is interesting, it can be enjoyable. A true artist will "work" at his art even if he doesn't need the money he can get for it. Fortunate is the man whose job provides a decent living but who also has a job that he likes to do. Yet such statements as I have quoted from Ransom's "Introduction" could not be popular. In a society so thoroughly committed to secularism and progress as ours was by 1930, they could not appeal to the man in the street—nor, as a matter of fact, to the intellectuals. Mechanization had indeed taken command.

An acute observer of our contemporary culture, Eric Voegelin, has remarked that "the contemplative critics of Western Culture had discerned the disintegration of society behind the facade of progress" and that "the progress of science and industry is no substitute for the order of society." But such contemplative critics, few if any of whom are on the political left, usually turn out to be poets and men of letters, writers like Paul Valéry, William Butler Yeats, T. S. Eliot, and, though this name may come as a surprise to some, William Faulkner.

They have been impressed with the basically unchanging character of human nature throughout the ages. They were never deluded into the notion that science (the "hard sciences" using an objective method for testing hypotheses and capable of making accurate predictions) could deal with ends and goals. Applied science, technology, could indeed provide the most efficient means to reach predetermined goals. But it could not as science select the proper goals. Marxism did not attract such thinkers as these, though in the thirties it did attract to one degree or another most of the other intellectuals.

Consequently, few people of the period were able to see (or are able to see now) the real point that Ransom and his fellow Agrarians were making. The Agrarians never questioned the ability of a technological society to produce goods for the consumer but were much concerned with the bearing of a technological society on the nature of the good life. They asked that we consider what the good life is or ought to be.

This matter is almost completely overlooked. It was assumed that any fool knew what the good life was. He at least knew what he wanted. Give him an abundance of material goods and he was free to choose for himself. The nature of the good life—the importance of a choice of goals and ends—hardly required discussion. Technology had given man the means to secure almost anything he wanted. Such was the unspoken assumption of those who attacked or ignored the Agrarians.

Man at last was coming to control nature. Here again Ransom had something to say. The exploitation of nature implicit in industrialization was disastrous to the good life. Mankind, of course, had to make use of nature. Indeed, had to prey upon nature. A return to Adam's happy life in the Garden of Eden (or that of the happy denizens of the Golden Age of the Greeks) was irrecoverable. Even so, man must indulge in no rape of nature; rather his relation to her should more nearly resemble a marriage involving respect and love. Ransom's own figure was that of a truce: no warfare against nature, no demand for unconditional surrender, rather a reasonable accommodation in which man could live in harmony with nature.

In one sense this was the most important item in the Agrarians' agenda, so deeply embedded in their thinking that they did not give it the prominence that it deserved. They did not, for example, use terms later to become familiar, such as "environmental protection" or "preservation of our natural heritage." Yet had they done so in the 1930s, it would have done little good. Even today, the "dead" lakes of Canada and New England, impure water supplies, and noxious air have not yet brought much vigorous response from the national administration.

A few years later Ransom had ceased from any special agitation for what he and his friends had called Agrarianism. It was a pity that they had so named it, for the name played into the hands of their opponents who jeered at them for not practicing what they preached. Clearly none of them were trudging behind old Beck, the plow mule, down on the farm. (By such logic as this, of course, their opponents would have to be called Industrialists and would have been required to take their places in a factory production line, or more humbly, tuning automobile engines at the local garage.)

Yet, Agrarianism was for Ransom no idea picked up as a kind of fad. It was a proper extension of his thought processes—an application to daily life of his philosophy—his conception of a proper vocation for a large, perhaps the largest, segment of mankind. He gave up prosecution of the case because in spite of his concern for philosophy and what it had to tell us about the satisfactory life, Ransom had a powerful streak of pragmatism in his nature. One test of an idea, and an important one, was whether it could be put to work. By 1945 or perhaps earlier, he had decided that the people would not accept Agrarianism. It had no political future.

In the 1950s or 1960s, I remember that he told me with reference to Agrarianism that the younger men deserved their chance to bring about their own notions of what a society should be. He doubted that those new ideas would result in success and happiness, but they would be put in force nevertheless. This was said with no trace of cynicism, as if he hoped that he would live long enough to see their failure and utter his "I told you so." Ransom was a generous man, and he had something of the calm of the old philosopher who is a bit detached from the fray.

I think, however, that Ransom for a time genuinely believed that the South might be willing to accept Agrarianism as a viable politico-economic program and that the Roosevelt administration might see fit to implement aspects of it. His early contributions to the cause had a quality of real enthusiasm.

How deeply the championship of Agrarianism was rooted in his thinking is abundantly displayed in a book that also appeared in 1930, his *God without Thunder: An Unorthodox Defense of Orthodoxy.* Here again the contest described is that between an abstracting rationalism and a loving comprehension of the concrete world as revealed by the senses and warmed by the emotions of the human being. Ransom makes it a contest between science on the one hand and art and religion on the other, but the science that he sees as rapacious and aggressive is not the contemplative science of, say, pure mathematics but the science that can be applied in working technologies. This "science" gives man power over nature and produces in man a dangerous hubris; art and religion on the other hand reflect the total experience of the human being, including an enjoyment of nature, and imply a sense of man's dependence on a powerful and mysterious entity that he must accept with awe but also may love and worship.

The book is full of challenging and often persuasive interpretations of such things as the story of Adam and Eve in the Happy Garden or the story of Cain and Abel or the Greek story of Prometheus, and it certainly gives a convincing account of the dilution of the Christian faith in the twentieth century.

As he had summarized it in a letter to Allen Tate some months before: "Little by little the God of the Jews has been whittled down into a spirit of science, or the spirit of love, or the spirit of Rotary; and now religion is not religion at all, but a purely secular experience. . . ."

What had caused the damage? In this same letter to Tate he writes: "The N[ew] T[estament] has been a backset as a religious myth; not its own fault, as I think but nevertheless a failure: it's hurt us."

Ransom's logic is thus pushed inexorably: any lessening of the mysterious power of an inscrutable God is dangerous for mankind. The claim that man was also a God, however hedged about with reservations, will almost certainly encourage man to believe that mankind can aspire to godhead and the Ruler of the Universe is after all knowable, not mysterious, and awesome, really a Big Friendly Brother, and probably just the spirit of brotherhood itself. For Ransom, such a view is a misconception, and a dangerous illusion for mankind to hold.

This view seems to leave Ransom with a primary audience of Orthodox Jews and just possibly Moslems. Though Ransom was later to say that his own position was that of a Unitarian, he must have known by 1930 that most American Unitarians were far too "liberal" in their theology to find any appeal at all in what he was saying.

Quite consciously, he was setting forth a program for the American South and for those whom he considered to be his own people. He makes this motive completely clear in his "Epilogue" to *God without Thunder*. His logic, he concedes, would recommend that the Western world "Enter the Synagogue, if the Synagogue might be so kind as to receive it." But the notion is impracticable, he believes, for "better or worse, man is a member of his own race or his own tribe. If there is not a religious institution that suits him quite near at home, he will have to go without one." So in turn Ransom has to reject the Greek Orthodox Church, Roman Catholicism, Anglicanism, and finally comes down to Presbyterianism, Methodism, and the Baptists. These last denominations, he writes, are "evidently close to my kind of community," even though he admits that they have tended "to secularize themselves more and more every day."

It is an honest statement in which the speaker faces the hard facts, but it is also a counsel of despair—not only because Ransom is aware of the difficulty of restoring the Protestant denominations to his orthodoxy, but for a far more important reason: because the choice is ultimately made not in virtue of his creed's ultimate truth but because it appeals to the needs of the members of the society in question. In short, human considerations turn out here to be more important than the claim of truth. But the Protestant might answer: This is the very reason I am giving up what you call orthodoxy. What I believe is more congenial to me as a member of a secularized society than are the beliefs of an earlier day.

I simply do not know enough about the personal beliefs of Ransom in his later mature years. The signs that we have would indicate that he believed in a kind of poetic materialism, perhaps not unlike that of George Santayana. He loved nature, and he evidently found in art a way of bringing mankind into a loving enjoyment of it, but he did not make the mistake of turning nature into a kindly and softhearted nurse. In *God without Thunder,* as we have seen, he comes close to identifying his god with nature itself, which is the source of both joy and sorrow but in which it is unpredictable. In 1929 in a letter to his friend Allen Tate, Ransom wrote: "The fear of the Lord is the beginning of wisdom; a big beginning, but only a beginning, of which is the love of the Lord. *Substitute nature* for the Lord *and he won't feel aggrieved* [italics mine]."

Walter Savage Landor's famous quatrain applies very well to Ransom himself if we omit the first line with its note of arrogance. Ransom rarely fought with anyone, though not because he felt that his antagonist was not a worthy opponent.

> I fought with none for none was worth my strife.
> Nature I loved and next to nature, art.
> I warmed both hands before the fire of life.
> It sinks and I am ready to depart.

Ransom had enjoyed his life and his last days were serene ones. The third line also applies most specifically to Ransom. He was a man who loved games, everything from golf and tennis to bridge and poker, and he lived in a cheerful happiness that had in it nothing either gross or gloomy. He did love nature and art, but he was no Platonic philosopher king, planning myths and rituals for his less exalted countrymen. He really tried to practice what he preached, attempted to live what he thought was the proper life of others in the community. Though his *God without Thunder* would seem to most people subversive of his father's faith, he dedicated the book to his father. His ties with his father remained close all his life. He attended Methodist services when his father preached. He even taught a Sunday School class, but it was noticed that when the Apostle's Creed was recited, Ransom did not join in the statement that he believed in "Jesus Christ, His only Son our Lord. . . ." When Ransom was asked why, he said, "Because I do not believe it." He gave up his church-going then, but the story is significant: he wanted to save his people and their culture and he would take part as fully as he could in their communal rites, but he had to be an honest man too. One has to acknowledge that at least he made a good try to fulfill his practical obligations as a member of his chosen community, though at the same time he had to honor the claims of intellectual truth as he saw it.

With Ransom's transfer to Kenyon College there was a waning of his interest in Agrarianism and in the religion that he thought was implied by it, a "traditional" religion of the sort described above. I think it wrong to say that Ransom ever "repudiated" Agrarianism, but he was no Don Quixote; he was too much the pragmatist for such a role as the Don's. Ransom still believed that he had been directing his lance against real giants that needed to be overthrown, but, though he was not mad, the bemused public at large could see in his endeavors only a tilting at some quite useful windmills. And since his society could not be talked out of this delusion, those giants were going to continue grinding away. After all, Ransom's efforts had always been in behalf of the society, not at all to show off his intellectual daring and dexterity. He quietly accepted the fact that the society had no intention of letting itself be changed radically. His churchgoing also stopped; a society that was committed to industrialism was happy enough to worship a God deprived of his thunder or to worship no God at all, since man believed that he was doing so well on his own newfound powers.

Though Ransom had for a long time been interested in the arts and particularly in poetry, he now came back to a consideration of the role of literature and the arts with a new emphasis. As the editor of a quarterly magazine, the newly established *Kenyon Review,* and with allies he could count on at *The Southern Review,* myself and Warren, there was an opportunity to present new claims for the importance of the arts. Ransom proposed that the two quarterlies should fire both barrels at once in an assertion of what was needed and thus salute the stirrings of critical thought. The *Kenyon* would publish five articles on this subject, and we at the *Southern* five others. Ransom himself in 1941 published his volume entitled *The New Criticism*.

When Delmore Schwartz asked Ransom why he didn't attempt to remodel a critic like R. P. Blackmur or Cleanth Brooks to fit the role of the "ontological critic" that he described, Ransom very properly refused to act on the suggestion. He had his own idea of what the proper critic should be, just as he had his own special conception of what poetry is. Nevertheless, he had many handsome things to say about some of his fellow critics, especially his younger friends, and no one could have been kinder to me or more concerned to help promote such a venture as *Understanding Poetry*.

Yet the truth is that for all of Ransom's philosophical interest in the nature of poetry as a special kind of verbal discourse, his ultimate concern, I have always been convinced, has been the function of poetry within society. Like Plato he was finally interested in what good, if any, the poet did for the republic, or for the society as a whole. Even Aristotle, who made his definition of tragedy a matter of its possessing a special structure in its presentation of an action, nevertheless added in his concept of catharsis, which had to do with his interest in the effects of poetry on the citizen at large. Ransom had imbibed deeply from the classics when he had read "Greats" at Oxford.

The study of the arts and of poetry, Ransom felt, might help ameliorate the plight of the individual living in a secularized and increasingly industrialized society. It might renew for him some sense of a fullness of the life of the spirit, otherwise denied by his daily life. Literature might give him back at least something of the sort of thing that he sorely needed.

Sheer rationalism turned the world into an abstraction—a set of logical relationships that were enormously valuable for securing the means for living—but the whole man craved a full world, sensuous, concrete, stimulating to the emotions and engaging man's total being. As the world became more and more abstract, we more and more needed art, and great art that would render real life acceptable.

Narcotics, violent stimulants, exciting distractions, such as those given by cheap and superficial art, could provide only temporary escapes from the boredom, the monotony, and the hardships of so much modern life.

This sense of what genuine art could do for society thus deeply influenced Ransom's theory of art. For example, a poem represented a statement of a sort and thus possessed a logic that involved a rational process. But a genuine poem went on to introduce all sorts of items not directly relevant to the "logic" of the poem. They delayed the movement toward the object—they gave glimpses of the real world that we know in its fullness. They turned something as abstract as a road map into something more like an oil painting of a landscape.

Such is my own analogy. Ransom, however, has supplied one of his own. The structure of a poem, which organizes it and represents its logic, corresponds to the path that would lead from where I am to my elected destination. But as I walk along the path, I am induced to stray from it from time to time, to look at a spray of wildflowers that caught my eye, or a small waterfall that has come into view just outside the path, or any other interesting though "irrelevant" item along the way. My walk with its practical concern has become thus a richer and more humanly rewarding experience.

A poem for Ransom, then, has a structure (the logical element) and a texture (sensuous, concrete materials that are irrelevant to that structure). Thus, there is a dualism that Ransom argues must be finally overcome if the poem is not to be reduced to nonsense. Yet the irrelevant material has an importance: it reminds us of a world much richer and more comprehensive than the abstractions to which we so often reduce our experience in order to accomplish a particular task or goal. No wonder Ransom chose as a title for his finest and most eloquent collection of critical essays *The World's Body*. His thesis there is that we must not let that marvelous and wonderful entity be reduced to a diagram. If we are deluded into thinking that by such reductive analysis we can possess it and use it as we please, we shall end up by destroying our own humanity.

Ransom brings religion and poetry very close together. Indeed, they become almost identical. Ransom's position seems to me essentially that of Matthew Arnold—granted the vast differences in their approach to the problem and the differences in the tone of their writings. (Yet the index to Daniel Young's life of Ransom has not a single reference to Arnold. Perhaps I do overestimate that likeness.)

For me, and I believe for others, the difficulty with Ransom's account of poetry lies in its basic dualism. The distinction between structure and texture seems very like the age-old split between content and form, a split which implies that metaphor, diction, rhythm, stanza form, and such other devices have only a "decorative" function, whereas clearly they can affect powerfully any ideational content, changing "what the poem really says." Indeed, as I. A. Richards reminded us some sixty years ago, if you change the way something is said, you have changed to some degree what it says. To take an extreme case: "That was a fine thing to do" can change its meaning from high commendation to withering disapproval, depending upon the tone of voice in which it is uttered. Good poets have the means to control the tone even when they are not present to read the poem in their own voices. Furthermore, if the concrete particulars ought to be irrelevant to the logic of the poem as a whole, are they more effective in proportion to their irrelevancy? What is the optimum irrelevance? The examination of any actual poem will show that there are vast differences between the degrees of irrelevance of the concrete items (the texture) to the thrust (logical structure) of the poem. Thus, Donne's celebrated comparison of the souls of a pair of lovers to the legs of a geometer's compass gets a high mark in the irrelevance scale, but most readers (and not merely modern readers) have found it a very effective way of bringing the poem to a satisfying close. But one can find many figures in Abraham Cowley's poetry that are on an absolute scale no more irrelevant than Donne's comparison and yet are felt to be absurd and ridiculous. I shall cite here one of Cowley's less absurd comparisons. The following stanza is from his *Hymn to Light.*

> First-born of Chaos, who so fair didst come
> From the old Negro's darksome womb!
> Which, when it saw the lovely child,
> The melancholy mask put on kind looks and smiled . . .

Or to come at matters from the other direction: why is Wordsworth's comparison of a young girl to the beauty of a star "When only one / Is shining in the sky" so much more effective than that well-worn comparison "Her eyes were like stars"? Stars are stars, and it is hard to see why one star is more completely relevant (or irrelevant) than two stars. I can't think that the matter is so simple that it turns upon the fact that a whole girl is less like a star and therefore more irrelevant than that the girl's two eyes are more like a pair of stars and therefore more nearly relevant. Wordsworth's comparison actually draws on the whole context of the poem and helps make the point of the poem: the girl in question, though unknown to the world at large and one who would be as little noticed by a passerby as "a violet by a mossy stone," is for the man who speaks the poem the only star in his firmament, not like Milton's beauty the "Cynosure" of all eyes, but surely for this speaker, his only true North Star, or better still—since the planet of love, Venus, is the first star in the sky in the evening, and for a while the only star that shines there—the star of love.

In short, the simile that Wordsworth uses is an important element in what the voice in the poem is saying: it helps define precisely what is being said and is actually highly relevant to the poem. It is not a truly irrelevant element.

What seems to me most worth saying in this general connection is that the structure-texture thesis will not account for Ransom's own poetry. He is indeed a very fine poet. The note that runs all through his poetry is a defense of a concrete and mysterious world in which all of us have been born and not an abstract and limited world that man can put to his own use. But there are many variations on the theme and many quiet lyrics that are only peripheral to this theme of cultural crisis: a child confronted for the first time with the fact of death; the deep love for one's native land, not lessened or deepened because of the unmistakable signs of its decline; a circumstance in which physical pain and mental anguish are weighed one against the other and the one used to buffer the other; the charming but, nevertheless, foolish confidence of youth. Many of these are "simple" poems, the matter of every day; but seen as cameo presentations of the universal human predicament, they take on power. No wonder that Thomas Hardy was one of Ransom's favorite poets; and Ransom's poems are just as intensely out of the "upper South" as are Hardy's poems out of his Wessex.

Yet the details of these poems of Ransom's are so completely relevant to the import of the poems that without them the poems would be so abstract as to be almost meaningless. Consider one of Ransom's best-known lyrics, "Bells for John Whiteside's Daughter." Little girls die unexpectedly every day, and because they seem so full of life their sudden death will seem especially desolating: but in this poem sudden death seems particularly desolating, for in this poem a generalization, an actuarial statistic, suddenly becomes alive and catches our attention and engages our feelings intensely. Yet the emotion evoked is not irresponsible; it is quietly measured to the occasion.

How is it done? Well, no one can fully explain the magic of a truly fine poem, but one can hope to call attention to some obviously salient points. There is the presence of the geese in the poem. The poem has only twenty lines all told, but nine of them have to do with the child's chasing the geese from the shade of the apple trees to the pond. The geese are "lazy," "sleepy, and proud." They cry out in their own "goose" language, of course, "Alas," but under the rod of the "little Lady," they "scuttle" away to the pond.

As the geese are described here in the poem they are creatures out of a child's fairy-tale world, sufficiently like human beings to take on the qualities of old, rather stuffy human beings, but they are recognizably geese, in their language and in the way they clumsily move about.

Tricking and stopping, sleepy and proud

and later as I have already remarked, they

            scuttle
Goose-fashion under the skies.

I don't know what "tricking" would mean here. The poet has exercised his liberty as a poet: for the *Oxford English Dictionary* knows it not in any sense that would fit a particular kind of perambulation. Maybe Ransom means that the geese keep deceiving the viewer's expectation, seeming to start one way, then stopping, and going another. Anyway, most of us, if we follow the child's perceptions as she "harries" the confused geese, do accept the word.

Are all the details about the geese irrelevant to the poem? I don't think so. This passage brings to life the earlier statement in the poem about the "speed in her little body," and the "lightness in her footfall." It helps explain why (in the first stanza) we are told that

> It is no wonder her brown study
>   Astonishes us all.

Moreover, the episode in which we watch her "tireless heart" in its play also unobtrusively makes another point: she has now, indeed, moved from a world of play and fancy into the studious concentration of the typical philosopher—little girls do not characteristically fall into "brown studies." The little girl is also moved out of childhood's world of talking beasts and into a world of stern reality. In the last stanza, the poet comments once again on her "brown study," as she lies there "so primly propped."

Wordsworth in one of his best-known poems addresses the child as "Thou, best philosopher," and we know from the context in what sense he meant it. Ransom's poem barely hints at the association. Even so, the child in her "brown study" has something to tell us about our destiny as human beings or at least is able to make a point that we already know all too well: Death is no respecter of persons. Death makes no promises as to how long we are allowed to live.

Though I don't want to worry the point of relevance or irrelevancy, I do hope that I have shown why I hesitate to accept Ransom's structure-texture account. In this poem, as so often, what Ransom has dubbed "irrelevant" seems to be doing all the really important work in the poem. We may summarize the meaning of the poem in a prose paraphrase, and such a paraphrase may have its uses in any shorthand description of a poem, but no paraphrase, however carefully made, can be a substitute for what the poem essentially is. I would prefer to say that the real poem is not so much a "logical structure" as a "dramatic rendition" of a total experience. That such experiences are organized for us by a good poet, novelist, or dramatist, I would cheerfully accept. They do not give us simply a jumble of detail, even though a poem like *The Waste Land* seemed such to some of its earliest readers. But how useful is it to describe the organization of a poem as logical when its essential unity seems to be the coherence of a dramatic experience or that of a well-told tale? For the poem (or novel or drama) cannot be reduced to a logical statement or statements without the loss of its very substance. In fact, Ransom in his *Selected Poems* of 1963 writes: "Poetry is still the supremely inclusive speech which escapes, as if unaware of them, the strictures and reductions of the systematic logical understanding." This seems to be a much more accurate statement of the case, and I would like to think that it was Ransom's final revision of his structure-texture account.

Yet any difficulties with his account of the makeup of a poem that I have had in the past do not compromise my experience of the poems he writes. Let the master call his metaphor, his daring uses of diction, his subacid ironies, and his general handling of tone—let him reckon them all as irrelevancies if he likes to think of them so. I find that they actually render his poems brilliant evocations of a mood or make a striking observation or more often constitute a rich and persuasive commentary on human life. Moreover, when they do become something like a pronouncement, the material that determines the voice of the speaker converts it from what might be the glibness of the daily columnist or the harangue of the backwoods prophet or the complaints of the newspaper contributor to a measured utterance of dignity, maturity, and wisdom. Control of tone through various rhetorical devices provides the credentials that imply that the speaker possesses experience, some knowledge of the world in which we live, a proper sense of humor, and no inflated sense of his own worth.

One hears that voice over and over in Ransom's poems. Often it is tinged with irony, sometimes with a rueful self-knowledge, but rarely, if ever, with an arrogant confidence in the rightness of what he says. The range of subjects and occasions is large. The incident may be a trivial lovers' quarrel between two adolescents, but not trivial for *them* ("Parting, Without a Sequel"). It can be a wounding and bitter outbreak between a married pair ("Two in August"). I have been told that the pair involved in this poem are two cats, male and female; and the poem is, detail by detail, entirely susceptible of that interpretation. Yet knowing this leaves the poem nevertheless a highly interesting and even poignant commentary on troubled human relationships.

In "Blue Girls" the speaker watches girls "twirling their blue skirts" on the grounds of a girls' college or finishing school. They are absorbed with their looks, their growing up into womanhood, and bored with their classroom exercises. The poem has been described as a bitter commentary, but it is nothing of the kind. The young women are not wicked, but young and thoroughly human and, of course, occupied with matters close to their own affairs; and their beauty is *fragile*. The observer is not censorious but feels the poignance of their pride and hopefulness. He is not being sarcastic, therefore, when he says (but, of course, not audibly to them)

> Practise your beauty, blue girls, before it fail;
> And I will cry with my loud lips and publish
> Beauty which all our power shall never establish
> It is so frail.

The poem ends with a continuation of what he could tell these delightful young creatures. He could tell them something of one of their teachers, known to them as a

> lady with a terrible tongue,
> Blue eyes fallen from blue. . . .

who was once

> lovelier than any of you.

Ransom is a realistic poet, an ironic poet. But far from being immune to beauty or the attractiveness of the world of the senses, he is able to capture the power and attraction of the world often almost magically. He does so in retelling the story of Judith of Bethulia, who when her city was besieged by the Assyrian king, Holofernes, volunteered to make her way outside the city to his tent, to get him drunk and kill him. She does so and brings back the conqueror's head to prove that she has finished him off. The next day the Jews attack their now-demoralized enemies and destroy them utterly.

A Hebrew elder is imagined to be speaking the poem. He says:

> Beautiful as the flying legend of some leopard,
> She had not yet chosen her great captain or prince. . . .
> And a wandering beauty is a blade out of its scabbard. . . .

Nor by process of veiling she grew the less fabulous.
Grey or blue veils, we were desperate to study
The invincible emanations of her white body. . . .

The poem ends with Holofernes dead, but the Hebrew elders still have
their worries.

May God send unto our virtuous lady her prince.
It is stated she went reluctant to that orgy,
Yet a madness fevers our young men, and not the clergy
Nor the elders have turned them unto modesty since.
Inflamed by the thought of her naked beauty, with desire?
Yes, and chilled with fear and despair.

Ransom can produce a withering satire, though he ordinarily uses the
more gentle modes of irony. In "Three Mountebanks," however, he takes
as his targets three southern hot-gospellers. As the son of a Methodist
parson, Ransom doubtless knew what his father thought of that breed. I
know what my father thought of them. Yet even here, there is no realistic
surface. He distances them somewhat. The first of these Mountebanks
vaunts the merits of Fides, his hound of faith; the second, those of
Humphrey, his elephant of patience; and the third, of Agnes, his lamb
who demands everywhere to be sacrificed. The evangelical rhetoric is
brilliantly caricatured.

A few of Ransom's poems deal rather directly with the crisis in culture,
the confusion entailed by the loss of the old faith and its verities. "Man
without Sense of Direction" and "Persistent Explorer" are two such poems.
The former describes a man "Who cannot fathom nor perform his nature."

And he writhes like an antique man of bronze
That is beaten by furies visible,
Yet he is punished not knowing his sins. . . .

His problem is essentially that of J. Alfred Prufrock or one of Eliot's
Hollow Men and springs from the same source, but the poem is not in the
least like Eliot's, and I am not sure that Ransom was aware of any likeness.

Ransom's "Persistent Explorer" puts the cause of the Explorer's problems rather boldly. In his explorations he has come upon a mighty cataract. The ancient Greeks would have recognized it as a sacred spot. For such a Homeric Greek a goddess would have provided a theophany as she did to a mountain shepherd of that time. But no supernatural vision occurs to the modern explorer. As Ransom puts it

The cloud was, but the goddess was not there.

For him

It was water, only water, tons of it
Dropping into the gorge, and every bit
Was water—the insipid chemical H_2O. . . .

Furious the spectacle
But it spelled nothing, there was not any spell
Whether to bid him cower or rejoice.

Science as such is dispassionately neutral. One can build neither ethics nor aesthetics on it and certainly not a religion.

Yet the joke—if it is on anyone—is on the Explorer himself. And so

no unreasonable outcry
The pilgrim made; only a rueful grin
Spread over his lips until he drew them in;
He would not sit upon a rock and die.

He refuses to give himself up to romantic despair. He will keep up his exploration. He will seek to find a country of the mind in which the human being can discover a more satisfactory habitation. Such was indeed the course that Ransom took during the rest of his life, but primarily in his discussions of literature as a special kind of activity that enjoyed a privileged status in relation to mankind's other activities and that served a very important function in the total human economy.

Prose, written in a characteristically graceful and persuasive style, was the principal medium for these lucubrations and speculations. Ransom's days as a poet were pretty well over with the publication of the collection entitled *Two Gentlemen in Bonds* early in 1927. He wrote very few poems afterward.

After 1934, Ransom wrote only one more poem, "Address to the Scholars of New England," in 1939. But he continued to revise his poems, and in his last collection in 1974 he rewrites eight of them, printing the new version side-by-side with the original poem and adding comments in which he explains the reasons for the revisions he makes. That he should have done so is a very interesting phenomenon, particularly since most of Ransom's friends—I think I'm correct in saying this—preferred the earlier versions. I think that the older philosopher tended to take over from the brilliant younger poet and that the logic of the argument officially dismissed what the muse had originally offered through inspiration. The reader, of course, will have to decide for himself. In any case, no harm has been done. If the revisions improve the poems, so be it; if not, the originals exist, and for those, like me, who usually prefer the original versions, a comparison with the altered version at least serves to call attention to certain felicities of word or metaphor or rhythmical device which contributed to the magical effect that we treasure.

We have had no other poet quite like Ransom in English, and we are not likely to have one in the future. He was an original, and he came from a special culture that may well be disappearing. He was thoroughly southern, though he does not fit any accepted southern stereotype. In his manner, however, he did, and *Time* magazine, for example, always referred to him as "courtly." The courtliness owed nothing to a landed aristocracy. The truth is that courteous manners were widely disseminated in the South and were the everyday habits of people of modest means. Ransom's middle Tennessee had never had a plantation economy. It was a "furnishing" state for the lower South, growing wheat, tobacco, and corn and breeding horses, mules, and cattle for export to the lower South, which was heavily committed to cotton culture.

Ransom, himself, was also basically evangelical in religious matters but firmly committed to learning. The Methodists set up colleges everywhere: Vanderbilt, Duke, and Emory, for example, all began as Methodist foundations. The classics were still regarded as essential to a sound education, and in Ransom's day Tennessee was dotted with small classical academies where Latin and often Greek were taught as a matter of course.

When Ransom went to Oxford, he had already had a provincial version of what the Oxford students had had at the great English "public" schools like Eton and Winchester.

It has been said that Ransom's speech had been slightly Anglicized. This is nonsense. He did use the British pronunciation of a few special words, such as "decadent." But his dropping of the final consonant *r* or his suppression of it in words like *arm, forth,* and *sort,* he took to England with him. These pronunciations are or were until lately a regular feature of the southern lowland dialect. Ransom and I had got them with our mother's milk.

Yet Oxford did have a great influence on Ransom, and though he never aped English forms and manners, his mind was in great part formed by his Oxford education, and he came to admire English civilization—not that of London but that of Thomas Hardy's Wessex, where man and nature had come to an agreeable accommodation with each other and the life and the rituals of the people of the west country showed as much. I had heard Ransom talk about the matter in one of his classes and was much impressed by what he had to say.

Ransom also had inherited from his family and his regional culture a solid moral base. Though he was careful not to don the robes of the moralist, he had very firm notions of what was good and what was evil and was, on certain matters, almost squeamish—or at least so it would have seemed to the present-day world. Such was the case in spite of his complete emancipation from orthodox Christianity. He looked with gentleness and kindliness on the positions taken by such friends of his as Allen Tate and myself and was the close and intimate friend at Kenyon of Charles Coffin, a committed Anglican. But for him Christianity was at best simply a great myth that had been useful to mankind in the past but was of very limited utility today.

How may one sum up this highly talented and brilliantly accomplished man, on one level so apparently simple and straightforward and yet at the same time so complicated in his learning and in his theoretical interests? Another contradiction: on one level he impressed one as the pure thinker, detached and remote, in argument referring this matter to what Plato had said in "the Sophist" and to, on another point, what Kant had settled forever in his "Critique of Practical Judgement." Yet, on another level,

Ransom clearly wanted to see his ideas put into action: his schemes for a proper economic basis for a good society in the South; his notions of what could be done with the Christian church in our present society; his eagerness to get "Criticism, Inc." at work in our universities so that the great virtues of literature could be made available to society—all of these were matters in which Ransom was deeply concerned. He was certainly no idle dreamer; he was not even the detached seer whose job was to solve problems and leave the application of them, and even the dissemination of them, to others to work out.

I have never come to a real understanding of his character and personality, and I now do not expect to do so. But I can offer my tribute to an extraordinary man who did so much for me, and for other people like me, through his example as a genuine man of letters and through his direct encouragement. I was only one of many who owe him a great debt. Not the least of his gifts to me was to jolt me out of my jejune romanticism and to open my eyes to the world of reality.

11

The Primacy of the Author

⌒

A colleague of mine has published a book which he calls *Criticism in the Wilderness*. I am not surprised at his title. He might well have decided to call it *Criticism on the Battlefield,* for ours is a day in which the critics, notoriously a splenetic lot at best, have at each other with hammer and tongs. Competition is supposed to be good for business, and I dare say that sharp debate may be good for the perfecting of critical theory. But confusion is not very helpful for any of us.

What impresses me most, however, is what appears to be the disintegration of the very concept of literature. The concept is constantly having to be wrested from its enemies—and sometimes even from its alleged friends. When I was much younger, the attack on literature came particularly from the historian and the biographer, who seemed bent on making literature simply the expression of the author or, more drastically, an expression through the author of a particular culture or of a special climate of ideas. Today the main attack comes from the linguist and the psychologist. The consequence is that the notion of a specifically *literary* art has been called into question. Literature, an entity having a special ontological status and a special function, is under steady attack. The very definition of literature has become cloudy and indeterminate.

In the beginning of civilization, literature served all kinds of purposes. It preserved and transmitted the myths, legends, and authentic histories of a people, their religious beliefs, and even their customs and laws. We know that the Greeks regarded the Homeric poems as something resembling our Holy Scriptures. Literature was thought to be a rich manifold. The notion of a specific aesthetic function had not appeared. Thus, as one would suppose, in primitive cultures, the scientist, the priest, the physician, and the poet were often merged in one person. Even when the great classical theorists and our first literary critics come on the scene—Plato, Aristotle, Horace, and Longinus—they do not agree on what literature is and does. Moreover, they are all largely preoccupied with the practical effects of poetry on the human being. Plato warned against possibly dangerous effects. Horace was concerned with what use, along with its pleasure, literature might provide. Longinus stressed the power of literature to transport us into a more exalted realm of feeling. Even Aristotle, in spite of his admirable stress on the structure—the makeup—of a literary work, also speaks of a catharsis, a purging of the emotions of pity and terror, which tragedy accomplishes.

Let me hasten to say that I am not condemning the great classical authorities for their concern with what literature might accomplish for the human being who participates in it. I agree that literature does serve to discipline our emotions, that it can enlarge our sympathies, and that it may provide us with a special and indispensable kind of knowledge. Literature has always been a powerful force in any humanistic education.

Yet history and philosophy seem to touch more directly upon the springs of human actions. Literature, by contrast, is much more indirect. In saying this, I am not forgetting that the declared purpose of some poems is didactic. But even in these poems, an indirect presentation plays a more important role than ethical and philosophical admonition. For example, Milton tells us in the opening lines of *Paradise Lost* that his purpose is to "justify the ways of God to men," and there is no reason to doubt that this was what he hoped to do. But what we actually have in the poem is a wonderful interconnected story of events in heaven and hell and upon earth, with grand and awesome scenes brilliantly painted and with heroic actions dramatically rendered. In short, generations of readers have found that the grandeur of the poem far exceeds any direct statement of theological views. The point is underscored by the fact that some readers who reject Milton's theology altogether nevertheless regard *Paradise Lost* as a great poem. Even more telling is the fact that long ago William Blake found Lucifer to be the true hero of the poem and said that Milton was "of the Devil's party without knowing it." I disagree with Blake's reading of the poem, but Blake emphatically makes my point:

whatever Milton's intention, his poem did not, for Blake at least, justify God's ways to men.

Were the classical critics aware of the difference between literature (or "poetry," as they termed it) and philosophy and history? Indeed they were. Plato rather deplored the sensual appeal of poetry, and this was the basis for his celebrated expulsion of the poets from his ideal republic. Horace, the practical Roman, was willing to settle for the pleasure if it were combined with edification. My friend William Wimsatt has freely translated Horace's dictum in the *Ars Poetica* as follows: "Either a poet tries to give good advice, or he tries to be amusing—or he tries to do both. . . . A mixture of pleasure and profit appeals to every reader—an equal administration of sermon and tickle."

Aristotle makes an important and much quoted point about the relation of literature to history by calling literature more philosophical than history. That is, the knowledge that literature provides is more universal than that provided by history, for literature is not tied to the actual facts. If history is faithful, it has to record accidental and relatively meaningless events. But the tragic poet can relate a story in which the events that it records would probably, under the circumstances, have really happened. In the poet's account, events thus take on a certain inevitability. Not being bound to the literal facts, the poet can better observe the actual laws of human experience.

So in this regard literature has the advantage of history—at least of history conceived of as a factual chronicle. But literature has a certain advantage over philosophy too. It can clothe the general and universal knowledge that it imparts in concrete terms—for it is not forced to present it as an abstract generalization.

To sum up, literature is a fictional, not a factual, account of events, and so does not claim to record literal truth; but it can convey truth about human beings; or, perhaps more accurately, about reality as experienced by human beings.

Some such conception of the nature and function of literature is sufficient to guarantee for it an important humanistic role. It does provide us with wisdom, but its characteristic way of doing so is not through direct exposition, but through indirect means. It works through concrete particulars—through fictions and symbolizations, through myths and metaphors—and not—at least characteristically—through abstract statements. But in the course of the ages, this concept has from time to time been lost sight of, or has been directly challenged by man's changing conceptions of reality itself.

Space does not allow me to follow the whole course of events. But to one crucial event in our history I must give at least cursory attention, for that event had, and continues to have, enormous consequences. The event had to do with the nature of truth itself, or at least a differentiation of kinds of truth.

Early in the seventeenth century, Descartes made a distinction between the truth that could be told about the spatio-temporal world in which man lives and that other world inside his own skull. The world outside could be measured accurately, and generalizations about its nature could be tested with instruments. Indeed, it was possible to arrive at objective truth about that world. But the inner world of dreams, wishes, emotional experiences was another matter. This inner world was not subject to measurement in the same way. So, as someone put it long ago, Descartes cut the throat of poetry. How? By showing that man's inner world was hopelessly subjective. Such, of course, was not Descartes' intention. Nor did the consequences of Descartes' distinction become at once visible. But more and more it was science that went on in a triumphant march and poetry that began to languish. The poet seemed condemned to the role of the ineffectual dreamer. He produced, to be sure, some very pretty works of art, but how did these poetical fictions relate to the world of objective reality?

Poetry, of course, did not die because of Descartes' unintentional throat-slitting. In the early nineteenth century, the Romantic poets fought back, insisting that the world was not simply a colossal machine and that not everything in it could be explained in terms of cause and effect. Nevertheless, the problem for the defender of poetry had been radically altered.

By Victorian times, the problem of truth and belief had become so acute that Matthew Arnold felt it necessary to redefine the situation. Arnold invested literature with a definite philosophical character. Arnold was to make it very plain why such a role had become especially important for the serious writer in the modern world. Science had cut away the underpinnings of religion, and the task of transmitting and sustaining ethical and other values would have to be assumed by literature itself. For literature, and especially poetry, would have to supply the goals and ideals for the good life.

In sum, science could serve as technician-in-chief to civilization. Science could indicate the best means for securing the ends to be sought in a good life, and literature could teach mankind what those proper ends were. Arnold had, in effect, reduced the old triad—science, literature, and re-ligion—to a dualism: literature and science. One should add that in this dispensation, philosophy as well as religion had been pretty well swallowed up by literature. It is small wonder that Arnold held that the prime func-tion of literature was to provide a criticism of life and that the greatest figures in the literary pantheon whom he praises—Homer, Dante, Shake-speare, and Milton—are praised for their "truth and high seriousness."

I must remark that Arnold, in my opinion, placed on literature a burden that it can scarcely sustain. But on this occasion I shall be primarily concerned with the fact that, in assigning literature a quasi-philosophical function, Arnold called in question a conception of literature that allows us to distinguish between the poet and the priest or the poet and the philosopher.

In the teaching of literature, the Arnoldian emphasis dominated the American classroom as late as the 1920s. It was certainly a powerful note in a number of the undergraduate literature classes in which I sat. In the graduate schools, however, another, though complementary, influence showed itself. This emphasis was on the role of literature as expressive of a whole culture: literature as report on cultural history.

This realization came to a focus in the nineteenth century in the work of the great French critic Hippolyte Taine. On the English-speaking com-munity, its great impact had registered through Taine's masterpiece, *The History of English Literature*. Literature, Taine showed, furnished a con-crete and detailed exemplification not only of the fashions, customs, and rituals of culture, but of its ideas and concepts, political, religious, and philosophical. The three main heads for Taine's account of any culture he defined as *race, milieu,* and *moment.* In America, this emphasis on litera-ture as the product of environmental forces received further emphasis from the historical methods developed in the German graduate schools of the nineteenth century. We may need to be reminded that we borrowed our Ph.D. degree from Germany as well as the graduate seminar. Surely Taine's method was a thoroughly sound one and yielded valuable results, but as mere evidence of the nature of a culture, poems, plays, and novels are not *necessarily* any more important than are sermons, newspapers, private letters, memoirs, and other such direct comments on the affairs of the day.

No one, I believe, can fairly object either to using the literature of an epoch to provide knowledge of its culture or to using knowledge of a culture to throw light on the literature itself. But does such study in itself offer a full or even the best way to study a poem or a play? Thus, if the value of Sophocles' *Oedipus the King* were exhausted in what it can tell us about the culture of Periclean Athens, why should we call it literature at all? What distinguished it from any other datum of the period that sheds its bit of light on the culture out of which it came? Haven't we always meant by *literary art* some transcendence of the cultural environment that produced it?

There is a related question of great importance for literary criticism. Is a knowledge of the sources and genesis of a work of literary art—knowledge, say, of the life of its author or of the culture that produced him—sufficient to account for the meaning and value of the work? Thus, a detailed knowledge of the eighteenth century and of the life of Colley Cibber surely will not reveal why his *Love's Last Shift* is inferior to *The Rape of the Lock,* from the pen of his contemporary and enemy, Alexander Pope. To make that judgment of value, something more is required. If we say that no objective value judgment is possible, the very concept of literary art disappears. The distinguished art historian Ernst Gombrich put the issue well. He said with reference to the importance of evaluation: "The neglect or denial of values seems to me the greatest danger in that trend toward the dehumanization of the humanities. . . ."

With reference to literary history and aesthetic values, allow me to use a personal instance. Long ago I was a member of a graduate course in the English literature of the eighteenth century. It was an excellent course and I profited from it. But it was primarily a study of eighteenth-century culture—the history of its reigning ideas, the lives of its more prominent authors, and of their relations to each other. Apparently, the professor teaching this course assumed that all of us knew how to judge and read a poem, and therefore needed no instruction in this matter. But if that was his assumption, he was woefully wrong. Our undergraduate instruction in literature had left us more or less ignoramuses. I remember one big blonde woman in the class who would go to the library and dutifully look up the literary reputation of whatever writer we were at the moment studying. But alas, sometimes she would fail to find a suitable opinion, especially if the writer in question was not a famous one. In such cases, she put the question to me: "Cleanth, is Sir Richard Blackmore any good or not?" And I, in my brashness and overconfidence, would give her a pat answer, an answer which she would dutifully accept. This young woman was not stupid. She had simply never been given instruction in criticism, and I must admit that, in confessing her ignorance, she was more honest than the rest of us.

Emphasis on the background and genesis of a literary work has often led the student away from the work into various bypaths. Source-hunting is one of them. It is discovered that the writer borrowed his plot from so and so, or modeled his main character on the life of a person whom he well knew, or was so much impressed with Sir James Frazer's *Golden Bough* that he made use of specific features of its symbolism. Source-hunting has not gone out of fashion in our own day. Such locating of sources and symbols can, needless to say, be illuminating, and at worst, source-hunting is probably a harmless pastime. But to be truly useful, it needs to be related to the meaning of the work and some basis of probability established for the writer's actual use of it. Aimless source-hunting and symbol-mongering is a nuisance to the serious reader.

Our intense interest in the genesis and development of a literary work stems in good part from an imitation of historical methods. We are properly taught that the best way in which to come to an understanding of the French Revolution, say, is to find in what historical events and social and ideological movements it was rooted. But we possess a more inveterate habit that accounts for our insistence on stressing the life of the author as the prime way of accounting for what a poem or novel means. We want to find what the author *intended* his work to "say." In their now celebrated essay entitled "The Intentional Fallacy," Monroe Beardsley and William K. Wimsatt discussed this particular issue, with the result that they stirred up a controversy that still goes on. I want now to review briefly what they had to say. From the very first, their essay has been widely misunderstood. It and its companion essay, "The Affective Fallacy," have become notorious as expressing the credo of the so-called New Critics and their alleged obsession with seeing the work of literature as standing naked, shorn of an actor or an audience—just standing there in beautiful isolation. "The Intentional Fallacy" is often interpreted to mean that Beardsley and Wimsatt considered the author to have been a kind of inspired idiot who had no intention at all in writing the poem; that the poem somehow mysteriously wrote itself; or, less radically, that one need pay no attention to the author's intention, even if it is ascertainable—in short, that the author's purpose is not worth bothering with.

The Beardsley-Wimsatt position, of course, does not involve any such absurd view of the relation of the work to its author. What it does do is to take into account the fact, long acknowledged, that writers sometimes write better than they know, that oftentimes more than *conscious* design is involved, and that the writer does not always tell the truth, the whole truth, and nothing but the truth about what his specific intentions were. Surely, such assumptions as these can be conceded without holding that the writer has no intentions at all, or that he does not, in the usual case, know his intention better than anyone else. In any case, there is nothing stated in "The Intentional Fallacy" that denies that a poem or novel or play lacks a teleological element or that it is idle to try to seek it out.

A number of years later, in 1968, Wimsatt published "Genesis: An Argument Resumed," in which he replies to some of the objections to the earlier essay and provides a convincing clarification of his position. In what follows I shall try to restate it, though, of course, in my own terms. The reader of a literary work normally begins with the presumption that his author has realized his intentions, more or less completely, in the work that he has written. But the wise reader expects to find that evidence in the work itself—that is, evidence that the author has really succeeded in "saying" what he presumably wanted to "say." Evidence to be found in the text is firsthand evidence. Remember what that great novelist D. H. Lawrence said: "Never trust the teller: only trust the tale." Placed beside Lawrence's admonition, what Beardsley and Wimsatt ask seems downright modest.

Then what about such evidence of an author's intention as may be gleaned from letters, diaries, recorded remarks of what he told a friend on such and such an occasion? Wimsatt would argue—correctly, I believe— that evidence of this sort does not have the same value nor occupy the same status as the evidence to be found in the text. Why? Because evidence of this sort is an expression of hopes and plans, not necessarily accomplished aims. As Wimsatt puts it, "The intention [as it is given in documents] outside the [work itself] is always subject to the corroboration of the [work] itself." Unless it can be found to be attained in the work, the intention has literally not been realized, and so tells us nothing about the meaning of the work itself, however valid it may prove to be as evidence of what the writer at some time or other *meant* to say or perhaps thought he had succeeded in saying.

Let me provide a simple illustration. In Faulkner's *Go Down, Moses,* Isaac McCaslin rejects his inheritance because he feels that the property is tainted by his grandfather's sin. Isaac's wife, however, sees no reason for him to reject his inheritance and tries to persuade him to accept it. So does Isaac's cousin, to whom the inheritance eventually goes by default. When a student at the University of Virginia asked Faulkner about the wife's motives, Faulkner replied that her motives were those of a whore; that is, she had married Isaac for his plantation. But in the novel it is stated on the authority of the novelist—not merely by one of the fictional characters—that "she loved him." Furthermore, this statement is quite in accord with the other statements and narrated events in the novel. What are we to say then?

In this case, we have to appeal the verdict from Philip drunk to Philip sober—that is, from the author talking about the novel he had written many years earlier to the novel itself, in its full elaboration and articulation. Faulkner had simply forgotten what he had earlier written. There are other instances of Faulkner's forgetfulness that could be adduced. Moreover, there is plenty of evidence that he sometimes simply preferred to remember events in another way—as one of his fictional characters, V. K. Ratliff, tells us that he himself does. The fallacy here would be for us to take the author's declaration of what he meant, made under whatever circumstances, as more valid than evidence of *achieved* intention as revealed in the work itself. The latter is firsthand evidence and has priority over evidence gathered from any source outside the work—secondary evidence or, as lawyers would put it, "hearsay evidence."

Evidence of this sort may indeed have some value. It can give us hints of where we are to look, and it frequently predicts correctly enough what we are likely to find accomplished. But when it contradicts what is in the work, the realized intention is decisive. Besides, the secondary evidence is often woefully inadequate or even completely lacking. Shakespeare, for instance, has left us no indications of what he intended to say in his plays outside the plays themselves.

Wimsatt's rich and subtle essay, "Genesis: An Argument Resumed," discusses the whole matter of background and historical conditioning, as well as such matters as the problem of the author's sincerity. Here, I can do no more than allude to these issues, and therefore I urge that anyone who has a serious interest in this topic read "Genesis" in its entirety. Yet I must reiterate one of the several important distinctions that Wimsatt makes in this later essay. He points out that if we are concerned with *biography,* it is perfectly proper to use what the literary work can tell us about the author. (At the very least, the work tells us that the author was able to conceive and articulate it; it may tell us more.) On the other hand, if we are concerned with *literary criticism,* it is illicit to go from the author as recorded *outside the work in question* to the work. Using the example of Thomas Gray's "Elegy in a Country Churchyard," Wimsatt points out that if there were no way of knowing who the author was—if the poem, untitled, had simply been discovered in an eighteenth-century commonplace book—we might make some thoroughly intelligent guesses about the author: that is, we might be able to work back from the poem to the author; we might even guess that the author was Thomas Gray. But the meaning of the poem does not in the least depend upon knowing that Gray was in fact its author.

Why spend so much time on intentionalism? Because the fallacy is very much alive and well. Wimsatt and Beardsley might well quote from *Macbeth:* "We have scotched the snake, not killed it." The book *Interpretations: An Essay in the Philosophy of Literary Criticism,* by P. D. Juhl, for example, emphasizes the idea of the author's intention. Juhl defines the word *intention* by saying: "I am using the term in the sense of an author's intention in writing a certain sequence of words—in the sense, that is, of what he meant by the words he used." But David Hirsch, in his review of the book, puts this shrewd question: "But how are we to decide *'What he meant by* the words he used' except by determining what 'the words he used' mean? And how do we determine this except by considering context, syntax, and lexicon?"

How do we indeed, except by such considerations? In fact, the real damage done by intentionalism is its temptation to the reader to play down the importance of the context, syntax, and lexicon—and, I would further specify, the metaphors, the rhythms, and the shifts of tone in the work that the author has produced for the reader's attention. Such factors, I repeat, constitute evidence that has priority over any other evidence from the author, including specific statements of what he somewhere said or wrote that he intended to do.

Nevertheless, some of you may still wonder why I have devoted so much time to this particular aspect of the critical problem. I must do my best, therefore, to indicate why I regard this as a key issue. In the first place, a decision on this point is crucial for a definition of what is *literary* study as distinguished from, say, the study of biography or history or the particular character of a culture. Yet some of you may still have your doubts. You may want to ask whether there really is, in fact, any such thing as literature as such. Are not so-called literary texts to be regarded *simply* as events or verbal manifestations of a particular culture? Shakespeare's *Macbeth* is certainly a historical event, and indeed it is a manifestation of Elizabethan culture. Nobody denies that. But it is also possible to regard it as having an aesthetic dimension. It is possible to compare *Macbeth* as a work of art with other plays of the same period and with still earlier plays, such as the *Agamemnon* of Aeschylus, or with much later plays, such as *Desire under the Elms.* If there is a proper study of literature *as literary art,* our decisions on the issues raised by Wimsatt will determine what is proper evidence for such study and what is not.

To take another instance, let us ask why we are interested in the lives of the poets. The career of John Keats is primarily worthy of our study because he was a great poet, and not the other way around. Shorn of his poetry, this young medical student who died so early in his life would probably have dropped out of our sight completely. Yet if it is the poetry that keeps the memory of him alive and that has generated biography after biography, it is important to inquire into the nature and quality of the poetry itself so that we can see what we mean in calling it "great."

So far I have referred to two areas of literary study: a study of the literary work as such and a study of the author who brought it into being. But a study of a piece of writing and a study of the writer who fashioned it do not exhaust the possibilities for study. A third area is the study of the reader and what various readers actually make of a given work.

There is also a fourth area, which might be regarded as the substratum supporting all the other three: the linguistic medium used by the writer, constituting as it does the very fabric of the work and the means by which the reader appropriates it. The linguistic medium has come in for intense study in recent decades: attention has been directed to what language essentially is, how it transmits its messages and meanings, the nature of its meanings, and in what sense, if any, language can be said to relate us to the world around us.

Of the four types, the study of a literary work as an aesthetic object is the hardest to define and maintain. There is the constant threat that it will be absorbed into history and biography or be devoured by reader psychology or by linguistic theory. Literary judgments, as we have seen, still labor under the cloud of subjectivity. By contrast, powerful objective documentation can be invoked to guarantee the "facts" of the author's life or the development of the literary conventions involved in his work, and of the history of ideas dominant in his epoch. These refer, or at least seem to refer, to facts that are objective and can be substantiated. But how do you prove that the judgment of the literary critic is right or wrong? In fact, can you really "prove" that Shakespeare is a better poet than James Whitcomb Riley? It might not be wise to leave that verdict up to a poll of present-day readers. Consider, for example, what the American public puts on the best-seller list each week.

I have indicated how, in the opening decades of our own century, a study of the author and the historical forces that had played upon him thoroughly dominated English studies. As the century wore on, a revulsion against this heavy stress on the author came to characterize much of the literary criticism in both Great Britain and America—a revulsion that came to be called the "New Criticism." The name was ill-chosen—and was not, as I have often pointed out, chosen by the so-called New Critics themselves. In any case, they were not a cohesive group marching under one banner. Probably their only common trait was their reaction against the reigning historicism and their renewed respect for the structure and the inner workings of the poem or novel or drama in question.

In sum, these critics were not concerned merely with the maker or the making, but with the thing made. Yet surely, if the work in question is really a work of art, then the art displayed in the choice of words, their placement in the total structure, the establishment of a particular tone and the various shifts from it are important matters, for together they define and refine the meaning of the work.

Moreover, a poem is not simply a bit of ornamental prose. Metaphors, for example, are not to be regarded as merely illustrative or decorative in function. The poet sometimes makes use of established symbols, but he often develops within the poem his own symbolism, and, in a sense, the whole poem becomes a complex symbol, as particular scenes, objects, and events, under the pressures of the context in which they are placed, suggest more universal meanings. With the application of such critical methods and insights, some previously disparaged poems came to be seen in a new light and took their place in the established canon, and even some poems already established in the canon revealed a new richness of meaning.

I do not want to claim too much for such new ways of reading developed by this rather loose and heterogeneous group of critics, but they have some real accomplishments to their credit. In any case, they exerted an enormous influence on the teaching of literature in this country. But any method can be vulgarized and mechanized, and such was the lot of the so-called New Criticism. Analyses of poems were devised for the sake of analysis. Symbol mongering and extravagant extrapolations of metaphors occurred too often. Yet, every method is liable to debasements and extravagances. They have already appeared in the use of even newer methods of criticism.

The study of the author's life and a study of the origins of the work are well worth undertaking in their own right, but if they are substituted for a thoughtful examination of the work, they become a threat to any literary criticism that is concerned with matters of art. To confine oneself to a poem's status as a historical document is equivalent to striding through a picture gallery with one's eyes riveted on the guidebook and paying only casual attention to the pictures themselves. We may become so engrossed with the author's dates, place of birth, biography, and position in the canon that we hardly look at the work he accomplished.

There is also a threat from another direction. We may become so much engrossed with the effects of the work of art—on ourselves or on the population at large—that we are again diverted from any serious contemplation of the poem or novel or play itself. This possibility is not simply a theoretical one. It is very much at hand, and I have given a good deal of attention to this matter elsewhere. The reader is indeed important: after all, it is the reader who completes the transaction that goes from the author through the work to the reader. But in such study, psychological and sociological concerns can become primary and make the work itself simply a means to that end.

The third threat comes from the linguist, the specialist in language itself. For with a criticism of language that denies that language has anything to do with reality, we are back to Descartes' ghost locked up in a machine. Or perhaps it is language itself that becomes the machine, its wheels in motion, yet coupled with nothing outside, the gears that make it move something outside itself having been stripped. This third threat is the most dire of all to a humanistic view of literature.

I hope that it is plain that, though I want to make primary the study of a literary work of art *as a work of art*, I am not at all committed to what goes popularly as "art for art's sake." Rather, I regard the contemplation of literary art as providing us with *knowledge*—knowledge of ourselves in relation to reality as human beings may know it, and a knowledge which gains special value from being disinterested and fully contemplative.

12

English Literature

A Subject Matter? A Discipline? A Special Amalgam?

*L*et me begin by saying a word about some of the options in my frankly indecisive title. There are formidable objections to regarding literature as a mere subject matter. I prefer to think of it as providing a discipline of the sensibility—a special way of apprehending reality. But though I prefer such a conception, it gives rise to all sorts of misunderstandings—as I well know from personal experience. To define literature in this fashion is to risk being called a mere aesthete and even an escapist who refuses to face the harsh facts of life.

In choosing between literature as subject matter and as a mode of perception, one comes up against the age-old split between content and form, a split which easily transposes into the split between head and heart, intellect and emotion. If we make literature primarily a subject matter, then we risk putting it into competition with history or sociology. If, on the other hand, we insist upon its formal properties, we may seem to suggest that it is mere rhetoric; that is, a pattern of verbal manipulations contrived to persuade people to act in certain ways. Regarded as essentially rhetoric, literature is reduced to verbal frippery except where it has been applied to some serious use, as, for example, propaganda for a worthy cause.

The split between form and content goes a long way back in our culture—at least as far back as the time of Descartes' distinction between the world outside us, a world amenable to mathematical description, quantitative and objective, and the world within us, a world that is qualitative and subjective. Once this distinction had been fully grasped, science proceeded, with accelerating speed, to win its great victories. I will not say that poetry thenceforward languished—though there is the celebrated saying that Descartes cut the throat of poetry. Yet a confusion about the role of poetry did certainly ensue. It persists to this day. It occasions questions such as: Does poetry tell the truth about our world? Or does it merely entertain us? Does it have anything to say about reality, or is its role to allow us to escape the pressures of reality?

I shall not pretend to settle the theoretical question here. In my title I have suggested no more than a sort of compromise between the views that literature is a subject matter and that it is a mode of sensibility. This is at best a rough-and-ready solution; yet, it is not entirely devoid of merit if we are talking about the place of English in the university curriculum. As a matter of practical fact, the imaginative reordering of experience does seem, as a matter of history, to be associated with certain kinds of subject matter. It is no accident that the great poets and the great fiction writers have tended to stress certain areas of human life and to deal with certain aspects of the human predicament. Love and war, solitude and society, faith and doubt, the return to nature or the building of the city— these tend to be the sorts of human experience which, if they do not absolutely define or delimit literature, are obviously associated with the typical literary masterpiece.

Yet whether or not literature is more than an amalgam, I am disposed to regard literature as yielding a special kind of knowledge. The knowledge imparted by literature is not—or at least is only adventitiously and incidentally—scientific or historical knowledge. It is knowledge—I am tempted to join the poets in saying—of the human heart. Writers as diverse as William Wordsworth and William Faulkner have said as much. But to put matters thus may seem to beg questions of all sorts: the statement that poetry is knowledge of the heart may be dismissed by the more tough-minded as itself a poetic statement; and if it is, is it proper to use a bit of poetry in order to define poetry? Furthermore, even those who are willing to accept a poetic definition when given by a poet, might draw the line at accepting it from a nonpoet.

Let me, then, fall back on an argument better suited to a philologist and professor of literature. Let me suggest the following definition: a literary work (the greatest, at least) contains a wisdom that savors of experience—that savors life lived. My use of the term *savor* is, by the way, not entirely an idle flourish. Etymology supports me here. The Latin word for wisdom is *sapientia,* and it comes from the same root as does our word *savor.* In fact, the Latin verb *sapio,* from which both are ultimately derived, meant in the first instance to *taste,* and only later took on the meaning of to *discern* or to *understand.* The *Oxford English Dictionary* records instances of *savor* in its earlier meanings of *wisdom, perception,* or *understanding* as late as the seventeenth century. Milton makes Adam allude to the connection in *Paradise Lost.*

Those meanings of *savor* are now obsolete, but their present obsolescence does not trouble me. Indeed, I want to push back behind the Cartesian revolution and to produce evidence that taste, experience, understanding, and wisdom were once closely associated with one another. As a matter of fact, the earlier meanings are not altogether obsolete even today; "a man of taste" does not mean a gourmet: it means a man of discernment and discrimination.

In short, I want to call attention to a day before knowledge had been made abstract, specialized, purged of emotion, and divorced from the senses. Knowledge in its human totality and concrete wholeness literature was once thought to give; and this sort of knowledge, I suggest, it can still provide for us today, if we can learn how to read it.

I can state this definition of literature more abstractly: the knowledge afforded by literature is oriented to man as a total sensibility, not just to man as thinker. It describes a concrete, not an abstract world. The world of which literature speaks has a structure that embodies human values. Literature is dramatic, not clinical; it is a portrait in oils, not a diagram; a landscape done in perspective, not a map.

Yet even if you agree with me to call literature "wisdom that has the savor of experience," you may feel that this definition is rather empty. What good does literature do? How does it help us deal with present-day realities or live fully in our present world? In what I have already said, I have hinted at an answer and I propose to move immediately to particular texts for illustrations. Literature is incorrigibly concrete. Why should not a justification of its place among university studies be concrete too? If, by using a special instance and the citation of particular poems and stories, I risk narrowing the application of what I am saying, I believe, nonetheless, that such is the right method here and the most effective way to exhibit the value of literature as a university subject in its fullness.

Let me begin with a particular instance. If the student knows how to read a poem or a novel, and if he has done sound reading in modern literature, he will be better able to understand not only himself as a man of the modern period, but the present state of the civilization that has nurtured him. I and presumably most of my readers have been molded by the culture of the West. The relationship between that culture and our own intellectual and emotional selves is very close. To understand one is to go far toward understanding the other. Such understanding might even be called useful knowledge.

What, then, do the literary masters of the present day tell us about the state of our civilization? What seismic cultural shocks do our contemporary poets register? If they do register tremors, where do the tremors show the cultural fault lines to lie? I press this issue, for many of our poets and prose writers have, each in his own way, indicated stresses and strains in our cultural fabric—indeed, our major writers have for a century now been much concerned with what one might call a crisis in the culture.

I hasten to say that one could investigate under this rubric various problems and topics. I think of such topics as the new world of the psyche as revealed by depth psychology; the increasing secularization of society; the altered rhythms of work and leisure under the impact of urbanization and industrialism; the changed status of nature and the natural; the passing of the cult of the hero, the rise of the anti-hero, and the death of the gods; romantic love and the sexual revolution; the sacred and the profane in our twentieth-century dispensation. I shall choose just one topic and try to deal with it in some detail, for the topics I have mentioned are all interrelated, and in dealing with one we shall touch upon all. All have to do with man's altered view of himself as he is forced to look at himself in the light of his cold and clinical new knowledge, against the backdrop of a neutralized nature. One surely does not exaggerate if he describes the consequence of man's altered view of himself as having resulted in a crisis in our culture.

I propose for the purpose of this discussion to examine what our contemporary poets have to say about just one aspect of this crisis, especially as it concerns history in its relation to nature. W. H. Auden's brilliant little poem "The Fall of Rome" is pat to this purpose. The title itself points to a past crisis that led to the dissolution of a great civilization of the past. The poem is explicitly about history, but the poet also has—particularly at the end—some comments to make about nature.

If we can read this poem with any real perception, it turns out to be not merely about the fall of Rome but about the fall of any civilization, including the possibility of the fall of our own. In fact, if you can put up with a little wordplay on the subject of nature and history, we might describe this poem as follows: it is a "natural history" of the winter season of any historical "organism."

One notices, for example, Auden's deliberate mixture of the past and present. The Roman Empire had piers but no abandoned trains; it made use of temple prostitutes, but not of pink official forma. In Auden's poem, ancient Rome and modern New York (or London) mix and merge. There are further echoes of our own, as well as an ancient, time: in a falling empire sex is nearly always given special importance. Caesar's double bed is indeed warm, and the temple prostitutes are kept busy even if they have no mind or taste for the "Private rites of magic" that interest some of their more decadent clients. In such a cultural breakdown as this poem describes, sex has a special attraction, for it seems to offer a privileged access to reality—it offers a return to something immediate and at the core of being. A related aspect of a culture in decay is the boredom of the "unimportant clerk." He (and obviously many others in his situation) feels divorced from the natural and spontaneous: life has become a monotonous and meaningless round.

Why, in the last two stanzas, does the poet suddenly shift to the natural scene—away from the life of men to that of birds and beasts? Because birds and beasts have no empire, no culture, no self-consciousness, no history. The life of natural creatures is blind and instinctive. It answers to physico-chemical laws, to herd instincts, and such training as the doe may give her fawn or the she-bear her cubs. But choice and responsibility in our sense do not exist. Empires may rise and fall, but the reindeer follow, as they always have, their immemorial migrations across the arctic tundra. The birds are, as Auden puts it, "unendowed with wealth or pity." They need no currency, amass no bank accounts, and have no reason to feel human pity—certainly not for man, who for them, if they notice him at all, is simply a strange, sometimes disturbing presence.

Auden's poem draws no moral: it does not ask us to feel this or that about the situation. But its very makeup will suggest to the attentive reader a situation worth his contemplation. Yet the tone of the poem is not solemn, but witty, detached, almost playful. With this poem we have come a good long way from Wordsworth and the early nineteenth-century Romantic poets, though it is plain that the Romantics, in their day, were addressing themselves to the same basic situation that Auden depicts. Wordsworth and Coleridge sensed the fact that civilized man had somehow broken away from nature. The old relationship had been lost, and Wordsworth insisted that it needed to be restored.

It might be useful at this point to develop a little further the contrast between nature and history. The world of nature is governed by laws that are absolute and unbreakable. If I, in a fit of despair, dive off the top of a ninety-foot tower, I will not break any scientific law. I will simply fulfill the law governing the rate of falling bodies. Indeed, no scientific law can be broken: that it cannot is the proof that it is really scientific. The world of history, on the other hand, is cluttered with laws that are broken every day. We constantly break laws governing the relationship of parent and child, family and clan, state and nation. We constantly break the laws of logic, of aesthetics, and of ethics. Yet, such laws cannot be dismissed as worthless because so prone to fracture, for no human society of which we have ever heard has developed without the support of such rules. In this area we find ourselves in the human dimension of promises and vows, police regulations, oaths of office, constitutions, traffic ordinances, the rules of etiquette, and the canons of good taste. All such laws are fragile— even the laws condemning murder and treason; yet can a society function without them? For man is neither an automaton that can be programmed to certain precise activities, nor is he merely an animal that can get along with instinctive drives and a modicum of conditioning. Man is that most peculiar animal that possesses the capacity to become a saint but also the dire likelihood that he will turn out to be only a rather drab and ordinary sinner. What he can't be is simply a good lion or a good bullock or a good goldfinch. The word *good* changes character when we apply it to the world of natural creatures.

In the Christian synthesis, nature and history stood in a specific relationship to each other: God had made nature, including man, and God was the lord of history. God had, in the beginning, created both man and nature good; but in the Fall, man had violated his bond with God.

God had, to be sure, given man a second chance. Man could be redeemed, but he was, nevertheless, a fallen creature, not innocent and not perfectible by his own unaided effort. Furthermore, man's loving rapport with nature had been broken also. Man now had to prey upon nature; even so, it behooved him to respect it and not to attempt to master it with ruthless brutality. If he could no longer live on the bounty of nature as a happy and unselfconscious natural creature, at least he ought to take what he needed from nature, not arrogantly or carelessly, but with a loving respect.

In our modern world, with the breakup of the Christian synthesis, nature and history have tended to fall apart. History has been subsumed under nature, or else nature has been subordinated to history. Thus, man sees himself as a natural creature who, nevertheless, can create his own history. Men who are obsessed with their own historical aims and purposes tend to regard nature as merely the arena in which they act, or as the source of the raw materials available for their designs and purposes. Nature has been stripped of its awe and luminous quality. As for God, he is either dead—that is, is an obsolete illusion—or he has become internalized as simply an aspect of man's own consciousness.

With reference to this matter of modern man and nature, I call your attention to a charming but powerful little lyric by Robert Frost. The poem is entitled "Come In." As the speaker tells us, he is, on this evening's walk, out for stars, not for thrush music. Nevertheless, he pays some attention to the song of the thrush and is responsive to its melancholy beauty. The song of the bird, issuing from its dark forest covert, almost seduces the hearer into thinking that it is the voice of nature itself, and that nature, sympathetic with man's sorrows, invites him to join her in her lament for the tears of things.

Thus the poet establishes the standard Romantic situation in which nature seems to stretch out a sympathetic hand to human kind. But the poet of "Come In" turns out to be a hard-bitten modern. He quickly recovers himself; he refuses nature's invitation, and reaffirms his original purpose, to go out and look at the stars. He responds to the bird almost gruffly: "I would not come in." But then he suddenly remembers his manners and modulates his tone. "I meant," he tells nature, or himself, or perhaps just us readers, "I meant not even if asked, / And I hadn't been." The last line gathers up beautifully the force of this little poem and gives it its power. For though this last line sounds like a kind of throwaway—an afterthought tacked on to the main matter—it actually makes the poem. Of course, nature hasn't asked the hearer to come into her dark and lament. Nature, no more than the evening thrush through which the observer for a moment fancies he hears her speaking, is not even aware of the man who is walking by. Nature, that quasi-mystical identity, is as blind and indifferent as she is beautiful. The hard fact—as the speaker of the poem finally reminds himself—is that man is alone in the universe, and if nature is not actively hostile, she is certainly quite indifferent to his presence. Insofar as he is simply another biological mechanism like the bird, an organism answering to nature's laws like any other biological mechanism, he is indeed a part of nature. But his awareness and self-consciousness are a peculiar trait apparently not found in other natural creatures. To quote Scripture here: "The foxes have holes, and the birds of the air [including the evening thrush] have nests; but the Son of man hath no where to lay his head"—nowhere, that is, to lay his head in the domain of nature. Man's head (that locus of dreams, imaginings, transcendencies) sticks up out of nature. It exceeds the physico-chemico-biological world.

In moving on from Frost's poem, let me call attention to the fact that what gives it its piquancy, its bite, its claim on our attention, is not its account of man's relation to nature as such, but the way in which that relation is dramatized, the way in which the human being who is imagined to speak the poem assimilates the truth in a response that is wry, ironically self-deprecatory, but not self-pitying or sentimental. The quality of that response is itself a most important aspect of the "knowledge" that this poem conveys.

An early poem by T. S. Eliot, one that has puzzled a good many readers, turns out—unless I miss my guess completely—to be concerned with this same situation: that of man up against a nature that has lost its mystery and its numinous quality, and stands revealed in all its sublime indifference equally to man's blandishments and to his violence.

The poem is entitled "Sweeney among the Nightingales." Sweeney is the Boston Irishman who appears in several of Eliot's early poems and in two fragments of a play. He is rough-hewn, no charmer, and certainly makes no pretense to being an intellectual; but Sweeney is no fool, either. In this poem Sweeney has got into some sort of dive or joint and is suspicious that the women—bar girls, presumably—are out to get him drunk or perhaps to use knockout drops and roll him for his wallet. But Eliot does not move into Sweeney's problem directly. Instead, he begins with an elaborate rhetoric and some almost rococo fanfaronades. In fact, he approaches his subject matter with all the portentousness that an epic writer might have used in Homeric times or in the Elizabethan age, as he leads up to this episode in his hero's life.

> Apeneck Sweeney spreads his knees
> Letting his arms hang down to laugh,
> The zebra stripes along his jaw
> Swelling to maculate giraffe.
>
> The circles of the stormy moon
> Slide westward toward the River Plate,
> Death and the Raven drift above
> And Sweeney guards the hornéd gate.

The key to what Eliot is doing is given—as so often in Eliot—in an epigraph placed at the beginning of the poem. It is a line he quotes from the *Agamemnon* of Aeschylus. Agamemnon, having just returned from the Trojan War, is murdered by his wife and her paramour. Dying, he cries out: "Alas, I've been dealt a mortal blow within [the house]." How would an intrigue against someone like Agamemnon or anyone else be presented nowadays, when nature has been neutralized, the gods all proclaimed to be dead, and man has become simply the wisest of the beasts? Under these circumstances, is it possible to have a tragic death at all?

We notice that Sweeney is described completely in animalistic terms. He is "Apeneck Sweeney." There are "zebra stripes along his jaw"; and when he laughs, these swell to "maculate giraffe." Later in the poem, a silent man in mocha brown is described as "the silent vertebrate in brown" and the bar girl named Rachel has "murderous paws" with which she tears at the grapes. Though a second bar girl is not described as an animal, the poem manages to turn her into pure mechanism. She becomes an automaton.

So all the portentousness of the ominous "stormy moon," the movement across the sky of constellations such as the Raven, and in the next stanza gloomy Orion and the Dog, constitute simply an ironic and mock-heroic background for the action.

Are Sweeney's suspicions of the bar girls justified? Were they really after his wallet? We never find out, for the poet is not interested in the outcome of this little episode. What he is interested in, and evidently expects us to be interested in, is the contrast between intrigue in the days of the heroes and demigods when nature itself seemed to suffer with man, the sort of intrigue about which Aeschylus wrote, and a cheap intrigue in the secularized world of today in which nature is drained of any meaning beyond its mere physico-chemico-biological character.

But what about the nightingales that figure so prominently in the title of the poem? They obviously represent nature, which is the indifferent backdrop against which men's little comedies and tragedies take place. The nightingales sing as sweet an obligato to the plot against Sweeney as they sang three thousand years ago to the plot against Agamemnon, the leader of the Greek host. Moreover, they are just as indifferent in their offerings—with the delicate songs or with the liquid droppings that they let fall. They have no sympathy with man and no tie with him.

Eliot is not here preaching a solemn sermon or sighing because we don't live in the age of Homeric Greece, nor is he making fun of Apeneck Sweeney and his likes. He is, if I understand him, canvassing, with some detachment and ironic contemplation, a situation which exists and which has very deep implications for us all. But he is not trying to dictate our response. Like the ideal artist as described by James Joyce, he stands behind the facade of his artwork, quietly paring his fingernails, serene and indifferent. His poem is allowed to speak for itself, and the meaning is left for him to hear that has ears to hear or that has eyes to see. Poems are not sermons or bits of propaganda or scientific formulas. They are dramatizations of situations. They have been created by the imagination, and if the reader is to realize them fully, his own imagination must be engaged. Yet surely this is why they contain not only knowledge—imaginative knowledge—knowledge of what it is like to live in a certain kind of world—but if we are up to gleaning it—wisdom as well.

Let me now provide a final example from William Butler Yeats, his never-too-much-to-be-praised "A Prayer for My Daughter." As the poem makes plain, the poet is in his tower home near the west coast of Ireland. It is a stormy night and the sea wind is blowing in off the Atlantic as the poet is watching over the cradle of his infant daughter. He is strangely troubled in mind, for he has an intense foreboding of the time of troubles that lies ahead for our civilization, and is deeply apprehensive as to how his daughter will fare in the turbulent and disordered world of the future. The poem was written in 1919, and we may confidently claim that Yeats indeed foresaw, as in a prophet's vision, the rise of Fascism and Nazism, the Second World War, and the troubled and disastrous times that have followed it.

Any sensitive reading of the poem will show that Yeats has developed a brilliant and rather elaborate symbolism. For example, the sea wind blowing in off the Atlantic, out of the "murderous innocence of the sea," is a destructive natural force. Yeats uses it, however, to describe threatening historical forces. The future is foreboding. Hence he prays that his daughter may find a life like that of some green laurel tree, "rooted in one dear perpetual place," able to resist the violent storms of history.

He wishes for her beauty, but not too much—not the kind that can make a stranger's eye distraught. As Yeats had bitterly learned from his long, unrequited love affair with Maud Gonne, women who are beautiful overmuch cause trouble to themselves and to everyone else. Helen of Troy was such a woman, and even the goddess Aphrodite "that rose out of the spray" made a poor choice for a husband—the bandy-legged god of the forge, Hephaestus or Vulcan.

The matter in which the poet would wish his daughter chiefly learned is courtesy. The light that he hopes will shine in her eyes is that of "a glad kindness." He prays that she may never, save "in merriment begin a chase, / Nor but in merriment a quarrel." Some readers have mistakenly concluded that the poem is an expression of Yeats's prayerful hope that his daughter might remain sweet, simple, and ignorant. But in wishing that his daughter may "think opinions are accurst," he is certainly not asking that she never entertain *ideas*. On closer inspection, it becomes plain that

Yeats is making use of Plato's distinction between ideas, which are absolutely true and which for him constituted reality, and opinions, which are no more than probably true and which are the occasion for arrogance, disputes, and intellectual hatreds. In fact, remembering Maud Gonne, who wanted to free Ireland not by the dissemination of ideas but by violence, including dynamite, the poet exclaims:

> Have I not seen the loveliest woman born
> Out of the mouth of Plenty's horn,
> Because of her opinionated mind
> Barter that horn and every good
> By quiet natures understood
> For an old bellows full of angry wind?

The woman with the opinionated mind and her bellows "full of angry wind" is imitating the wind howling off the Atlantic, "out of the murderous innocence of the sea." She is aping in her human dimension the violence of nature. She is acting out of her instincts and not out of a disciplined humanity.

The poet asks for his daughter a different kind of innocence, one which comes whence Plato taught that it came, out of the depths of the soul and the soul's fundamental knowledge of its self. As the poet puts it, if one is able to lay aside all opinionated hatred, his "soul [may recover] radical innocence." A radical innocence is a rooted innocence, like that of the laurel tree, rooted in one dear perpetual place. Such a soul learns that it is "self-delighting, / Self-appeasing, self-affrighting, / And that its own sweet will is Heaven's will." So taught, so disciplined, the poet's daughter can, "though every face should scowl / And every windy quarter howl / Or every bellows burst, be happy still." Thus, if his daughter can recover that radical innocence of the soul, which differs so profoundly from the murderous innocence of the sea, she can, relying on her inner resources, withstand even the wars and disasters that lie ahead in the troubled future.

The last stanza of the poem has bred certain misconceptions. Careless readers are prone to interpret Yeats's prayer that his daughter's bridegroom may bring her to a house "Where all's accustomed, ceremonious" as a wish that his daughter may marry well and thus be protected from the hardships of the world. But it is not a wealthy bridegroom from a great house that the poet wishes for his daughter. Hers may well be a modest home, provided that all is "accustomed" and "ceremonious." For the poem ends in a great hymn to custom and to ceremony, to life as ordered ritual. The poet in a bold closing assertion argues that innocence and beauty are not, as men usually think of them, the casual gift of blind nature; rather, they come from order and discipline. As the poem ends he exclaims:

How but in custom and in ceremony
Are innocence and beauty born?
Ceremony's a name for the rich horn,
And custom for the spreading laurel tree.

This is Yeats's least romantic—and most classical—poem. It is indeed Platonic, for it locates true beauty, not in the dower bestowed by the careless largesse of nature, but in a quality derived from learning and self-discipline. It is consequently an expression of humanity and not simply of nature.

Let me recall what I have said earlier about the relation of history and nature. What is the relation of the two in this brilliant poem? Nature here is indifferent to man, as it is indifferent in the poems earlier examined, from Auden, Frost, and Eliot. Yet for Yeats, nature can still provide symbols of something that is thoroughly and deeply human. The laurel tree rooted in one dear perpetual place becomes a type of the life he would wish for his daughter. Conversely, if nature can provide analogues for disciplined humanity, history can be seen as a kind of *natural* process, with all of the meaningless chaos that we sometimes attribute to the storms of nature. Yeats's poetry is full of this notion. He sees history running through its cycles—through the springtime of a culture, its summertime of blossoming, its autumn of rich harvest, and its winter of desiccation and death. There are hints of this in "Prayer for My Daughter." The sense of the poem is that Western civilization is in for a hard time and that the individual can do nothing to change history. It is this prophetic vision that, as the poem opens, causes "the great gloom that is in [the poet's] mind."

Do we have to conclude, then, that Yeats regards history as violent and senseless as the world of nature and as little answerable to man's purposes and needs and beliefs? Does he write in complete despair about the human enterprise? I think not, though it is interesting to remember that Yeats did not believe in progress, and certainly not in the millennialists' dream, so dear to many in North America, the dream that holds out the prospect of man's building, through his own efforts, the perfect society. Yeats obviously reposes his hope in the individual soul.

Does this mean, then, that Yeats has reinstated God? Again, no. Certainly not the Christian God. But he does believe that man can find in the depths of his self eternal truth, and that the purified and disciplined soul can survive the vicissitudes of history. Such faith resembles to a degree Christian transcendence, though perhaps it is best to put the emphasis where I earlier suggested: on a kind of Platonism in which the individual soul, through a process of anamnesis, can recover the eternal truths and thus achieve its salvation, even though most men are deluded by shadows and other false appearances and are consequently subject to all the ills and misfortunes of nature and condemned to a meaningless history.

I began by asking whether modern literature could throw any light on events of our own time such as the crisis in culture in which we experience the breakup of the Christian synthesis, with man now reduced to nature, and human history having become a natural process; or else, nature transformed into a mere extension of the human enterprise and man, as the new lord of history, prepared to fashion a new heaven and a new earth. In other words, pure naturalism or millennialism or a mixture of both.

Obviously, the poets and novelists of our century have been very sensitive to these issues, though they have reacted to them in various ways. On the whole, they have not tried to generalize the issues or to attempt solutions. Marxism, Freudianism, Existentialism, death-of-God theology, millennialism, ecological destruction of the planet—all these issues in some form or another are treated in modern literature, in essence or in potentiality. But our literary men have their value, in the production not of philosophical studies or political treatises, but of fictions and myths— in providing not solutions, but diagnoses, of the cultural malady.

Even the avowed Christians among them, such as Auden and Eliot, tend to dramatize the situation rather than to prescribe a remedy or to recommend certain values. Actually, I have taken pains not to stack the deck. Along with the avowed Christians, there are non-Christians among the various writers that I have presented. I could have added to them such artists as John Crowe Ransom, Wallace Stevens, and James Joyce. The significant matter common to all of them—whatever the differences in their philosophical commitment or their final attitudes—is that Western culture has been profoundly shifted and that the aftershocks of this major earthquake continue to be felt.

I have noticed that some of our most perceptive psychologists and historians listen very attentively to our best literary artists because they are aware that the artist has a special sensitivity to shifts in cultural attitudes, and that he also has the gift for finding an ordered pattern where others may perceive only aimless confusion.

It is not statistical information or recipes for action that we ought to expect from literature. What we can get is a kind of inward knowledge—a knowledge finally of our deepest selves. We can, through literature, come to understand better our times as well as ourselves and, not least important, to understand better the relation between ourselves and others, the dead as well as the living.

With awakened imaginations, we may be able to see man's present triumph (or perhaps it is better to call it man's present plight) in the long perspective of history. If that view is calculated to moderate our pride, it can also give us some comfort in reminding us of basic continuities and unchanged verities. In short, if the knowledge that literature can give will not necessarily enable us to save our society, it may at least save our own sanity.

Such knowledge is precious and, even if not peculiar to literature (as I think it actually is), can be acquired most practically through an enlightened reading of our literature, past and present. But we must never mistake it for mere information or for a compendium of rules and axioms. Its secret power is that it awakens and develops our own powers—our imaginative powers that enable us to respond to reality, to make the proper discriminations in apprehending the truth in any situation, and to discipline our own sensibilities so that we can enact with wisdom and delight our assigned role in the drama of human existence.

13

Science, Religion, and Literature

❧

One of the wisest men of our day has addressed our special cultural condition thus: "I am persuaded that in our time the battle between the powers of good and evil is pitched in Man's mind even more than in his heart, since it is known that the latter will ultimately follow the former." Note that he is careful to write "even more than in his heart," for no wise man can ever discount the importance of the heart in matters of this sort. Nevertheless, I think that Owen Barfield, for that is my wise man's name, is correct in holding that the battle between good and evil in our time, because it is a battle of ideas, is being fought primarily in men's heads.

Two thousand years ago Saint Paul saw how important was the struggle for men's minds. There is, in his Epistle to the Ephesians, a relevant passage, his exhortation to the congregation at Ephesus to put on the whole armor of God in the conflict that they had to face. In chapter 6, verses 11–12, he tells them to

> Put on the whole armor of God, that ye may be able to stand against the wiles of the devil.
> For we wrestle not against flesh and blood but against principalities, against powers, against the rulers of darkness of this world.

When Saint Paul specifies that the real enemy is not flesh and blood, that is, other men, he makes it plain that this is to be a battle of ideas.

I need not remind you that a celebrated, even notorious battle in defense of Christianity was fought in Dayton, Tennessee, a half century and more ago. Many thoughtful Christians today cannot regard the result as a victory for their side. They believe that the battle was fought on grounds disadvantageous to the cause, that the strategy was misconceived, and that the tactics were woefully inadequate. Note that I am not faulting for any lack of ardor or zeal those who believed that they were defending religion. The mistakes were of the head, not the heart. In any case, the war goes on, and whether or not you call the encounter at Dayton a victory, that encounter did not rout its supposed enemies. I repeat: the war continues.

Yet I do not intend to rattle the bones of the past. I am concerned with the present and the future. Moreover, I am even hopeful. I am convinced that in our day a strong case can be made for Christianity. But we may need to change our strategy by attempting to see just what it is that we oppose in science. We may be surprised to find how little we do oppose in authentic scientific theories and procedures, and so then desist from desperate charges against entrenched positions that cannot be won. We might do so by according to science its truth in those matters where it is indeed genuine, and direct men's attention to those areas in which science as such has no real power of determination—where *as science* it does not depose. Those areas are vast and most important to humanity itself. Such in general is a strategy with which we might hope to win men's minds. If we chose to pursue it, we might find that many scientists, including some of the most distinguished of them, would not oppose us but welcome us as friends.

Having said this, I must make two things clear before going forward. The first is this: it may seem that I am suggesting that Christians capitulate, concede that they are beaten, and accept with good grace whatever meager bone the scientists will throw them. This is not at all what I mean. The role of Christianity as I see it remains all important. There is a vast need to be satisfied and an opportunity to be exploited. Moreover, in the course of action that I would suggest, Christianity stands to give up nothing proper to her true mission.

The second matter in which I could have been misunderstood is this: I may have given the impression that I bring ideas that are fresh and new. I make no such claim. The strategies that I shall suggest have not originated with me. What I propose is much more modest. It is to do no more than clarify issues, trace the history of the questions at issue, and to call attention to some of the great thinkers of our time.

I mentioned that I would try to set forth what might be called the history of the question—of this supposed conflict between science and religion. I suppose that we could find hints of it in the earliest history of man as we know him, but our purposes here are best served by going no further back than Descartes. What I would call attention to is his distinction between the world outside man—the world of space-time as we have come to know it—and the inner world—the world inside a man's head—the world of desires, wishes, dreams, and valuations of all kinds, including spiritual values. The world outside man is susceptible of exact measurement, Descartes showed, and in doing so, he made possible the extraordinary progress of the physical sciences which has accelerated triumphantly ever since. But what about that elusive but fascinating interior world that is the domain of man's soul? How do you measure a thought or weigh a wish? No scientific triumph was possible in this realm. That aspect of it gave trouble and has given trouble ever since. For example, is modern psychology a hard science? Isn't it still highly speculative, and don't psychiatrists with equally good credentials often give diametrically opposed testimony in every law court in the land?

Descartes was a sincere Christian. Indeed, he honestly believed that his work reinforced Christian faith. But it is plain that it did not, in the same sense that Descartes has been said to have cut the throat of poetry. Because the man in the street respected the truth that the scientist had to give him about the space-time world, he came to ask whether the poet dealt in truth at all. Didn't the poet simply express, for instance, his own personal dreams and fancies?

Later still, a philosopher was to describe what Descartes had done as locking up a ghost in a machine. Not only was the space-time world as described by Descartes a mighty machine, but wasn't man's own body, by the same token, a machine too? And what was the connection between this machine and that pale insubstantial spirit or ghost that apparently lived within the round box of a man's skull?

There is no need to blame Descartes, of course. If he had not made the breakthrough for modern science, someone else eventually would have done so. It was, as we say, in the cards. The development of modern science was inevitable. Furthermore, we owe a great deal to science: it has conferred immense benefits on mankind even if in atomic weaponry it makes possible the greatest perils of mankind.

Many of you, I am sure, will feel as I did some time ago, when a surgeon performed an operation on me. I was very glad that he was able to consider my body as a rather delicate and highly complicated machine in which something was out of kilter and in need of the repair that he was competent to make.

By the middle of the nineteenth century the chasm between the outer world and the inner man had widened so much that the poet Matthew Arnold, who was also a serious student of contemporary British culture, became very much concerned about what he rightly saw was a matter of critical importance. His poem "Dover Beach" was one of the fruits of his pondering on the matter. In this poem the speaker is at a window looking out on a moonlit night. He listens to the tide going out at Dover Beach and says:

> Listen! You hear the grating roar
> Of pebbles which the waves draw back, and fling
> At their return, up the high strand,
> Begin, and cease, and then again begin,
> With tremulous cadence slow, and bring
> The eternal note of sadness in.

The sense of sadness for this listener is deepened by his hearing in it symbolically the ebbing of religious faith. The Sea of Faith, which was once at the full, is now, he reflects, withdrawing from "earth's shores," and the poem closes with something very like despair. To the speaker of the poem, the world has come to lose all meaning, for the world which had seemed so various, so beautiful, so new, has, as he now sadly reflects,

> . . . really neither joy, nor love, nor light,
> Not certitude, nor peace, nor help from pain.

So wrote Arnold the poet. As a critic of culture, he dealt analytically with the same cultural situation. Arnold's essential position may be summed up as follows: the advances of science had made it impossible to believe in religion. For religion had attached itself to certain facts and these supposed facts had been challenged by science. Yet mankind still needed values such as religion had formerly supplied. What then to do? Arnold's plan was essentially this: science would show us the most effective means to secure the ends we seek. Art, and particularly literature, would, on the other hand, present the ends, the values, to be sought. Thus Arnold reduced science, religion, and art to a pair of opposites, science and art—art replacing religion which, Arnold believed, had been rendered null. For if science had demolished the supposed facts to which religion adhered, literature fortunately adhered to no facts. It made no positive truth claims. Literature, or poetry, as Arnold called it, was a relatively pure symbolism. In accepting literature, the reader accepts a world of as-if, of make-believe, of fiction. Thus, its authority could not be undermined by the intrusion of the objective truths of science. Arnold accepted, in effect, the distinction that Descartes had drawn between man's outer and inner, or objective and subjective, worlds. But he went further than Descartes in explicitly giving up the realm of religion by regarding it as finally mere poetry.

It is my belief that Arnold asked literature to shoulder a burden that it is incapable of bearing. Literature has its own task to perform, an indispensable task, but it cannot serve as an anchor for man's ethical being or as a reliable guide for his conduct. Later I shall have more to say about the true mission of literature and its importance for any civilization. At this point, I simply want to assert firmly that it cannot, as Arnold hoped, replace the function of religion. As T. S. Eliot, one of the most important of our Christian intellectuals, put it some years ago, if one cannot accept a religion, then he will simply have to do without. There is no substitute for it.

Where shall we then find our values in this modern world, if literature and art cannot be our resources? Not in science, I would say. It may be significant that Arnold himself never made that claim. Why not? Because in practical matters, science can tell us what is the most efficient means by which to bring about a certain end. But we have no right to ask it to make—as science—a choice of ends. Yet the choice of ends is the most important thing we ever do. The machines which are the results of applied science are, in their power and complication, quite marvelous, and, of course, extremely useful. But they provide in themselves no moral directions for their proper use. An airplane can fly needed diphtheria antitoxin into a snowbound village, but it can also drop a bomb on that same village. Its efficiency as a machine—that is, as a means—remains unchanged whether we regard the mission it accomplishes as humane or fiendish. The machine is sublimely neutral, indifferent as to the end we wish to accomplish through its use.

The so-called laws of science are not like the laws that constitute the criminal code or that regulate the transfer of property. They are actually definitions. You couldn't break them if you tried. If, in a fit of deep depression, I decided to take my own life and to that end jumped off the roof of a tall building, I wouldn't break a single scientific law, even if I broke every bone in my body. I would simply fulfill the law of falling bodies. In deciding to kill myself I would certainly break ethical and religious laws, and any state or municipal laws that forbid suicide. Such laws as these can be broken. That's one of the reasons we have law courts and build jails. The point involved is important: we cannot look to science *as science* to dictate the important choices that we are forced to make.

Now all this ought to be clear enough. Yet for the man in the street, it is not clear. He has learned to look up to science as the source of all kinds of technical wonders and also as the source of thoroughly tested, objective truth. In this matter, the advertising agencies have not been very helpful. Advertisers would like to steal a bit of science's honestly won prestige for their own products. Thus we have toothpaste ads proclaiming that this brand is recommended by doctors, or picturing a white-jacketed gentleman in a laboratory surrounded by his test tubes, and underneath the picture a caption that reads: "Science tells us. . . ."

Now this kind of conduct is not at all fair to the careful and accurate scientist who makes no claims that he feels he cannot fulfill and, if he makes ethical judgments, makes no claim that they are the findings of some scientific experiment.

Surely, however, it is plain by now that I have no quarrel with science or with the scientist as such. But the impact of applied science on the man in the street has been pervasive, and it has had—through no fault of the genuine scientist—the effect of skewing the whole notion of what modern science is and what it does. There is also the impact of the so-called social sciences, such as sociology and psychology. Granting the importance of a careful study of the areas with which they concern themselves, their findings are, as yet, not in the same class as those of, say, chemistry and physics.

Years ago, I heard I. A. Richards shock a group of sociologists by saying that all of sociology, except its statistical studies, was poetry—by which he did not mean that the sociologists' pronouncements about society were worthless. They might indeed be wise and informed judgments, but then so might be some of the judgments on society made by Chaucer or Shakespeare. I think, however, that I ought to add in fairness, not so much to sociology as to Richards, that Richards meant to be a little mischievous in his statement. He wanted to rustle the dovecotes, and he certainly did so.

More to my point, however, is the following illustration that I take from the work of one of our ablest contemporary novelists, Walker Percy. Percy, by the way, has had his scientific training, with a bachelor's degree in biology, and an M.D. for his medical training. He knows what science is and does, and surely has no quarrel with it. Yet he is a Christian church-man who takes his religion most seriously.

In the course of his second novel, entitled *The Last Gentleman,* he makes a distinction between "the anteroom of science" and "the research laboratory." In short, the average man in our country gets his science by hearsay, usually out of the Sunday supplements, and knows little or nothing directly about scientific method and the nature of scientific proof. Small wonder that he is not clear on what genuine science really says and what it does not undertake to say.

Allow me to pursue this matter further still, for it is an important one. Sunday-supplement science and the astrological charts aside, what science in its applied forms has done is to condition our thinking about almost every aspect of the world around us and even of ourselves. The ubiquity of machines, their increasing complication, and their importance to us in our daily lives has meant that we become habituated to mechanical models. We tend unconsciously, if not consciously, to think of the universe as a great machine, of the animal and vegetable world around us as not made up of living organisms, but of mechanisms, and even of our fellow human beings as machines too.

This tendency to treat even human beings as if they were superior machines has blurred the line that divides the animate from the inanimate. The distinction, however, is crucial, for in our modern world there is little left of the life of the spirit, whether in human beings themselves or in the universe, if we think of everything in mechanical terms.

I want for a moment to return to the division that Descartes opened between man's outer world which can be accurately measured and analyzed by scientific methods, and man's inner world which is by definition filled with thoughts, desires, volitions, and valuings—entities impossible to measure or analyze by scientific methods. By our time this fission has grown to a yawning chasm. If we try to deal with that inner world through scientific methods, we commit ourselves to a rigid behavioristic determinism, or, more desperately, we come to regard that inner world as an illusion: that is, we come to think that men cannot make real choices, since their choices have already been determined in some cause-and-effect process. So the ghost locked up in a machine becomes even more vaporously ghostly, for the twentieth-century world does not believe in ghosts—either the Holy Ghost or ghosts that are unholy.

The way out of such an impasse seems to me clear: we must not allow ourselves to become victims of what logicians call a "false option"—that is, feel that we must choose science and reject religion, or else accept religion and reject science. We can accept both if we come to understand what each deals with and what their relations are to one another. That relationship is often obscured. Our educational system is at fault here, though confusion in this matter tends to be general in our culture. Yet since science has to do with means, then each practical pronouncement of the scientist begins with a proviso: to wit, *if* you want to achieve such and such a result, then this is the only means, or perhaps this is the most efficient means. That proviso is rarely uttered, but it is always implied. Science cannot, as science, tell you what end you ought to pursue.

Yet we must remember that the goals that religion sets up—and of course I have in mind preeminently the goals set up by Christianity—are not susceptible of scientific proof. That is, they are not objectively verifiable in the sense in which that term applies to chemistry, physics, and mathematics. The test tube and the electron microscope are not relevant to them.

In sum, the exact sciences have eliminated the personal equation, the very matter of so much consequence to literature and religion. But in eliminating all of the human equation they have also eliminated all of the human dimension—the whole realm of human valuation. Since this is the realm occupied by our deepest impulses and basic values, its loss would be of great consequence to every one of us. It is in this same area that we find our ultimate goals. A life lived in the pursuit of poor ends or no ends at all is a life hardly worth the living. To recur to the plight in which Descartes left man's soul, the state of being a ghost locked up in a machine, we must reject this as a model. For the human being, the real world, the world that counts, is not that of a machine, however marvelously engineered. Reality cannot be adequately described in terms of mathematical abstractions. These are true enough as far as they go, but the human enterprise involves much more, and a different order of being.

Both religion and literature concern themselves with a world structured in terms of human value. Hence they have much in common. Indeed, it is easy to see why Matthew Arnold felt that literature, and especially poetry, might suffice to provide values for mankind. Religion, with its embarrassing encumbrances, could be dispensed with.

Yet, for all their similarities, religion and literature are not the same thing, and demand from us different grades of belief. Moreover, it is by different standards that we judge the value that we place on them.

It is fairly easy to demonstrate this second point. Not all verse that claims to be Christian poetry is poetry at all. Even some verse that proclaims a Christian message is, if considered as poetry, rather shallow and shabby. Conversely, some poems that are clearly not Christian may qualify as good poetry. There is indeed some great Christian literature and it can serve us well—to nourish the Christian in his religious experience and as a witness to the non-Christian of the majesty and power that most of us will be primarily interested in. But it is important to recognize that some definitely non-Christian poetry may also be of value to the wayfaring Christian in this twentieth century.

In any case, we will want to get our facts straight and our principles clear. For those of us who are teachers, it is especially important that we do not hurt our cause and sin against the truth by damning as having no literary value some very fine poems and novels on the grounds that they are not Christian.

I believe that contemporary non-Christian literary works, including some that have been extravagantly praised, are very faulty, but it would be pertinent to say that their real fault is that they are incoherent, confused, sentimental, or simply empty of any significant human meaning. Those are the grounds on which they could justly be condemned.

I have perhaps overwhelmed you with generalizations. In any discussion of literature it is always sounder to make use of concrete cases and particular illustrations. Let me, then, quote from two poems on the loss of faith in the modern world. The first is by Thomas Hardy, who was one of a number of Victorians on whom the discoveries of science made a shattering impact. Nevertheless, it is plain that Hardy missed his faith, and some of his poems mourn its loss. But the following, entitled "In Tenebris (I)" expresses his settled conviction of the absence of God. I shall quote only three stanzas.

> Wintertime nighs;
> But my bereavement pain
> It cannot bring again;
> Twice no one dies! . . .
>
> Birds faint in dread;
> I shall not lose old strength
> In the lone frost's black length:
> Strength long since fled. . . .
>
> Black is night's cope;
> But death will not appall
> One who, past doubtings all,
> Waits in unhope.

In its grim monosyllables it is an eloquent statement of the dignity of an austere stoicism. The man who speaks the poem is one who has moved on "past doubtings all," not on into a realm of hope but into the blankness of "unhope," a rare, obsolete word that Hardy has chosen to express the speaker's final state of mind.

Now compare this poem with a poem by Allen Tate, entitled "Last Days of Alice." The title may seem odd until it dawns on us that the poet is likening the situation of modern man to that of the little heroine of *Alice in Wonderland* and of *Alice through the Looking Glass.* In both stories the little girl's dream takes her into a fantastic world that is utterly absurd by ordinary standards—white rabbits who wear waistcoats and consult pocket watches, members of a pack of playing cards coming to life, and the knights, kings, and queens of a set of chessmen working their way across a landscape laid out neatly in the design of a chessboard. Those dream worlds, though utterly bizarre, have their elements arranged in perfectly logical fashion.

Tate is intimating that the world as revealed by modern science is of a like sort. Thus, a lectern, which is solid enough to hold up my papers, turns out to be, under rigorous scientific analysis, largely empty space. The physicist can break it down into protons, neutrons, electrons, and other electrical particles. When he has finished his precise description of what a lectern is, we find that we are not dealing with substances at all in any usual sense, but with quanta of electrical energy.

So much for the disappearance of sound, color, smell, taste, and palpability from this highly abstract world. What has further disappeared along with a substance is a sense of purpose, meaning, or value in any terms that have relevance to the human being, for the world revealed is clinical, abstract, and quite detached from good and evil.

Let me quote Allen Tate's description of this world into which modern man has penetrated:

Alone to the weight of impassivity
Incest of spirit, theorem of desire,
Without will as chalky cliffs by the sea,
Empty as the bodiless flesh of fire. . . .

The beautiful line "Empty as the bodiless flesh of fire" is very much to the poet's purpose here. The matter described by the physicist in his ultimate analysis is "empty" in the sense of insubstantial. But it is not a dead, passive thing. It has the energy and vitality of fire. The description of a "bodiless flesh" as corrosive as fire itself catches immediately the terrible beauty as well as its anti-human character.

An earlier comparison in the poem, that in which the world described by the physicist is likened to that encountered by Alice when she managed to slip through the mirror into the strange world on the other side of it, suggests an additional point. Alice's looking-glass world is in a sense a product of her own mind. In short, Alice's world came out of her own head as she gazed into the mirror over the mantel. So in a sense also the completely logical but sometimes fantastic and terrifying world of modern science came out of man's head too.

In revulsion from a world so alien to the human sensibility and apparently so devoid of human values, the speaker of Tate's poem in its closing stanzas cries out in terror and near despair. His cry is a prayer to the Christian God to take him and the rest of us back into his governance, even at the risk of coming under his condemnatory judgment.

> We too back to the world shall never pass . . .
> Being all infinite—function depth and mass
> Without figure, a mathematical shroud
>
> Hurled at the air—blessed without sin,
> O God of our flesh, return us to your wrath
> Let us be evil could we enter in
> Your grace, and falter on the stony path.

What are we to make of the phrase "blessed without sin"? Simply that modern man is without sin (and therefore in the old sense blessed), but not through having had his sins forgiven. Rather, it is that in the new dispensation the conception of sin has been abolished. Karl Menninger, the noted psychiatrist, some years ago published a book, the title of which is *Whatever Became of Sin?*

As you have perhaps already surmised, Tate's poem is the testimony of a man on his way back to Christianity rather than the utterance of a presently confirmed believer. Nevertheless, it is very apt for our purposes here.

My third poem is from a confirmed believer, yet it too reflects a battle with doubt and distraction. It is by the great seventeenth-century poet George Herbert, who once aspired to a brilliant career at the English court and had good reasons to hope that he might gain it. In the end, however, he entered the Church, and in the insignificant little parish of Bemerton ended a saintly life as a pastor and priest. Notice that the poem begins on a note of protest and rebellion.

The Collar

> I Struck the Board, and cry'd, No more.
> I will abroad.
> What? Shall I ever sigh and pine?
> My lines and life are free; free as the rode,

Loose as the winde, as large as store.
        Shall I be still in suit?
Have I no harvest but a thorn
To let me bloud, and not restore
What I have lost with cordiall fruit?
            Sure there was wine
Before my sighs did drie it: there was corn
       Before my tears did drown it.
Is the year onely lost to me?
       Have I no bays to crown it?
No flowers, no garlands gay? All blasted?
         All wasted?
Not so, my heart: but there is fruit,
And thou hast hands.
Recover all thy sigh-blown age
On double pleasures: leave thy cold dispute
Of what is fit, and not. Forsake thy cage,
       Thy ropes of sands,
Which pettie thoughts have made, and made to thee
   Good cable, to enforce and draw,
     And be thy law,
While thou didst wink and wouldst not see.
       Away; take heed:
     I will abroad.
Call in thy deaths head there: tie up thy fears.
     He that forbears
    To suit and serve his need,
       Deserves his load.
But as I rav'd and grew more fierce and wilde
      At every word,
Me thoughts I heard one calling, *Child!*
   And I reply'd, *My Lord.*

I think I hardly need comment on this poem, and I believe that even its seventeenth-century idiom does not obscure the drama of struggle, and, at the end, the quiet but powerful resolution of the speaker's problem.

Now all three of these poems seem to me excellent poems by literary standards, but the relation of each to Christian belief is, as we have seen, quite different. Nevertheless, as I shall argue, all three modes can provide spiritual nourishment for us. Literature that is not authentic, even that which professes to have a Christian content, can be debilitating and even corrupting. Some popular hymns that I could name, but shall not, have, I am sure, done real harm.

Let me summarize briefly some of the uses of genuine literature. Contemporary literature can set forth the perils and difficulties of our time; what it feels like to be an unbeliever; what the intellectual climate of our age is like; what some of the main obstacles to belief are.

Surely, if what I said at the beginning is even partially true, namely, that the principal battle for Christian belief has to be fought nowadays in men's minds, then the more that we know about the cultural and intellectual climate of the present day, the better. It is just here that modern literature can be of great service.

I do not mean, however, to suggest that our century has failed to produce some beautiful affirmations of Christian faith. Such expressions exist. But in my opinion some of the most valuable uses of literature for the defense of Christianity occur in work that frankly exhibits the trials of belief as the typical man of our century encounters them. Thus, we can learn to appreciate the joy of religious faith even by negative means— from its lack, from its very absence. Moreover, we test the quality of our own faith by acquainting ourselves with the strength of the opposition. I quoted earlier verses from Saint Paul's Epistle to the Ephesians in which he tells his congregation at Ephesus that the forces with which they had to contend were not merely other men, "flesh and blood," as he puts it, but "principalities and powers." It is for this reason that the Apostle tells his congregation to take up "the shield of faith," so that they may be able "to quench all the fiery darts of the wicked." He also tells them to take up the "sword of the spirit," but most of his exhortation has to do with defensive armor, "the shield of faith," the "breast plate of righteousness," and "the helmet of salvation." Saint Paul evidently knew that his followers were in for no pillow fight: the weapons of the adversaries were powerful. To plunge in naked, sword in hand, was not enough.

In conclusion, I want to refer once more to the function of literature. As I understand it, the primary function of literature is not to state doctrine, but rather to let us know what it feels like to be a certain sort of person or to hold a certain faith. Its true role is not to teach abstract ideas, but to dramatize the motions of the spirit.

After having devoted my life to teaching literature, I am not, believe me, disposed to undervalue it. Literature can do marvelous things for us: it can act to civilize us, to broaden our sympathies for others, to make us understand our inner lives better, to enrich our lives, including our religious lives. In short, I think that it is indispensable to the human enterprise. But literature, in spite of all the benefits it can confer, cannot be a satisfactory substitute for religion. Matthew Arnold, great man that he was, was simply wrong.

14

T. S. Eliot and the American South

*I*n the years before Eliot took out British citizenship, his friend Sir Herbert Read was aware, he tells us, of "the struggle going on in Eliot's mind" between the claims of England and his native America. In the essay which Read contributed to *T. S. Eliot: The Man and His Work,* he does not state what he believes was the decisive factor in Eliot's ultimate decision; instead, he simply prints the following excerpt from a letter that Eliot wrote to him on April 23, 1928.

> Some day [Eliot wrote] I want to write an essay about the point of view of an American who wasn't an American, because he was born in the South and went to school in New England as a small boy with a nigger drawl, but wasn't a southerner in the South because his people were northerners in a border state and looked down on all southerners and Virginians, and who so was never anything anywhere and who therefore felt himself to be more a Frenchman than an American and more an Englishman than a Frenchman and yet felt that the U.S.A. up to a hundred years ago was a family extension.

Just how seriously are we to take all this? Is Eliot simply being playful with his friend? Even if the account contains its grain of truth—and I believe it does—it also clearly contains a good measure of exaggeration. Nevertheless, it is Eliot's first and indeed, so far as I know, his only reference to his having a southern connection. I think it very likely that the boys at the Milton Academy in New England did tease the new boy from St. Louis about his southern drawl. That statement has the ring of truth, for in the 1890s St. Louis may well have been a good deal more southern in accent than I judge it to be today.

Read also writes that "on one or two later occasions in a mood of solemn gaiety [Eliot] would sing a ballad like 'The Reconstructed Rebel. . . . '" Unless I am mistaken, this is a song of defiance from the lips of a thoroughly *unreconstructed* southerner. It begins:

O, I'm a good old rebel
Now that's just what I am;
For the "fair land of freedom"
I do not care a damn . . .

and it states that "Three hundred thousand Yankees / Is stiff in Southern dust," and follows with such bloodthirsty sentiments as

They died of Southern fever,
Of Southern steel and shot,
I wish it was three million
Instead of what we got.

If Eliot in his mood of solemn gaiety was trying to adopt the most extreme caricature of the hard-bitten, never-say-die southerner, he couldn't have chosen better. Auden, too, was drawn to the ballad, apparently for similar reasons. I remember that he used to lick his chops over it.

Eliot's singing this song does not, of course, prove very much of anything about his relation to the American South. But the Page-Barbour lectures, which he gave in 1933 at the University of Virginia, can tell us a great deal about what he thought of the South. The lectures were published in 1934 under the title *After Strange Gods*. The first lecture, addressed specifically to the Virginians, is a carefully considered statement of ideas and principles that are integral to Eliot's later work and thought.

In this first lecture, he says that he had never visited the South until he crossed the Potomac in 1933 on his journey to Charlottesville. Though in his 1928 letter to Read he does claim to have been born in the South, we remember that he immediately goes on to qualify this statement by telling Read that his parents were northerners living in a border state; for Missouri, though it can claim one of the stars in the Confederate Stars and Bars, is in fact more accurately described as a border state in which the Union sympathizers were very numerous and soon gained control.

At any rate, Eliot makes it quite clear that he regarded this visit to Virginia as his first to the South whose tradition he meant to discuss as having proved special and important on the North American continent.

The close relation of these Page-Barbour lectures to Eliot's developing ideas is confirmed by his statement that he was taking this first visit to the Old South as an apt occasion for a reformulation of his early essay, "Tradition and the Individual Talent." In that essay he had been concerned primarily with the individual writer. Obviously he meant now to discuss tradition in its larger terms as affecting a whole society. Because Eliot saw in the American South an example of what he meant by a tradition still alive and relatively coherent, his lectures in Virginia would offer a proper occasion for such a reformulation and for an extension of such an examination. True, Eliot avoided mere flattery. He described in more guarded terms the cultural situation as it now existed: he told his audience that he expected to find in Virginia "at least some recollection of a 'tradition' such as the influx of foreign populations has almost effaced in some parts of the North, and such as never established itself in the West," though he immediately added that "it is hardly to be expected that a tradition here, any more than anywhere else, should be found in health and flourishing growth."

So much for the opening paragraphs of Eliot's first Page-Barbour lecture. But before I go on to cite and quote from some of the other things he had to say about Virginia and the South, it may be wise for me to answer a question that may already have arisen in your minds.

Just how seriously can we take the compliments that Eliot addressed to his southern hosts? Eliot is known for his civility and his courtesy. Besides, a lecturer is not only tempted but licensed to give a certain amount of praise to his auditors, especially if they comprise people of another nationality or even of another pronounced regional difference. An American addressing a British audience or a Japanese audience is aware of this, and will usually take some pains to appeal to traits that he and his audience share. Eliot does show his acute awareness of his cultural difference from his hosts. Thus, at one point he tells his Virginia audience that a complimentary remark that he had just made "should carry more weight for being spoken by a Yankee."

Nevertheless, I believe that what Eliot says in *After Strange Gods* on the subject of southern culture he did mean very seriously; and especially what he had to say about tradition, about the relation of the region to the nation, and about the nature of culture and the character of the good life. But he speaks as a realist. In fact, in his first lecture he fully recognizes the intense pressure on the South to change its ways and the difficulties that it would find in preserving its own identity. It is not too much to say that *After Strange Gods* amounts to a grim warning rather than an invitation to self-congratulation.

How can I be so confident of this estimate? Because of two considerations. The first is that Eliot had evidently read with deep interest and sympathy *I'll Take My Stand,* which had been published three years earlier. So he was well aware of the analysis that a group of southerners had recently made of the present plight of, and future prospects for, the region.

In short, the Yankee visitor, now a British subject, had not simply succumbed to the charm of Charlottesville and Mr. Jefferson's University of Virginia. Very early in his first lecture he refers to *I'll Take My Stand* by name, and throughout the course of that first lecture he refers to Agrarianism and to what he chose to call the neo-Agrarians.

Yet he could not have been unaware of the fact that many southerners thoroughly disagreed with the Agrarians and that the University of Virginia itself could hardly be considered to be a stronghold of the Agrarian movement. For instance, Stringfellow Barr, a historian at Virginia and a close friend and associate of Eliot's host at Charlottesville, Scott Buchanan, had in 1930 debated John Crowe Ransom as the spokesman for the twelve contributors to *I'll Take My Stand* on the merits of the Agrarian position. The debate, by the way, had been held in Richmond, and had attracted many literary people and public figures from Virginia and elsewhere. This circumstance does not, of course, impugn in any way the sincerity of Eliot's tribute to Scott Buchanan in the preface to *After Strange Gods.* Eliot there thanks Buchanan "for conversation and suggestions" out of which, he tells us, his Page-Barbour lectures grew. But it should make plain that in his first lecture, Eliot knew that he could not take for granted that he was preaching to the converted and had no reason to assume agreement from his listeners when he praised the virtues of the older southern culture.

There is a second and far more cogent reason for taking seriously Eliot's praise of the South's regional culture. Fifteen years later he would publish his *Notes Toward a Definition of Culture,* a much more elaborate formulation and development of the position he sketches in the first of his Page-Barbour lectures. In spite of the modesty of its title, the *Notes* constitutes a detailed elaboration of Eliot's ideas on the nature of a culture and the mode of its transmission from one generation to another. Its third chapter, entitled "Unity and Diversity: The Region," has a particular relation to what Eliot told his Virginia audience about the relation of southern culture to American culture generally considered. Naturally, in the *Notes,* a book that was calculated to the longitude of Great Britain, the regions with which Eliot is principally concerned are Ireland, Wales, and Scotland. But the principles involved apply fully to the relation of America's most self-conscious region, the South, to the United States as a totality.

So it was not the tradition-laden atmosphere of the Old Campus at Charlottesville, Jefferson's beautifully planned arrangement of buildings and grounds, that drew from Eliot as visitor indulgent comments on regionalism and culture of the South's older day. On the contrary, Eliot obviously did see in the American South at least some residue of habits of mind and of a traditional way of life which he regarded as having universal value.

To take a particular instance of links between what Eliot said in the Page-Barbour lectures and what, years later, he included in his *Notes* on culture, consider these two passages.

He told his Virginia audience in 1933:

The Civil War was certainly a disaster . . . from which the country [and here he means the whole of the United States] has never recovered, and perhaps never will: we are always ready to assume that the good effects of war, if any, abide permanently while the ill effects are obliterated by time.

In the later book (1948) he writes:

The real revolution [in the United States] was not what is called the Revolution in the history books, but is a consequence of the Civil War;

after which arose a plutocratic élite; after which the expansion and material development of the country was accelerated. . . .

Eliot then proceeds to mention other consequences of what he regards as the "real revolution," consequences that he regards as deleterious to the development of a flourishing culture. Thus, in the *Notes* he not only confirms his earlier statement but indicates what he had meant in saying that the American Civil War was a disaster, not merely to the South, but to the whole of the United States.

That Eliot regarded as fully relevant to the American South his discussion of the relation of the cultures of Ireland, Wales, and Scotland to the dominant culture of England becomes fully clear in the following passage from his first Page-Barbour lecture:

> No one, surely, can cross the Potomac for the first time without being struck by differences so great that their extinction could only mean the death of both cultures. . . . to come into Virginia is as definite an experience as to cross from England to Wales. . . .

Eliot argues that a national culture would be poorer if it were strictly uniform in its makeup. Variety among its various parts constitutes a stimulating force. A strict uniformity lacks the richness and depth that come from a measure of diversity. Thus, in obeying the natural instinct of human beings to realize themselves, the people of a region are actually nourishing the national culture. If a regional culture is suppressed or obliterated through some facile notion of cultural uniformity, everyone loses.

Eliot provides a concrete illustration by pointing out the ways in which the poets and fiction writers of Scotland, Wales, and Ireland have enriched the literature written in the English language. It would be easy to make the same case for our southern writers. Imagine the impoverishment that American literature would suffer if one subtracted from it Katherine Anne Porter, Eudora Welty, William Faulkner, and R. P. Warren. If these writers had kept silent or, almost as damaging, if they had ignored their southern cultural material and tried to imitate scrupulously Washington Irving, Henry James, or Sinclair Lewis, American literature would not be what it now is.

Eliot's *Notes Toward a Definition of Culture* is a closely argued book. I shall make no attempt at a full examination of it here. It will serve my present purpose well enough simply to call attention to some of the issues in which it closely resembles the Agrarians' *I'll Take My Stand.*

First, both books call for resistance against economic determinism. Our reasonable goals and ends ought to determine our means, rather than the most efficient means forcing upon us the ends we are to pursue.

Second, both see a very close relation between a people's religion and its culture. Indeed, in a very meaningful sense the culture is an extension and expression of a people's ultimate values—something that neither Eliot nor the Agrarians hesitate to call by its true name: religion.

Third, both emphasize an actual community in being. No amount of planning or social engineering can create a community. The community is the reality with which one must deal. It cannot be ignored, and if it is destroyed the possibility of developing a genuine culture may well be destroyed with it.

Fourth, the transmission of cultural values is best done through the family, and the family must be preserved.

In the interests of economy I have stated these matters in my own terms, but I believe that I have not too much simplified what is said in the "Introduction: A Statement of Principles," of *I'll Take My Stand,* and in the essays by Allen Tate and Lyle Lanier. I am equally confident that I have not distorted Eliot's views as expressed in his *Notes,* though I have obviously left out much that is in that rightly freighted book.

I must now turn back to *After Strange Gods.* One large question about that book still remains to be answered: Why did Eliot never allow it to be reprinted? It is, I believe, the only one of his books that has never been reissued. I think that I know the answer, and if I am correct, his decision not to reprint it had nothing to do with his approval of regional cultures and regionalism, but with what he had to say in the second and third Page-Barbour lectures.

In writing a book entitled *After Strange Gods,* with its provocative subtitle, *A Primer of Modern Heresy,* Eliot was risking trouble and almost certainly inviting misunderstanding. The phrase *After Strange Gods* is itself provocative. It has a definitely biblical ring, though I have not been able to find this exact phrasing in either the Old Testament or the New.

The phrase would seem to be an amalgam of a number of texts found in the Scriptures, texts which reproach various persons or peoples for going "a whoring after" gods other than the true God, and of several other texts which carry a similar reproach for seeking after "strange gods." I expect that the phrasings "after other gods" and seeking "strange gods" simply fused in Eliot's memory. The amalgamation probably sounded so right that he didn't take the trouble to look it up. I, for example, was so certain that "after strange gods" was an exact quotation that I was shocked when I couldn't find it listed in Cruden's *Concordance*.

Yet the title would probably not have aroused so much hostility had Eliot not added his subtitle. By declaring his book to be *A Primer of Modern Heresy*, Eliot was here surely trailing his coat as if inviting a fight. Our age in particular is sensitive to anything that smacks of heresy-hunting. We associate it with intolerance, some priestly group turning over a victim to the secular arm for dire punishment. In a permissive age, the person who even appears to be himself intolerant can expect to be treated with intolerance.

Worst of all, in his second and third lectures, Eliot illustrated his statements about the heresies of the age with examples from the works of living (or only recently deceased) writers, writers such as Katherine Mansfield, D. H. Lawrence, and Thomas Hardy. With these illustrations the fat was indeed in the fire.

It did not avail that Eliot pointed out that he was not in this instance judging their literary art—which he conceded to be great—but was writing as a moralist, concerned with the moral disorder of our world as reflected in their art. Nor did the fact that Eliot made it plain that he regarded Lawrence and Hardy, for example, as distinguished literary artists, even though their fiction revealed the disorder and growing cruelty of the world in which they and he lived. Nor did it apparently help very much that he made a related judgment of the mind and sensibility of his old mentor at Harvard, Irving Babbitt, and of Ezra Pound, his warm friend, whom he tells us in his second lecture is "probably the most important living poet in our language."

Eliot had actually given rather precise notice of what he was planning to do in this book by quoting as a long epigraph a passage from Theodore Hacker's "Was ist der Mensch." Here Hacker writes of the chaos revealed in present-day literature, though he attributes it to tendencies in our age and not to evil in our writers. He cites them because their art furnishes a faithful mirror for what is going on in the culture.

Surely this is also the use to which Eliot puts the works of the contemporary writers whom he invokes. Perhaps he believed he made his purpose plain when he wrote in his second lecture that he was not concerned here "with the author's *beliefs,* but with orthodoxy of sensibility and with the sense of tradition. . . ." He also mentioned in this second lecture the "alarming cruelty in some modern literature," but the general context indicates that he meant the alarming cruelty of our world as reflected in modern literature. If so, this is very close to Yeats's remark on the "growing murderousness of the world"—certainly not an unwarranted observation.

Most damaging of all, Eliot made a remark in his first lecture that seemed distinctly anti-Jewish: unity of religion, he wrote, made "any large number of free-thinking Jews undesirable." As far as his argument is concerned, *free-thinking* is the key phrase. Thus, even the ultra-conservative Old South got along with its God-fearing Jews very well. There was perhaps less anti-Jewish feeling in the Old South than anywhere else in the United States. "Free-thinkers"—whatever the final merits of Eliot's argument—would have been the accurate term. And if free-thinking was the issue, whether the ancestors of the free-thinkers were of the Jewish, Catholic, or Protestant faiths would not matter. Yet Eliot, in the light of his later statements, must have bitterly regretted what he had earlier set down.

As a matter of fact, the anti-Jewish passage aside, the argument advanced in the last two lectures could not be expected to thrive in the intellectual climate of the 1930s or, for that matter, in that of the later twentieth century. In any case, whatever has merit in Eliot's position is better stated in the *Notes,* with the appropriate reservations and qualifications to be found there. Clearly Eliot later on preferred to write *Notes Toward a Definition of Culture* than to reissue *After Strange Gods.*

There is an additional epigraph on the title page of *After Strange Gods* which so far seems to have attracted no notice at all. As we know, Eliot liked to employ epigraphs. He frequently uses them to preface individual poems, including even some of his short lyrics. The epigraph I am concerned with here amounts to two and a half lines of verse from Sophocles'

Oedipus Rex. As usual, Eliot prefers to quote the Greek original, but I shall set down here Bernard Knox's translation. My own Greek is too rusty these days to provide a translation entirely accurate, much less elegant. The Greek seer Tiresias speaks as follows: "Go think this out, and if you find that I am wrong, then say that I have no skill in prophecy."

We have encountered Tiresias before in Eliot's poetry. In *The Waste Land* Tiresias is made to witness the lovemaking that is not loving or fulfilling or life-giving, but sterile and meaningless.

(And I Tiresias have foresuffered all
Enacted on this same divan or bed;
I who have sat by Thebes below the wall
And walked among the lowest of the dead.)

In the notes to *The Waste Land* Eliot tells the reader: "What Tiresias *sees* . . . is the substance of the poem." I propose here that what Mr. Eliot sees in the modern world is indeed the substance of what he has to say about it, not only in *After Strange Gods,* but also in his *Notes Toward a Definition of Culture.*

Are we to conclude then that in *After Strange Gods* Eliot means to assume the mantle of the prophet Tiresias? Well, at least Eliot seems to see a parallel between Tiresias and himself. Both are conscious that their predictions are almost certain to be disregarded. The ears on which the words of each will fall are deaf indeed. If none are so blind as those who will not see, none are so deaf as those who will not hear.

Yet I mustn't make Eliot seem too serious here. He had an excellent sense of humor with which he is not often credited. His reference to Tiresias is so well hidden as to seem sly: only for the observant eye is the admission apparent. Though aware that what he is going to say will not be understood, he will make his statement anyway. In that matter at least Eliot has proved to be a true prophet: he has been regularly misunderstood.

Yet now the content of the prophecy is worth reexamining. Modern Western man, and especially his American version, is predisposed to *hubris:* an overweening pride in his own powers and achievements. Now he may be threatened by the very success of some of his most brilliant achievements. Eliot was probably aware that even his choice audience of traditional Virginians were also Americans and might stand in need of such a warning. To have solved, as Oedipus did, the riddle of the Sphinx does not mean that one knows the whole nature of man or that he can accurately read his own future.

It would be foolish to claim too much. Eliot was never the unregenerate southern rebel, and long, long ago he had put away his southern drawl in favor of an impeccable British accent spoken after the manner of Oxenford. His visit to Virginia in 1933 was apparently his last—not only to Virginia but to any other state of the old Confederacy (with the exception of a brief visit to the University of Texas in 1958). Nevertheless, his concern for the older southern culture was considered and genuine, and he established a lasting friendship with one of the most thoughtful of the southern Agrarians, Allen Tate. When Eliot's letters are finally published and the remainder of Tate's, that correspondence, though probably not extensive, may tell us a great deal about a warm and enduring relationship and one founded on common sympathies and understandings of our twentieth-century world.

15

The Past Reexamined

The Optimist's Daughter

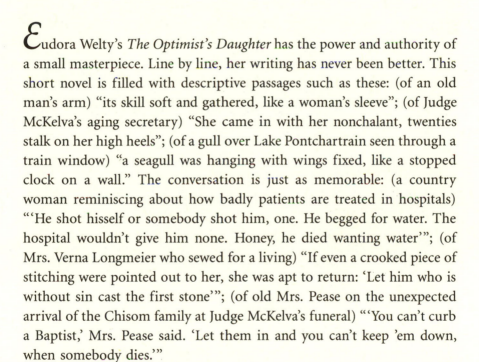

*E*udora Welty's *The Optimist's Daughter* has the power and authority of a small masterpiece. Line by line, her writing has never been better. This short novel is filled with descriptive passages such as these: (of an old man's arm) "its skill soft and gathered, like a woman's sleeve"; (of Judge McKelva's aging secretary) "She came in with her nonchalant, twenties stalk on her high heels"; (of a gull over Lake Pontchartrain seen through a train window) "a seagull was hanging with wings fixed, like a stopped clock on a wall." The conversation is just as memorable: (a country woman reminiscing about how badly patients are treated in hospitals) "'He shot hisself or somebody shot him, one. He begged for water. The hospital wouldn't give him none. Honey, he died wanting water'"; (of Mrs. Verna Longmeier who sewed for a living) "If even a crooked piece of stitching were pointed out to her, she was apt to return: 'Let him who is without sin cast the first stone'"; (of old Mrs. Pease on the unexpected arrival of the Chisom family at Judge McKelva's funeral) "'You can't curb a Baptist,' Mrs. Pease said. 'Let them in and you can't keep 'em down, when somebody dies.'"

Yet *The Optimist's Daughter* is much more than a tapestry of brilliantly evoked scenes from small-town life and dialogue in the southern idiom; it is a novel with a very definite shape. As a fictional structure it shows a surprising complication of development and a rich exfoliation of themes.

Laurel McKelva Hand, a widow in her early forties, has been summoned from Chicago, where she now lives, because of the illness of her father, Judge McKelva. Laurel's mother had died some ten years earlier.

Her father, now in his early seventies, had, a year and a half before, married a woman much younger than he, Wanda Fay Chisom, a shallow little vulgarian. As the story begins, we obviously do not know very much about Laurel, but we can sense her feelings as she listens to the conversation and witnesses the conduct of her father's second wife. Wanda Fay comes of the plain people; some would use a harsher phrase: common white trash. She is cheap, self-centered, aggressive, and completely unmannerly. Her tactlessness all too clearly manifests her lack of understanding and concern for other people.

Fay's conduct at the hospital before and after Judge McKelva's death is so outrageous that a reader not well acquainted with Miss Welty's work might be tempted to attribute her treatment of Wanda Fay to a contemptuous dislike for the southern poor white, but he would be badly mistaken. Eudora Welty knows the poor white inside out—knows his faults and his lacks, but his virtues too. In her stories and novels she has treated him in all sorts of modes: with considerate understanding as in that beautiful story, "A Piece of News"; with gusto and good humor in *The Ponder Heart;* with a loving admiration for the heroic dignity of the characters whom she depicts in *Losing Battles.* Her intimate knowledge of the way in which the southern countryman (whether sturdy yeoman or down-at-heels subsistence farmer) thinks and talks—indeed of the very cadences of his speech—bespeaks a fascination with, and a loving attention to, the rural whites of the South. She never degrades and dehumanizes them by reducing them to a stereotype: in Eudora Welty's fiction they are always individuals. Her depiction of the conduct of Fay McKelva— and Fay's conduct is perfectly awful—is not to be taken as a snobbish slap at the southern poor white. Miss Welty has intimated this point quietly but effectively by bringing into the hospital scene the Dalzells, a sizable clan of poor whites, who have come to wait out the operation on old Mr. Dalzell. The Dalzells are primitive, unlettered, and earthy in their thought and speech, but they are not sleazily cheap; they are not on the make; they have not cut their connections with the land; they are family-minded. Mrs. Dalzell has nothing of the utter self-absorption of Fay.

When the Judge's young widow and his daughter return from the hospital in New Orleans to Mount Salus, Mississippi, with his corpse, we move into—on one level at least—social comedy. We are aware of Laurel's feelings at the funeral, which takes place in the McKelva house, but Miss Welty does not subdue the scene to the tone of Laurel's grief. She expects her reader to attend to the social types and personalities, and there is a considerable human variety among Laurel's own friends.

Major Bullock, the father of one of the bridesmaids at Laurel's wedding, is not very bright, indeed something of a numbskull. Later it becomes plain enough that the Major has been making a number of trips to the sideboard to solace his grief. Mrs. Bullock ("Miss Tennyson") is no numbskull, but she has her eccentricities. So it goes, through a series that includes the Judge's secretary, the Presbyterian minister who is to preach the funeral sermon, his wife, crotchety old Mrs. Pease, and many another friend and, not to be left out of account, the very efficient undertaker with his "Baptist face." To complete the range of social types, there come into the house, at the last minute, and to Laurel's shocked surprise, Fay's family—she had earlier denied having any family left at all—including her mother, brother, sister, her grandfather, old Mr. Chisom, and several children. Fay's nephew, little Wendell, wearing a cowboy suit, is not too much overawed by his first funeral; Wendell can't wait to peer into the face of the corpse lying in the open casket.

Laurel had tried to prevent her father's body being put on display, but her objections are overborne, not merely by Wanda Fay and her unmannerly clan, but, rather disconcertingly, by some of Laurel's own friends. Miss Tennyson protests: "'But honey, your father's a Mount Salus man. He is a McKelva. A public figure. You can't deprive the public, can you? Oh, he's lovely.'"

The scene is a set piece of the sort that Miss Welty always does so well, but she has not created the scene simply because she does this sort of thing well, or to exploit regional folkways; it has its function in the story to be told. The funeral is in the most profound sense a social occasion. A closely knit community is here gathered around the bier of one of its more prominent members, not so much to mourn him as to celebrate— and with genuine affection—his achievements. The community means to do him honor, but as the Judge's friends, talking together before the funeral begins, exchange reminiscences about him, Laurel is shocked to find how many things about her father they have got quite wrong. They have described—apparently in good faith—virtues that she knows he simply never had, and they have failed to mention what she regards as his truly admirable qualities. In spite of the presence of lifelong friends and the company of her six bridesmaids, she feels that she is now really alone—driven back upon herself. She even tells herself that the community hadn't deserved her father any more than Fay had deserved him.

If Laurel is critical of the community's lack of any deep understanding of her father, this does not mean that she is completely comfortable at dismissing the community's implied censure of her. Though that censure is implied rather than stated, and given jokingly rather than seriously, some of Laurel's friends make it plain that if she had come home after her husband's death and stayed with her father, he would not have fallen a victim to Wanda Fay. Why, old Mrs. Pease asks, did she, in the first place, have to go away to Chicago and marry a boy from the great world outside? Why, now that her father is dead and her inheritance leaves her well off, does she want to return to her job in Chicago? Why not stay here with her friends?

Yet, though Laurel cannot accept the notion that she was personally responsible for what happened to her father, the question as to why he married Fay obviously troubles her. Fay violates—in her cheapness, her lack of feeling, her hard aggressiveness—every concept of womanly behavior that the Judge reverenced. We, as readers, witnessing Fay's violent behavior—attempting to pull her dying husband out of his hospital bed, and later, hysterically embracing him as he lies in his coffin—are made thoroughly sympathetic with Laurel's bepuzzlement. How could Judge McKelva have chosen this creature for his second wife? Neither the usual explanation offered—a lonely, old man, flattered by youth and what he takes to be beauty—nor the reason given by the Judge's servant—"'He mightily enjoyed having him somebody to spoil'"—satisfies the daughter. Not even the more charitable remark by Miss Adele, Laurel's first-grade teacher—"'She gave a lonely old man something to live for'"—really explains his choice.

Laurel has been more than shocked and puzzled by her father's strange second marriage: all her feelings about her father and mother and what their married life was have been terribly disturbed. She will not allow herself to ask: Did my father truly love my mother. Instead she says out loud to her friends: "'He loved my mother.'" But in the context of the story, her assertion before the world protests almost too much. We gradually come to understand that Laurel is a far more troubled woman than the opening pages had revealed. The novel thus moves from fairly broad satire and social comedy into Laurel's reexamination of the past. Bereft and alone, her review of her early life becomes urgent and almost compulsive: "In her need . . . Laurel would have been willing to wish her mother and father dragged back to any torment of living. . . . She wanted them with her to share her grief. . . ."

Laurel's dark night of the soul is literally that. Miss Welty has very skillfully cleared the stage for her retreat into the past and into herself. The pickup truck from Texas which had brought Fay's family to the funeral is returning to Texas that same evening, and Fay, on impulse, decides to ride back with her family for a short visit, planning to return on the day on which Laurel will leave for Chicago.

With Fay's departure, Laurel has the family house (which now belongs legally to Fay) to herself for the last time. As she wanders through it, she cannot help noticing the little changes in decoration, the telltale rearrangements of furniture and objects, that speak of the new wife and of the Judge's closing years. His desk is empty—emptied not only of his legal papers but of all the letters that her mother had written to him. But Laurel soon recalls that the destruction of the letters is not to be attributed to Fay. Her father never had kept her mother's letters; it was his habit to answer *any* letter promptly and drop it into the wastebasket. There was nothing in his desk of her mother for Laurel to "retrieve." But her father's letters to her mother have been preserved: Laurel finds them in her mother's little secretary which had been shunted away into the sewing room.

Laurel makes the discovery on the last evening that she is to be in her old home. She has had dinner with friends, and Major Bullock has escorted her home on this rainy night of early spring. Closing the door on the night, she enters the house and finds that a chimney swift—Laurel had acquired an irrational horror of swifts in her childhood—has got down the chimney and is now frantically flying about in the darkened house. She is terrified by the swoops and dartings of the bird, and finally, in desperation, shuts herself away from it in the little sewing room where she had sometimes slept as a child. Here she finds her mother's secretary and the letters that her mother had preserved—presumably all the letters she had received from her husband and from her own mother. Laurel spends the night reading those letters and at last falls asleep in a chair. Next day, with the return of morning light and of the old family servant, Missouri, who had known and loved her mother and father, Laurel manages to capture the bird and release it into the sunshine.

Does the bird merely represent the vague terrors of the night that beset Laurel? Or does the sooty bird, soiling with its meaningless lunges the curtains that Missouri had washed so carefully the day before, betoken the alien presence of Wanda Fay in the house, troubling its old inhabitants, putting a smudge on everything? Or does the bird, so eager to get out of this strange labyrinth into which it has fallen, resemble Laurel herself, trapped in the past that has suddenly become to her strange and problematical? Perhaps all of these suggestions apply, yet the author has wisely not directly hinted at any of them. Whatever we want to make of the bird episode, or even if we dismiss from it any symbolic import, we will almost certainly feel that the incident is beautifully placed and answers perfectly to Laurel's emotional situation: her sense of a disturbing element in the house on this gusty night of spring, one that creates in her mind anxieties and vague fears—for what troubles her, of course, is not the literal darkness, but the darkness of her past, which she now realizes she does not understand.

One of the most brilliant aspects of this novel is the way in which Laurel's mother, Becky, is made to rise up as a vivid presence out of her notebooks, school books, recipes, the letters her own mother had written to her from West Virginia, and the letters written to her by her husband. Becky was evidently a tremendously intense person. She was brave, as Laurel believes her father, for all his other virtues, was not. Becky was demanding—perhaps she demanded too much of her loved ones. She was hard on the Judge—in her own special way, as hard on him as Fay. Laurel remembers the last months of her mother's life, her failing eyesight, her pain in her last illness, and her reproaches to her husband. Becky actually called him a coward, presumably because he would not face the tragic possibilities of life, the tragic "irremediable things," as George Santayana has termed them. Judge McKelva, in his more "optimistic" view of the world, could not grant that anything was truly irremediable.

Laurel's commiserative understanding almost extends to Fay herself. At the funeral, Laurel, looking at Wendell as he begins to cry, thinks: "He was like a young, undriven, unfalsifying, unvindictive Fay. So Fay might have appeared, just at the beginning, to her aging father, with his slipping eyesight." And now on this night of self-examination and casting up of accounts, Laurel realizes that "Both times [her father] chose [a wife], he had suffered. . . . He died worn out with both wives. . . ." Laurel realizes further that whatever rivalry there was between her mother and Fay, it was not "between the living and the dead, between the old wife and the new; [it was] between too much love and too little."

Laurel is not trying here to justify Fay, but to understand her father and to realize that though her father did love her mother, the relation between them had never been an easy one. How could it have been in view of their polar opposition in outlook? Her mother, for example, had always been passionately attached to her mountain home in West Virginia, and in her last illness, when she mentioned the wild strawberries that she used to gather there, her husband had cried out: "'I'll take you back to your mountains, Becky.'" To which Becky replied: "'Lucifer! Liar!'" And Laurel remembers that in her last illness her mother had irrationally reproached her too: "'You could have saved your mother's life. But you stood by and wouldn't intervene. I despair for you.'" After her father's death, Laurel had thought: "I [do] not any longer believe that anyone [can] be saved, anyone at all. Not from others."

Yet in the deeper understanding achieved on this night—even in gaining some comprehension of why her father might have turned to Wanda Fay—Laurel never for a moment comes to doubt the significance and the importance of the relationship that existed between her mother and her father. If there was any element of torment in that relationship, and it is now plain to Laurel that there was, "that torment was something they had known together, through each other." Even when her mother "despaired" of her father and demanded of him "'Why is it necessary to punish me like this and not tell me why?'" she "still . . . held fast to [his hand and] to Laurel's too. Her cry was not complaint: it was anger at wanting to know and being denied knowledge; it was love's deep anger." Such a relation, if full of pain, is nevertheless profoundly human, and therefore infinitely valuable. Laurel has at last come to recognize and accept the relationship between her father and mother, and her numbed heart at last comes to life. "A flood of feeling descended on Laurel. . . . [She] wept in grief for love and for the dead. She lay there with all that was adamant in her yielding to this night, yielding at last. Now all she had found had found her. The deepest spring in her heart had uncovered itself, and it began to flow again." Throughout the first third of the book the reader could scarcely have guessed how badly hurt Laurel had been and how frozen had been her heart. Now, looking back from the vantage point of this crucial moment, all becomes apparent, and many of the earlier events in the novel fall into proper perspective.

This summoning back into vivid life of her parents and their long and, at the very end, difficult relationship, serves to recall Laurel's own brief and, as she remembers it, perfect love affair with her own husband. (He had been killed aboard a naval vessel in the Pacific in the Second World War.) "[Laurel] had gone on living with the old perfection undisturbed and undisturbing. Now, by her own hands, the past had been raised up, and *he* looked at her, Phil himself—here waiting, all the time, Lazarus. He looked at her out of eyes wild with the craving for his unlived life, with mouth open like a funnel's." The revivification of her parents' fulfilled, though sometimes tormented, life makes her realize with new poignance the fact that her own life with Phil was not, and never can be, fulfilled.

> What [she asked herself] would have been their end, then? Suppose their marriage had ended like her father and mother's? Or like her mother's father and mother's? Like—
> "Laurel! Laurel! Laurel!" Phil's voice cried.
> She wept for what happened to life.

Yet even if Laurel's night of memories and explorations of the inner self ends with the "deepest spring in her heart [having begun] to flow again," Laurel has not yet resolved all her problems, for she is not yet quite done with Fay. Fay returns a little earlier than she had been expected, and there is a final encounter between Judge McKelva's daughter and his second wife. Earlier on that morning, before Fay had turned up, Laurel had burnt every scrap of her mother's papers—the recipes, including one for "My Best Bread," the school notebooks, the letters written to her by her husband and those written to her by her own mother, Laurel's grandmother—everything, so that the slate is now wiped clean—or almost clean. She can now turn the house over to its legal owner without regret: "There was nothing she was leaving in the whole shining and quiet house now to show for her mother's life and her mother's happiness and suffering, and nothing to show for Fay's harm; her father's turning between them, holding on to them both, then letting them go, was without any sign." But when, looking into a kitchen pantry, she finds the breadboard so lovingly made by Phil for her mother and always kept clean and polished by Becky for her breadmaking—when she finds that board scarred and gouged (Fay had used it to crack black walnuts on)—it is almost too much. She bursts out to Fay, "'You desecrated this house.'"

At last she puts a question about the scene in the hospital room on the night of her father's death, the question that hitherto she had suppressed. She asks, "'What were you trying to scare Father into—when you struck him?'" Fay's answer is simple and, according to her lights, sufficient: "'I was trying to scare him into living! . . . I wanted him to get up out of there, and start him paying a little attention to *me,* for a change.'" Then Laurel tries to tell Fay about the breadboard—why it matters—but none of her explanations can make any impression on this woman. All bread "'tastes alike, don't it?'" Fay asks. And as for Phil's labor of love in making the board for Becky, Fay asks in perfect good conscience: "'What has *he* got to do with it? He's dead, isn't he?'" Fay goes on to tell Laurel that the "'past isn't a thing to me. I belong to the future, didn't you know that?'" Fay's estimate of herself is profoundly true and this, of course, is why she is not fully human. People to whom the past means nothing cannot be fully human. In this matter Fay resembles Faulkner's Flem Snopes and Jason Compson. They all lack the pieties that bind one generation back to another, the loyalties and the imaginative sympathies which affirm that all men are of one race and, further, that the living and the dead are of one race too.

(Fay's statement that she belongs to the future has a further significance. Though *The Optimist's Daughter* is not designed to be a tract for the times, it is, nevertheless, a document of our times. Fay represents a human type to which the future may indeed belong: the rootless, finally amoral, individual whose insistence on self-aggrandizement is not countered by any claim of family or clan or country. The true significance of

Fay's ethos is not a reflection of a particular class or section; she might just as well have been born in the Bronx or the Bay region of San Francisco.)

After her experience of the night before, however, Laurel is at no loss to handle the situation. She is aware that the past is nothing to Fay, but what she says to Fay is: "'I know you aren't anything to the past. . . . You can't do anything to it now.'" Nor can Laurel, as she now well knows, do anything to the past either. She does not speak this aloud to Fay, but she does say to herself: "The past is no more open to help or hurt than was Father in his coffin. The past is like him, impervious, and can never be awakened. It is memory that is the somnambulist. It will come back in its wounds from across the world, like Phil, calling us by our names and demanding its rightful tears. It will never be impervious. The memory can be hurt, time and again—but in that may lie its final mercy. As long as it's vulnerable to the living moment, it lives for us, and while it lives, and while we are able, we can give it up its due."

Other writers, of course, have come to this insight. Wordsworth, for example, wrote:

Thanks to the human heart by which we live,
Thanks to its tenderness, its joys, and fears,
To me the meanest flower that blows can give
Thoughts that do often lie too deep for tears.

The discovery is made over and over again, and is dramatized—through flower or breadboard—by each successive writer in his own appropriate fashion.

So Laurel can now put her mother's scarred breadboard "down on the table where it belonged," forgoing the quixotic gesture of taking it along with her. All that she leaves behind—family home, furnishings and all—is impervious to Fay and the future. What for her is precious in it is past any harm that can be done to it by anyone. She is now ready to take her plane back to Chicago and her job.

16

The Past Alive in the Present

ᕲ

The poets and novelists who made the Southern Renaissance in the twentieth century have received much praise from various quarters. But in my opinion, their most handsome compliment has come from Vann Woodward, the acknowledged dean of southern historians. In his *Thinking Back: The Perils of Writing History,* he has provided an absorbing account of his own career as a historian. Early in the book he tells us of what the emergence of this new and exciting literature out of the South meant to him as he began his study of southern history. He writes that "no Southern youth of any sensitivity could help being excited by the explosion of creativity taking place during the early 1930s—in fiction, in poetry, in drama."

Yet, more than a vague general excitement was present. On a later page Woodward states very specifically the aspects of that literary movement that impressed him so deeply: the past was not dead but very much alive in the present; the southern past was presented without special pleading, the deficiencies alongside the virtues; and a serious attempt was made to remove the veil that hid much of the real southern past. In short, the new poets and novelists of the South were telling the truth—something like the whole truth—about the southern experience, past and present. Then Woodward adds a further point: the perspective to which they had won might enable them to provide some valuable and necessary insights into the American experience as a whole.

To this last point I mean to return later, but I want now to develop further Woodward's praise of the new southern writers for their consciousness of the past's presence, alive and significant, in the present, a sense of lived history that gave continuity and resonance to their renditions, even of contemporary experience. Can one provide concrete illustrations from the Southern Renaissance? Yes, indeed—from Faulkner, for instance. But in the 1930s and 1940s the issue of the past in relation to the present was sadly confused by most reviewers and literary critics, both North and South. Many of them felt that Faulkner simply could not face the realities of the modern world. Needless to say, the issues that interested Faulkner were far more complicated than that. The past could prove a support or it could prove an intolerable burden. But it could not with impunity be evaded any more than the present could be dismissed, for the present had grown out of the past.

In *The Sound and the Fury* Quentin Compson is hagridden by the past, but in a special way. His ancestors have set a pattern for him that he cannot fulfill. They were men of honor whose behavior had established standards that he cannot live up to. In his desperation he comes to believe that his only escape is into death, but it is an escape from an intolerable present situation—not merely into the past, for it is his personal past that judges and condemns that present.

That this is the true account receives full confirmation from what we learn of Quentin in the novel *Absalom, Absalom!* One can, of course, argue that *The Sound and the Fury* and *Absalom, Absalom!* are two distinct novels and that the Quentin in one is not necessarily the same man as the Quentin in the other. But the problems of Quentin A and Quentin B are in essence the same problem: how to understand, and even more to shoulder, the burden of his past. That problem is given its personal urgency because he has failed to protect his sister's honor. In *Absalom, Absalom!* the fascination that the character of Henry Sutpen holds for Quentin is Henry's achieved defense of his sister's honor even if it demands killing his best friend. As for the past being alive in the present, Faulkner has presented it in the most powerful symbolism possible: Quentin's discovery of the emaciated form of Henry Sutpen himself. Henry had fled the country as a kind of Cain or Orestes and so, decades before, had become simply a part of the legendary history of Yoknapatawpha County. But on his midnight visit to the ruinous Sutpen mansion, Quentin sees Henry Sutpen, who has secretly come home—come home to die, as he tells Quentin. Hyatt Waggoner aptly describes Henry as a flesh-and-blood ghost, now living in a house long thought to be haunted. Could there be a more powerful symbol of the tragic past of long ago alive in the present? This memory of the withered body of Henry Sutpen lying on the yellowed sheets haunts Quentin. Months later, Quentin, lying in his dormitory room at Harvard, cannot put this vision out of his mind.

Yet, the past as a living force can exert its vigor in the mind of a southern boy under very different circumstances and for very different effects. Of Chick Mallison, in the novel *Intruder in the Dust*, Faulkner as author observes that "every Southern boy fourteen years old" is capable of reliving the moment just before Pickett's charge at Gettysburg as if the issue had not been already decided some eighty years before. For a boy like Charles Mallison, the moment becomes circumstantially alive: "The guns are laid and ready in the woods and the furled flags are already loosened to break out and Pickett himself . . . [is] waiting for Longstreet to give the word and its all in balance." Here again the long-past event is still very much alive in the present consciousness.

To call this passage, as one New York–based reviewer did, "literary, flamboyant, historically ridiculous in terms of America today" misses the point entirely. Faulkner himself, I have no doubt, had had the experience; I confess that I have had it, and I know many others who had. Make of it what you like, it is a cultural fact that has to be faced if we want to deal honestly with cultural history and to understand the psyche of the South in the first third of the twentieth century.

The fiction and the poetry of Robert Penn Warren are suffused with the sense of the past still alive in the present, a past that his characters fail to accept at their peril. The past must be accepted and, if possible, redeemed. For example, one of his most brilliant earlier poems is entitled "Original Sin," but Warren uses the theological term in his title as a metaphor for a deeply ingrained quirk in all men, however rational. We cannot live entirely by maps and schedules. They are never quite perfect enough. The best-laid plans of mice and men gang agley—break up on that hidden rock of experience. But what looks like a vicious perversity may in fact yield its blessedness. Life is more exciting and finally more wonderful because of the very fact of our hidden affections, blind urges, faiths that resist all rational attempts to extirpate them. Yet, the poem is not a celebration of the irrational. Of course, we have to try to be rational, but we must never deceive ourselves that it is entirely possible. Life is too mysterious for mere calculation to encompass. If what I have just set down looks like moralization, do not put the blame on Warren's poem. The poem is a dramatic rendition; in fact, its subtitle is "A Short Story"— not a philosophical treatise, but a narrative of one man's experience.

Perhaps Warren's full-dress presentation of this theme in verse is *Brother to Dragons.* The poem imagines what might have been the impact on Thomas Jefferson of the terrible news that two of his nephews, out on the frontier of western Kentucky, had murdered one of their slaves for committing a trivial offense and then chopped up his body on a meat block, in the presence of the other slaves, to intimidate them and to make sure that they would fear to report the crime. Though there is nothing among the Jefferson papers to indicate how he responded to such tidings, he must have known of the murder. The killers were the sons of his favorite sister, Lucy. Moreover, the news did get out to other people. To Jefferson, such news obviously struck at family loyalty and pride. But its impact on Jefferson had to be even more special. He had entertained high hopes for mankind, placed as he was in the New World and so given a new start. It was Jefferson who had invested so much of his moral and spiritual capital in man's natural reasonableness and goodness.

Since there is no extant information as to what Jefferson's reaction was, Warren has been left free to imagine it: the shock and horror, the revulsion against his great dream for mankind, and his final reappraisal of his beliefs. His sister Lucy pleads with her brother not to disavow his dream but to accept the past even with all its horror and shame and to try to build a better dream on the only firm foundation it can ever have: an acceptance of the past, the actual past. Lucy tells her brother:

> Your dream, dear brother, was noble.
> If there was vanity, fear, or deceit in its condition,
> What of that? For we are human and must work
> In the shade of the human condition.

Jefferson, accepting the past, even the wickedness disclosed in his own bloodline, concurs when his friend and kinsman Meriwether Lewis (of the Lewis and Clark expedition) exclaims:

>   nothing we had
> Nothing we were,

Is lost. All is redeemed
In knowledge.

Jefferson adds:

But knowledge is the most powerful cost.
It is the bitter bread.
I have eaten the bitter bread.
In joy, would end.

It would be a pleasure to quote passages from the work of John Crowe Ransom, Donald Davidson, and others who made the Southern Renaissance of the 1930s and 1940s, the writers to whom Woodward pays special tribute. Moreover, one could find plenty of further illustrations from the succeeding generations of southern writers, for the historical consciousness is still to be found among them, even among some of our youngest writers. But there is one more of the earlier generation whom we cannot fail to consider: Allen Tate. He has two special claims on our attention here. The first is that of the essayist who has written most explicitly and extensively on "the peculiar historical consciousness of the Southern writer." Woodward quotes this very phrase in his account of the "heartening effect" exerted on his own work by the writers of the Southern Renaissance. A second claim for special attention is Tate's fine novel, *The Fathers,* which treats in dramatic detail the traditional man and the antitraditional man. But the issue as presented in that novel is complicated—all the more so by the new ending with which Tate furnished his revised edition.

The problem—at least as it has presented itself to some readers—is this: assuming that Major Buchan is the essential traditionalist, the man who honors the past and would preserve its values, and assuming that his son-in-law, George Posey, is the man of the future on whom the traditionalist values rest lightly and who is ultimately interested only in making money, do not both turn out to be equally destructive of any stable society? One of them seems to be blindly locked into the past; the other, utterly contemptuous of it. It is easy to see why Tate wanted to make the two protagonists direct antitheses, each of the other. But do Major Buchan and George Posey exhaust the human alternatives?

Lacy Buchan, the major's youngest son, relates, many years afterward, an account of the destruction of his family: Major Buchan refused to see what was at stake, believed that Virginia could keep out of the impending War Between the States, disowned his son Semmes for joining the Confederate army, and only after his own house had been burned by a regiment of German-speaking Union troops came to see his folly and so hanged himself. If not a Lear, Major Buchan turns out to be a kind of Gloucester: deceived in this instance not by his bastard son, but by his son-in-law, and, like Gloucester, sacrificing his own son in the process.

Posey scorns all the forms of the traditional society as irrational and therefore ridiculous. When he wins the prize at the tournament and so is allowed to crown with a chaplet the young lady of his choice as Queen of Love and Beauty, he cannot make himself place it on Susan Buchan's head but unceremoniously drops it in her lap. When he is insulted by another man, he scorns to meet him in the duel that custom requires, and simply knocks him down with his fists. Later on, when the same man insults him even more viciously, he simply draws his pistol and shoots him down like a dog. No tears need be shed for the man Posey killed; by common consent he deserved his fate. But again, Posey scorns the traditional forms for handling such matters. He believes in direct action—even impulsive action.

It is easy to see why George Posey would have proved an attractive, even glamorous figure to any teenage youth brought up in what must have appeared to him a stodgy home in which nothing exciting ever happened. But how can Lacy, fifty years later, an elderly man, looking back on the disaster to his family, possibly utter the following laudation of Posey? "As I stood by his grave in Holyrood Cemetery fifty years later [that is, in 1911] I remembered how he restored his wife and small daughter and what he did for me. What he became in himself I shall never forget. Because of this I venerate his memory more than the memory of any other man."

Are these words freighted with an irony that I have simply missed? Remember that George Posey, in a sudden spasm of anger, had shot and killed Lacy's brother Semmes, that he had driven his wife, Lacy's sister, insane, and that in the last glimpse we are given of Posey's little child, she is babbling, "Papa make money, Papa make money." This is her comment on his nearly constant absence from home. Tate has provided a short preface to the revised edition. Its subtitle reads: "Caveat Lector." Is it meant to sanction a measure of irony—even sarcasm—in Lacy's final appraisal of Posey? In this preface Tate says that the revision "gives the reader two heroes: Major Buchan the classical hero whose *hubris* betrays him; George Posey, who may have seemed to some readers a villain, is now clearly a modern Romantic hero." Let the reader indeed beware, but of just what?

Thus far I have been concerned with the appropriateness of the ending that Tate has supplied for his novel. But there is a deeper and more general problem: just what constitutes a historical consciousness? More specifically, does Major Buchan, a man of the tradition, possess any historical consciousness himself? The answer here is not as obvious as it may at first appear. Major Buchan has difficulty in imagining any civilized society that is different from his own, that of a Virginia gentleman living on his own acres. He is obviously not a particularly reflective man, but if he were, surely he would affirm the basic continuity of the past and the present. As a matter of fact, a reflective person, including the typical literary artist, until rather recent times always has. The characters of Shakespeare's Roman plays are not vastly different from Shakespeare's contemporary Elizabethans. The mind-set of men of different races and ages was held to be essentially the same. Calibans, of course, were something else again, but Caliban as Shakespeare portrays him in *The Tempest* is not altogether human. But an Antony or a Caesar could be easily accommodated, *mutatis mutandis,* to the Elizabethan scene—British higher education found little difficulty in basing itself on the classics of Greece and Rome, not only in the seventeenth century, but almost down to the present day.

The historical consciousness as manifested by T. S. Eliot, Ezra Pound, and Tate himself is a much more sensitive and specialized cast of mind. These writers have felt that the changes that had begun to occur in twentieth-century culture had gone far deeper and would radically alter the whole human perspective. Specifically, they saw a challenge to the value system by which mankind had lived for millennia past.

Tate was later to find his general prescription for society in a return to orthodox Christianity, specifically as embodied in the Roman Catholic Church. In later life he became a Roman Catholic himself. But earlier and more generally he had stressed "the peculiar historical consciousness" that was the southern writer's rightful heritage and urged him to write without any evasion or defensiveness of southern history. The writer was to render the whole truth about his own region and about his country, the United States at large. Although this position began to be foreshadowed in his early essays, it came to its full and final expression in 1959 in "A Southern Mode of the Imagination."

Where does all of this leave Major Buchan? Did he have, as a southerner, a "peculiar historical consciousness"? My reading of the text of *The Fathers* makes it quite plain that he did not. Tate would have surely approved of the major's belief that men of the past were recognizably like ourselves and, I suspect, would have seen the worth of the major's love of manners and ritual. Yeats, in his great poem "A Prayer for My Daughter," has put the matter in a form that I believe Tate must have applauded:

> And may her bridegroom bring her to a house,
> Where all's accustomed, ceremonious.
> How but in custom and in ceremony
> Are innocence and beauty born?

George Posey, by the way, did not bring Major Buchan's daughter Susan to such a house. The last section of *The Fathers* depicts it as an abode of living death.

Yet, a true "historical consciousness" includes an awareness of change and of the need to cope with it. The major entirely lacks such an awareness. He lives in a kind of virtual present in which he cannot envisage real change as ever occurring. Moreover, the major is guileless and something of a sentimentalist. Early in the novel, George Posey charms the major out of his sense of outrage at what the major regards as Posey's breach of good manners. Posey puts his excuse so prettily and apparently so innocently and plausibly that the major relents at once. Late in the novel, after Posey has shot Semmes Buchan to death, he sends a letter of apology that wins the major's heart. As Major Buchan tells Lacy: "He shot your brother in anger, and he explained everything that had led up to it. I have been particularly impressed by his contrition." Major Buchan is obviously a special case. He is not typical of the southern landed gentry of his time: compare Lee, Stephens, Jefferson Davis, Mary Boykin Chesnut, and many another. Buchan has as little sense of history as has his son-in-law, George Posey.

Semmes Buchan, though no intellectual, at least saw what was happening to the country and to Virginia. Lacy's grandfather Buchan seems to me to have had an acute consciousness of history and a sound judgment of men. He, or at least his ghost, explaining matters to Lacy, gives an analysis of Posey's character that surely must reflect Tate's own: Grandfather Buchan knows about Posey's capacity for destruction, and from what it springs. George Posey, he tells his grandson, "is entirely alone. My son, in my day we were never alone, as your brother-in-law is alone. He is alone like a tornado. His one purpose is to whirl." It is a thumbnail sketch of the rootless, alienated man of our own day.

This magnificent novel through 203 pages (of the revised edition) renders with powerful drama a major universal theme. It is not merely a "southern" novel or even an antebellum novel. The essential problem is quite alive today. If much of our population is as well intentioned as was Major Buchan, it also shares his utter lack of a consciousness of history; as for George Posey, I suspect that if we look sharply about us, we could make out a goodly number of George Poseys among us. Our Poseys are as glamorous to our young Lacys and can beguile our Major Buchans as well as George ever did.

My denial of the historical consciousness to that obviously traditional man Major Buchan is not actually made in so many words by the text of the novel, and readers who regard Buchan as representing all that Posey is not may be somewhat bewildered, for does the author not set up these characters as polar opposites? In any case, to deny the "restorative" powers to Posey, as I have done, and to see him as a purely destructive force does clearly run counter to the last paragraph of the revised edition. (Neither does it accord very well with the concluding paragraph of the original version of *The Fathers.*) Most of all, my interpretation flies in the face of the long note that Tate supplied for the revised edition.

A full discussion of these matters must be reserved for another essay. Here it would constitute a further distraction from my main point: the historical consciousness exhibited by the writers who made the Southern Literary Renaissance, a movement in which Tate was a key figure and to which his own writings contributed so much—his essays, his poems, and *The Fathers* itself, save for that puzzling last paragraph.

17

The Primacy of the Reader

❧

I have often discussed what Monroe Beardsley and W. K. Wimsatt term the "intentional fallacy"—a fallacy referring not to a mistake made by the author but to one made by the reader or the critic. The critic must not take the intent for the deed. He may find useful clues as to what the work is about from sources outside the work, but if so, such intimations must always be tested against the work and validated there. In this case, special information, got directly from the horse's mouth, is insufficient. What counts is whether the horse (that is, the author) won, placed, or merely showed. In other words, how he fared in the race is what goes into the record book. Yet human nature being what it is and our habits about discourse being what they are, such a distinction will probably always be vulnerable to attack and difficult to defend. Most of us feel it more natural to talk about the author and what he sought to do rather than to talk about the makeup of the poem or novel constructed. Did not that truly great English critic, S. T. Coleridge, prefer it that way? In the *Biographia Literaria,* after leading us up to a proposed definition of poetry, he suddenly shifts the topic. It is really easier, he tells us, to describe the ideal *poet,* and this is just what he proceeds to do.

Though the old-fashioned historicism is still well entrenched and still powerful, there has come recently from a new quarter a fresh attempt to see the literary work as primarily an expression of its author. Harold Bloom, for example, has presented a renewed emphasis on the author in its most striking form. He is very much concerned with the poet, his characteristic energies and impulses, and what, according to him, is the poet's necessary resistance to the work of his poetic forebears: the "strong" poet (to use Bloom's adjective) succeeds in breaking free from a tradition that he finds suffocating and is able to make his own work fresh and new, whereas the "weak" poet can do no more than imitate work already done and better done. The relation of this concept to some of the Romantic poets of the early nineteenth century and to Sigmund Freud in the twentieth is rather obvious. Rebellious energy, according to William Blake, is the way to the only truth that we can experience, and the Oedipal attack upon the father is inevitable in literature as well as in life.

There is clearly an element of truth in such doctrines. A genuine poet is not only not content to imitate his literary masters: if he is a genuine poet, that fact will show itself in his forging a style that is definitely his own. But is the typical poet necessarily as self-conscious as Bloom would have him? And is he so anxious to replace the literary master from whom he principally derives? Such knowledge as I have of the history of English and American literature shows no such general pattern, nor have I found this impulse notable among the contemporary poets whom I have known personally. This is not to say that I am not acquainted with a few poets—I am thinking here in particular of one first-rate poet—whose ego drives are ferocious. The poet I have in mind, however, is not so much concerned to slay his literary father as to commit acts of mayhem on his brother poets; in fact, I expect that the competitiveness among men of letters is mostly with their living contemporaries rather than with their dead ancestors. In any case, what Bloom has called the "anxiety of influence" is surely not the basic or the typical motivation of the man of letters. Some of our very best writers seem to be the least infected with a sense of rivalry and jealous competition.

Yet, because of Bloom's intense interest in the writer as a man struggling to free himself from both literary conventions and the benumbing effects of an established tradition, Bloom, in his later writings, has become less and less concerned with the structure of a poem or of a piece of fiction. Mind you, Bloom is thoroughly capable of handling such matters when he chooses to do so; he can on occasion be the highly perceptive practical critic. Yet, since Bloom's heart is in what he takes to be the artist's necessary struggle to liberate his true self, the fabric of an artist's work becomes primarily interesting to him as evidence of that struggle. In short, Bloom is—at least in recent years—much more interested in the maker than in the thing that he has made, and he is interested in the maker principally as he exhibits himself as the ποιητής ᾿αγωνιστής — the maker combatant or, more literally, the "poet agonizing." Significantly, Bloom entitled one of his books *Agon*.

Denis Donoghue has summed up the situation aptly in one sentence: "Bloom's practical criticism is indifferent to the structure, internal relations, of the poem, or to its diction, syntax, meters, rhythm, or tone: it is chiefly concerned to isolate the primal gesture which the critical paradigm has predicted." That primal gesture, of course, is the stipulated defiance of the father, and the critical paradigm is the preordained and inevitable Oedipal conflict. Bloom's emphasis on the writer rather than the writing is, then, of a very different order from that of the older historicism that was regnant in the nineteenth century. Bloom also differs from the usual intentionalist in a more special way. The "strong" poet's general intention is ever the same: to circumvent the poetical father—to deny the father's intention, to twist it, or in some other way to evade it. In any case, Bloom's basic affinities are with the poet rather than the historical scholar, with Nietzsche rather than with Taine.

In *Agon*, Bloom tells us that he writes as a "Jewish Gnostic, trying to explore and develop a personal Gnosis and a possible Gnosticism, perhaps one available to others." In saying this, Bloom makes it clear that his fundamental motive is now philosophical and theological, not primarily literary. There is surely nothing wrong with this, but it is useful for us to realize that his principal concern is certainly not with literary criticism as such.

Gnosticism may seem remote to us. It is a view of reality which the early Christian Fathers attacked as a heresy, which we now know was not restricted to Christianity, and which indeed antedated Christianity. We also now know that the spirit of Gnosticism is very much alive in our own day. Eric Voegelin, for example, has devoted several learned volumes to a discussion of Gnosticism, particularly in its modern phases. Essential to the Gnostic view is the belief that the Creator God was a wicked demon or demiurge. The task of the enlightened soul, a soul possessed of the proper esoteric knowledge (Gnosis), is to reject this wicked and ill-made world and return to the true God who is to be found behind the facade of our daily experience. One aspect of the Gnostic religion is thus the cultivation of the secret wisdom which allows the emancipated soul to rejoin the true God. But another aspect is an active and practical rebellion against this world—an effort to remake the world in accordance with the secret wisdom.

I find, for example, both the mystical and the positivistic aspects in a Blake or a Shelley or an Emerson—to mention only three poets. One assumes that it is the mystical and individual aspect that Bloom finds attractive. Yet it is significant that in his new book he writes: "I have come to the conviction that the love of poetry is another variant of the love of power." Voegelin would agree that, ultimately, the love of power, however it may disguise itself, is part and parcel of the Gnostic mentality. Far from accepting reality, Gnosticism is ultimately disappointed with it and means to circumvent it, escape from it, or remake it to suit its own vision. We move toward the more aggressive, political mode when the love of poetry is seen as a "love of power"—not as contemplation, but as an assertion of the ego.

I want to turn now to an incursion into literary criticism that comes from the other side—from an exaltation of the reader. The most vociferous proponent of this view of the critical process is Stanley Fish, and although Bloom's concern is with the writer and Fish's with the reader, both are agreed on one point: they both disparage any hope of an accurate reading of a literary text. Bloom argues that the "strong" poet is forced to misread what his poetic forefather was trying to say; presumably the "strong" critic will have to do the same. For Fish, on the other hand, the reader so fully determines what a literary text is that he can be truly said to create the text; the reader transforms it from whatever the author may have meant by it. In both cases, the reading makes no pretense to arrive at what we used to call an accurate reading or a correct reading.

If Fish were doing no more than insisting upon the importance of the reader as an essential element in completing the literary transaction, few people would care to dispute him. A literary work that is unread obviously remains inert; it is merely *potential* literary experience until someone has *realized* it through a reading of it. Moreover, that readers differ in their interpretations of a poem, a novel, or a drama is scarcely news to anyone who has put in many years of trying to teach people how to read literature. In fact, the vast industry which presently produces thousands of volumes of literary criticism and scholarship, including textbooks, would never have arisen if literary works could be appropriated easily and if every reader agreed with every other in his interpretation.

The importance of the reader was in fact made abundantly clear in I. A. Richards's landmark book of 1929, *Practical Criticism*. As many of you will remember, Richards had his honors students in English at Cambridge University write brief accounts of some thirteen untitled poems. The results were startling, even to those who were prepared for diversity or for sheer incompetence. Among other things, the book made it obvious that a study of the poet's life and the various cultural forces that had shaped him did not in itself insure a reader's ability to deal with a poem on its merits: stripped of the convenient handholds of authorship and literary period, the typical poem proved to be a very slippery object indeed.

In 1958, much the same point was made in a little paperback volume entitled *Keats's Well-Read Urn*—a title that probably tilts a mischievous nod toward a book that I had published in 1947, called *The Well Wrought Urn*. In *Keats's Well-Read Urn*, the point about reader diversity was, because of two circumstances, made even more emphatically. First, the book dealt not with thirteen different poems, as in *Practical Criticism*, but concentrated on just one—"Ode on a Grecian Urn"; second, the readers whose interpretations of the poem were examined were not students, but well-established scholars and critics—some of them famous. In the course of this book, the editor, H. T. Lyon, summarizes or quotes, in all, some eighty-eight interpretations. Personally, I trust that in using the adjective phrase "well-read," the editor meant no more than "well-thumbed" or "worn by the hands of many readers," and I say this because some of the readings are not well done—in fact, some are quite inept, in spite of having been written by professional scholars and critics.

Although I accept the fact of diversity, I must thus insist that some readings are *better* than others, and I trust that a nearly correct or adequate reading of the "Ode," or of any other poem, is not just a will-o'-the-wisp: if the search for a correct reading is really hopeless, I see little point in continuing literary studies at all; if there can be no proper reading, one would have to counsel each reader to do what he likes and let the devil take the hindmost; if there is no substantive difference that distinguishes A's reading from B's, we would seem to be reduced to a rather stale

relativism. The notion that, instead of looking for the most nearly adequate reading among various possible interpretations, we should simply
choose the most interesting has in fact been urged by Stanley Fish and
others. I expect, however, that "more interesting" is a disguised way of
saying more accurate or adequate—a view which is urged more powerfully when we ask: More interesting to whom? To the schoolboy or to the
mature man? To the reader of *True Confessions* or to the reader of *The
Confessions of St. Augustine?* After all, there is interest and interest, and
the more gratifying kinds of interest are connected with *significance.*

Stanley Fish, however, insists on the inevitable variability of interpretation, and in his book *Is There a Text in This Class?* the author of the text
dissolves into a shadowy wraith; the author as a human being who writes
out of his experience has disappeared altogether. Perhaps Fish's most
extreme example of this phenomenon is simply a random assortment of
words, for the words he cites were not set down out of any desire to write
a poem—or indeed to fit into any syntactic relationship. It seems that,
one morning at Johns Hopkins, Fish had failed to erase from the blackboard the names of certain authorities listed there for a class in linguistic
theory. When the students from another course—this one in seventeenth-
century religious poetry—came into the classroom, Professor Fish chalked
a framing line around this little column of six proper names and wrote at
the top of the frame "p. 43." Then he mischievously told the members of
the class that they were looking at a poem of the kind that they had been
studying. Nothing daunted, the members of the class began to interpret
the assemblage of names in terms of Christian symbolism. The name
"Jacobs" brought to their minds the story of Jacob's ladder, regarded by
Christians as a type of the ascent to heaven. "Rosenbaum" ("rose tree"),
they assumed, must surely refer to the Virgin Mary, the rose of Sharon,
mother of the Man-God through Whom the ascent could be made.
"Ohman," the last name in the list, they variously interpreted as meaning
"omen," "oh man," or even "amen." With a little straining, therefore,
these three words could be fitted into a Christian poem about man's need
for salvation through the acceptance of Jesus Christ as his Lord and
Savior. I shall not go into further detail, such as the way in which Fish's
students fitted such names as "Levin" and "Thorne" into the stipulated
pattern. Let me simply sum up this piece of clever manipulation of words

by saying that this example proved—to Fish, at least—that readers do not *decode* poems. They *create* poems. Given their notion of what a poem is, along with their expectations about what they ought to be able to find, they proceed to find those expectations realized in whatever is singled out to be read as a poem.

Having witnessed this remarkable piece of verbal sleight of hand, one might be tempted to push Fish into logical absurdity by asking whether just any set of words would do—or even no words at all. But there is no need to do so, for Fish has already been there before us, insisting that the same results would follow even "if the paper or the blackboard were blank: the blankness would present no problem to the interpreter, who would immediately see it as indicating the void out of which God created the earth or the abyss into which unregenerate sinners fall, or in the best of all poems, both." All is grist to Fish's remarkable mill. Indeed, it works even *without* grist, grinding out poems just the same.

The example on which I have dwelt at some length (and upon which Fish has dwelt even longer) constitutes the proof, so he argues, that poems are really created by the reader. I must confess that, to me, it proves something very different—namely, the gullibility of the students who sat in Stanley Fish's classroom and the amazing docility of all too many students who sit at the feet of a teacher with a magnetic personality. How can students who are conversant with seventeenth-century poetry and who believe—I shall use Fish's own language—that poems are "more densely and intricately organized than ordinary communications" also believe that any odd lot of nouns, lacking any syntactic organization at all, can possibly be a seventeenth-century poem? If they had also been taught "to see connections between one word and another and between every word and the poem's central insight"—I am again using Fish's own words— they would be sure that this poem did not come from the likes of a Donne or a Herbert or a Marvell. Where in this jumble of words is the characteristic *logic* of the religious poets of the seventeenth century? Where is their involved figurative language? What the example proves to me is that the students in question cannot read a poem—or perhaps they diplomatically pretended in this instance that they could not do so.

Another key aspect of Fish's reader-oriented criticism is his special account of what the reading process actually is. For Fish, the process of reading is necessarily broken up into small units. It is not an unbroken flow—reading proceeds by jerks, in a process of starts and stops. Thus, in reading the following lines from Milton's "Lycidas"—

The Willows and the Hazel Copses green
Shall now no more be seen,
Fanning their joyous Leaves to thy soft lays—

Fish says that the reader is constrained to stop at "seen," so that he interprets the passage to mean that, now that Lycidas is dead, the willow and hazel copses will wither and die in sympathy with him and "will no more be seen by *anyone*." Of course, the reader *does* go on to read the next line and, in doing so, realizes that the willow and hazel copses will no longer be seen by *Lycidas*, for his music that once fanned their "joyous Leaves" will have ceased with his death. But Fish holds that the first reading (some kind of provisional reading?), though corrected in the next moment, remains as part of the reader's experience and so has to remain as a part of the meaning of the poem.

The argument here reminds me a little of Zeno's paradox of the race between Achilles and the tortoise: give the tortoise a bit of a head start, and the fleet-footed Achilles can never catch him, for by the time the Greek warrior has covered half the distance to the tortoise, the creature has moved on a certain distance, and by the time the runner has run half this new distance, the tortoise has moved a little further too; since one can carry this process on to infinity, the tortoise will always be ahead. The logic may be impeccable, but the conclusion violates both common sense and reality. The motion of Achilles is continuous, not start-stop, and so is my reading. If, from time to time, I mistake the meaning, either through my own obtuseness or through the author's clumsiness, I can correct the mistake and reread the passage in question. In saying this, I am not leaving out of account the possibility that the author perhaps intended for me to stumble and hesitate for a moment—intended for example, as a rhetorical device for providing a particular emphasis or introducing a deliberate ambiguity. Such a concession, however, does not affect my argument, for such a rhetorical device will also finally have to relate to a total and final effect of the work.

Fish, however, sets great store by his start-stop theory of what actually goes on in the reading process. He evidently believes that it supports his conviction that language is truly indeterminate and that it proves that the reader normally generates all kinds of out-of-the-way interpretations and meanings. For someone like Fish, whose specialty is coming up with the new and unexpected meaning even in familiar texts, such a method of reading becomes a very serviceable tool. His method of reading does generate new meanings all over the place.

Nevertheless, it is Fish's claim that his theories of reading and of the whole interpretive process do not commit him to a complete relativism. Why not? Because, as he says, our individual interpretations are not simply our own but are governed by the standards of an interpretive *community* to which every reader necessarily belongs. In this way we are somehow delivered from subjectivity; that is, we do not stand alone in our interpretation. Yet how much *objectivity* is actually afforded by this doctrine of interpretive communities? No one doubts that interpretive communities exist, or that they change from time to time. But the mere acceptance of that fact still leaves us with relativism—historical relativism of the sort that we have had with us for years past.

There is a further serious objection to be offered here. Fish's bulwark against mere subjectivity, even if it operates within the same period of literary activity, is far from watertight. How cohesive is any literary community? Doesn't it often show a bewildering diversity? Consider the various interpretations of Keats's "Ode on a Grecian Urn." The period covered by *Keats's Well-Read Urn* runs roughly from the 1820s to the 1950s. But if this span does not seem sufficiently compact to allow a fair test case, then let's limit the span of the interpretive community in question to a period from 1896 to 1930—thirty-four years, or about the span of one literary generation. Even in this more limited period, we find a great diversity of interpretations, not merely in niceties of detail but in fundamental points. For example, Lyon, the editor, writes as follows with reference to the famous concluding lines, "Beauty is truth, truth beauty?— that is all / Ye know on earth, and all ye need to know":

> Diversity of opinion could hardly be more extreme than in [the following] judgments. For [Robert] Bridges the final line redeemed a poor poem, for

[T. S.] Eliot they spoil a good one; for Sir Arthur Quiller-Couch they are ignorant and uneducated; for I. A. Richards [they are] that still ambiguous entity which he calls a pseudo-statement.

It can be argued that if, in a familiar and famous case, the doctors can disagree so radically as these critics do, one may well despair of achieving anything like a "right" reading, and I am not unaware of such difficulties. But note that such evidence also severely limits the amount of objectivity provided by one's belonging to a particular interpretive community. In fact, to get anything like a really cohesive interpretive community, we would probably have to confine it to a very small group indeed—to Professor Fish and his students, for instance.

Fish acknowledges that interpretive communities change, and of course they do. He also tells us that it is the virtue of his kind of criticism that, since there is no "correct" interpretation, there is no substantive loss if such a change does occur. I am not consoled, however, by an "objectivity" of judgment guaranteed in such terms, for it would then be possible to have literally dozens of interpretive communities of minuscule size, all existing side by side, and indeed from the last chapters of Fish's book, I get the impression that a strong-willed and magnetic individual can engineer such changes almost to order.

A British reviewer of *Is There a Text in This Class?* seems to have got the same impression. He writes:

> . . . What is significant in [Fish's] theory is how he identifies the class which he aggrandizes [that is, the new interpretive community]. It does not consist of aesthetes, independent thinkers, *amateurs des livres*, poets' poets, but it is the unified class of the faculties of university English departments, with special privileges [going] to the more ambitious and the most assertive. Fish's arbiter of critical truth is characteristically someone with students to teach, colleagues to convince, a hearing to gain for himself, and who, if he does well in all this, will be, in Fish's words, "a candidate for the profession's highest honors."

After one has made full discount for the British penchant for amateurism, with its distrust of American professionalism in criticism, and for British wariness of almost any critical theory of literature, one might find a large element of truth in this indictment. For it must be conceded that

Fish's reference to "a candidate for the profession's highest honors" does give off a faint whiff of the world of business success. It might almost have been spoken by a bright young advertising executive, confident that he can market any attractive new product. It suggests that, to such a person, the formation of a new interpretive community (one which will underwrite his new interpretive strategies) will present for him no problems.

I want to turn next to what is probably the most extreme form of reader-oriented criticism. Several years ago, Susan Sontag wrote an essay entitled "Against Interpretation." She writes well, and her essay, with its forthright title, created quite a stir. Clearly, she expressed the feelings of a great many readers who were fed up with what often seemed the sterile but noisy wrangling of the critics. Her argument, if taken literally, would sweep the whole board clean; she would protect the common reader and, especially, the innocent reader from the depredations of the professional literary critic, and she would do so by urging a moratorium on every variety of criticism. In effect she asks: Why don't we simply leave the reader alone and let him find his own enjoyment of the poem or the novel without worrying his way through the labyrinth of critical theory? Away with the whole pestiferous tribe of critics, she says, and in concluding her essay, she declares that what we need today is not a hermeneutics but an erotics of art.

One has to be sympathetic with her view of things: the discussion of literature, and particularly of literary theory, ought not to be allowed to overwhelm literature itself. Moreover, I agree that it may be useful for the reader to look at poems and novels with an innocent eye, to range about for himself, to experience the thrill of making his own discovery. Nevertheless, it would be naive to believe that the innocent reader does not sometimes require help. It is equally naive to believe that, if the meddlesome literary critics could only be suppressed, the reader would not be subject to other people's interpretations: the extermination of literary critics would still leave the book reviews, the publishers' advertisements, the chitchat of the cocktail party and the schools and colleges in all the courses in English except those restricted to grammar and composition. However tempting the notion of preserving the innocence of the common reader, it is hardly feasible. Long ago, T. S. Eliot remarked—not wholly in jest, I believe—that he would personally prefer to address his poems to people who could neither read nor write; in short, he would prefer a truly clean slate, a virgin reader, one who had not been given wrongheaded notions of what poetry is. I think I know what Eliot meant, but his proposal, which is even more drastic than Sontag's, is made ironically, for he knew that such an audience is impossible to find. The innocent reader simply does not exist: the popular culture of the day has already corrupted him.

The young reader can in fact usually profit from honest literary scholarship and from a literary criticism which tries to elucidate the text but which is sufficiently modest about forcing opinions on him. What is worse than useless to the novice reader is a criticism that is distracting or domineering or simply perverse and pigheaded. But how do we get rid of the misleading and the useless? You don't get rid of the counterfeiters by doing away with money; you don't burn down the barn to get rid of the rats.

Some decades ago, Randall Jarrell made a related point, lamenting the fact that more people preferred to read about poems than to read the poems themselves. It is a pity that this is true. But it is true. Publishers find it difficult to take on unknown poets, and their books of verse rarely sell. The editors of our university quarterlies find it easier to secure acceptable essays on poetry than excellent poems, and as a former editor of a university quarterly I can claim to speak from experience. Nor is the situation dramatically better with fiction. William Faulkner's name, for example, is now internationally famous and his books sell, but until he won the Nobel Prize, those same books certainly did not sell; the novels that we now acknowledge as his masterpieces were for a long time out of print, and he had to eke out a living by grinding out short stories of a more immediate appeal or by doing movie scripts in Hollywood. During this dark period in his career, it was a small group of literary critics who kept his reputation alive, among them critics like Malcolm Cowley and Robert Penn Warren, who in the 1940s led the way toward a popular admiration for his work.

No, I don't believe that Susan Sontag's erotics of art can replace an interpretation of art, although I wish that I *could* believe it: how much simpler it would make everything if we could simply persuade people to love to read and then let nature take its course.

It is possible to distinguish among an author-oriented, a work-oriented, and a reader-oriented criticism. I have admitted the legitimacy of all three, as indeed I believe every reasonable person must, for each orientation has its special appeal and use. A literary criticism that stresses the author is especially appealing because it is humanly attractive. We respond to personalities, especially if the life lived by the subject was particularly sensational or glamorous. I myself confess to having a real weakness for biographies, but the life of an author whose work is third-rate may also be a pleasure to read. Yet to argue that such an author's work is first-rate simply because his life was exciting is to abandon literary standards altogether. If there is such a thing as literature (some thinkers would seem to argue that there is not), then its nature and the standards by which we judge its worth are important, and we must try to discover them, however difficult it may be to do so.

Moreover, important as the reader is and however various readers are in their reactions to the same set of words, I do not think that we can put the meaning of a text at the mercy of the lowest common denominator of any set of readers, or that we ought to throw up our hands and say that the text means simply what anybody thinks it means. If we take this despairing view of matters, then we must actually give up the vaunted claims of literature as a humanistic discipline.

To sum up: The author surely counts—we don't want our poems and short stories assembled for us by computers. And the reader also counts, for it is he who brings the literary work to full life in his own mind. Yet neither the study of the author's biography nor that of the reader's prejudices, mental sets, and inherited value system is sufficient to establish literary value.

Consider the following tiny four-line poem:

Western wind, when wilt thou blow,
The small rain down can rain?
Christ, if my love were in my arms,
And I in my bed again.

Since the poem is anonymous, there is here no need to trouble ourselves about the life of the author. Since it was apparently written before the

Enlightenment, Professor Bloom himself would presumably argue that "anxiety of influence" had not at that time arisen, although I must say that I do not fully understand just why the Enlightenment made all that much difference. Nor do I understand why the modern manifestations of Gnosticism show themselves after the Enlightenment, but that is another matter which I do not mean to get into at this time.

Yet even if this little poem has no known author, it yields a great deal. It has, I believe, a determinable meaning, and it shows itself to be authentic poetry. But does it manifest to the *common* reader its value as poetry along with its meaning? I think that it does, although the average reader may need some help in his reading. For one thing, he may need some assistance with the antiquated grammar, particularly in the second line. For another, he may be puzzled by the reference to the rain. I can imagine his asking: What has the rain to do with the speaker's wanting to clasp his love in his arms? Why the rather special attention to weather conditions? Wouldn't the person who speaks here long to be with his loved one if the countryside were as dry as a chip and the sky cloudless, with moon and stars clearly visible?

Questions like these deserve answers. The scholar-critic, therefore, might have to provide a note on geographic and meteorological conditions. The scene is presumably England, where the west wind brings a warm and gentle rain picked up from the Gulf Stream. In short the speaker of this little poem is not praying for a downpour or a cold blast or a tempest: the fine rain is the gentle all-night rain that gives life to the plants in the fields, and the drought that the speaker prays it will break may well be also an aridity and deadness in his own heart. There is yet another suggestion. The invocation of the rain sets the stage for the imagined scene that closes the poem. The speaker imagines not only his loved one in his arms, but himself at home, in his own bed, with the gentle rain falling outside to curtain off the lovers from the world.

If the student or the plain reader feels that too much is being made of details like these, he might be asked to consider what happens if we omit the first two lines and so get rid of the rain. Such omission would, of course, forfeit the rhyme, *rain-again*, but something more important would be lost from the poem. The omitted lines provide a frame for the outcry of loneliness, but it is more than just a frame: these lines provide a context in which we may imagine further the plight of the man who cries out. He is alone, and in his frustration, he appeals to the forces of nature. We do not know why he is away from home or what circumstance has separated him from his loved one, but these first two lines, with their concrete particularity, stir our imaginations and give a sort of dramatic substance to the cry that ends the poem. And there is one more point. The domestic detail of "And I in my bed again" anchors the poem to reality: this man is not merely lonely but homesick. Nor is the loved one merely a romantic dream girl, a fantasy of youthful desire: he has held this woman in his arms before, and in his own bed. His yearning is thereby made more poignant and more real.

Will the reader accept all this? Not necessarily—nor should he have it thrust upon him. He ought to accept only what he can absorb. But the concrete suggestions may cause him to take the poem seriously, ponder its details, and try to make sense of them for himself. In fact, he may come to realize that poems are not simply prettified nonsense but actually make sense. A fine contemporary British poet has put it well: Prose makes sense in only one dimension, while poetry makes sense in two or three dimensions. Discursive prose is thin and spare; poetry is thick and rich. Discursive prose is practical, communicating its message or stating its formula without much—or even any—use of the imagination. But poetry is the creation of the imagination, and it stirs the imagination of its reader. This is one of the reasons it can nourish the spirit and strengthen our own sense of being total human beings.

18

Literature in a Technological Age

Over two centuries ago, a young man, scarcely an elder statesman then—he was only thirty-three—was asked to draft a formal declaration of the independence of the American colonies from the government of Great Britain. He began:

> When in the course of human events it becomes necessary for one people to dissolve the political bands which have connected them with another, and to assume among the powers of the earth, the separate and equal station. . . .

But I need quote no further. You will remember the clarity and power of that noble utterance. Recently Professor Ross Baker of Rutgers University translated Jefferson's prose into a jargon not at all unfamiliar in our own day. His account goes like this:

> When at a given point in time in the human cycle the phase-out of political relationships is mandated, a clear signal needs to be communicated to the world as to why we are putting independence on-line.
>
> Truthwise, it has been apparent for some time that human resources should be accorded equal treatment, and that they are eligible for certain entitlements, that among them are viability, liberty, and the capability of accessing happiness.

It is an amusing parody, and a useful one, for it is not too outrageous as a caricature. Every day we read prose nearly as bad. Moreover, Baker's parody has the authentic formaldehyde stink of the synthetic prose of a technological age: gutless, bloodless, thoroughly inhuman. Wordsworth called the poet a man speaking to men; this is the utterance of a robot speaking to God knows whom. But could he be speaking to us?

The enormous Atlanta airport has under it a miniature subway train to get passengers from one concourse to another. I asked someone the other day why the recorded voice directing traffic on the subway was so robot-like. I was told: because people could be counted on to take it seriously. When that inflectionless baritone ordered people to get back from the car doors, they got back. I got back; you can't argue with a machine. In this instance perhaps a machine voice was well chosen. But in our ordinary affairs we don't want to become mechanized by our machines.

Jefferson's noble style reflects a humanistic education. His declaration is not only stirring and resonant; even the rhythms contribute to the impact of what is declared. But it is also an exact and lucid statement. Accuracy is not sacrificed to elegance.

Jefferson, of course, lacked our modern office equipment. He had no electric typewriter, let alone a word processor. He had only an ink pot and a goose quill pen. But he had something more important: imagination, sensitivity, and a well-stocked and disciplined mind. He knew the value of words and how to arrange them to achieve their most telling effect.

Jefferson's society was in general short on machinery, but it was very long on the essentials of a true culture. That his world of colonial Virginia was relatively small was an asset. Society was compact and cohesive. Life was highly personal. Finally, every educated person had had a humanistic education. That was practically the only education to be had. Everyone had read the same basic stock of books.

The Latin and Greek classics dominated education in Virginia and in the Old South generally. My own curious first name goes back to that period. A great-grandmother of mine evidently admired the Greek philosopher Cleanthes, and so started that name on its course through the family down to me. What a burden it was for a thirteen-year-old boy who had to wear glasses. Jefferson's own reading, of course, went on beyond the classics to include also the historians, scientists, and men of letters of a later time: Dryden and Pope, Shakespeare, Voltaire, Molière, and Rousseau. Like Francis Bacon, Jefferson took all knowledge to be his province.

My theme here, however, will not be "Carry me back to old Virginny"— that is, to colonial Virginia. We cannot go back, and few of us, I suppose, would choose to return. Nevertheless, we might, while retaining the advantages of our marvelous technology, hold fast to the cultural values exemplified by Jefferson. The humanist is not concerned to do away with machines, but to direct them to proper ends, for machines cannot direct themselves. The ends must be chosen for them, and one hopes chosen by wise human beings.

The problem is where to find wisdom. I propose that in our time the humanities—history, philosophy, and literature—may be a source well worthy of our attention. They contain the funded wisdom of the past, and that past is not to be dismissed. Here I shall be stressing the claims of literature rather than those of philosophy and history, not because I disparage the latter disciplines, but simply because literature is the discipline I know best. Yet before discussing the role of literature I must say a brief word about the state of our language. For language is the door through which we enter into literature—and indeed, into philosophy and history, and all other learned studies as well.

Since I mean to be brief, I shall have to be blunt. Neither reading nor writing flourishes in our blessed United States. Certainly good and even great prose is being written today, and, I should add, some very great poetry. Some of it even gets read. But in important respects we are an illiterate nation. A large section of our population cannot read at all, and many of those who can read do not read books.

The two reports recently sponsored by the former secretary of education, the Honorable T. H. Bell, "A Nation at Risk" and "Involvement in Learning," present some very grim statistics. They tell us that 23 million of our adults are functionally illiterate; that almost 40 percent of our seventeen-year-olds are incapable of drawing proper inferences from written documents; and that only 20 percent can write a persuasive—I think they must have meant to say a "coherent"—essay. I know too many Ph.D.s who cannot write a *persuasive* essay. As for our college students, the reports speak of the great number of dropouts, of declining scores in the tests administered to those who stay, and of the shift of most of them from the humanities into purely vocational courses. They record what amounts to a disaster, and one of Pearl Harbor dimensions.

These findings, however, do not come as a surprise to those of us who teach English language and literature. When I began my college teaching fifty years ago, the breakdown in the teaching of these subjects was plain to be seen. Why, then, did we not speak out? We did, but few—even in the academic community—wanted to listen. We had no privileged platform from which to speak. An English instructor's complaints about the state of English studies were to be expected. Naturally *he* would suppose that what *he* was doing was very important. At my first teaching post I quickly discovered that the English department was regarded as a "service department." That is to say, our real job was to patch up the spelling and grammar of students who were going into really important studies such as electrical engineering or biology.

Such undervaluation reflected then, and continues to reflect now, the attitude of the whole society. English grammar for most of us was a dull study, even a nuisance, and nobody could be blamed for finding the spelling of English irrational—it is.

When the study of the language itself is in trouble, the consequences for literature are obvious. Moreover, even if the student has learned to read, and the proper books are available for him on the library shelf, the benefits of reading do not automatically follow. The moral of the old proverb about the horse that can be led to water but cannot be made to drink still has force. How does one induce the student to drink deep from the well of English undefiled? By extolling the wonderful taste of the Castalian spring from which, in the past, generations have slaked their spiritual thirst? I think not. A magnetic teacher or an enthusiastic parent who has proved in other matters the accuracy of his judgments may succeed with such a method. Few others can. The student wants to be told what literature is good for.

Literature does yield a very real pleasure, but a pleasure not easy to describe to the uninitiated. Moreover, how can this rather specialized pleasure compete with those obvious pleasures with which our society showers the population? These obvious amusements promise instant gratification and call for little or no effort, and for almost no prior preparation. The average student is quite content, thank you, with the pleasures he already enjoys. Why take up others?

The greatest handicap under which literature suffers, however, is that literature is so often badly taught. It is the easiest subject to make a stab at teaching and one of the hardest to teach well. Many a person never recovers from the taste that he got of poetry, say, in the fifth grade. The one enduring lesson that he learned there was that he never wanted to be bothered again with this insipid stuff.

The great problem is the character of the age itself. A technological age—especially an extremely brilliant and successful one—has difficulty in finding a proper role for literature. Such a society sees literature as a diversion, as a mere amusement at best; and so it is classed as a luxury, perhaps an added grace to adorn the high culture which the technology has itself built. Yet such homage obscures the real importance of literature and of all the humanities. It classes them as decorative extras, luxuries, whereas in truth they are the necessary complement to our technological and industrial activities.

For over a century the problem of the real relation of literature to science, theoretical and applied, has been with us. In fact, the very development of an industrial society raises the question of the value of literature.

In a famous poem Matthew Arnold tells how, on Dover Beach, he had listened to the "melancholy, long withdrawing roar" of the outgoing tide, and in it had found an emblem of the ebb tide of religious faith. Science was clearly destined to become technician-in-chief to civilization, but what about the values by which mankind lived? What was there to take religion's place? Arnold prescribed literature, and especially poetry. Poetry was invulnerable to science, for it had no factual underpinning for science to sweep away. It was fictional, a creation of the imagination. "More and more [Arnold wrote in 1880] mankind will discover that we have to turn to poetry to interpret life for us, to console us, to sustain us. Without poetry, our science will appear incomplete, and most of what now passes with us for religion and philosophy will be replaced by poetry." With such a concept as this, no wonder that Arnold could claim that "the future of poetry is immense," for in effect he was entrusting to poetry the direction of the whole human enterprise.

How has Arnold's prophecy fared? Not so well, I should say. Though our intellectuals are still influenced by it, the ordinary citizen is hardly aware of it, and if he were, would be puzzled by its specifications. He wonders why science, this beneficent magician, cannot tell us what to do as well as how to do it. In any case, he would be utterly baffled by the notion that fictions conceived by the imagination and not tied to the facts of this world could possibly interpret for us the facts of life.

I believe that in asking poetry to replace religion and philosophy, Arnold laid upon poetry a burden it cannot possibly bear. As we should expect, the religious intellectuals of our time, such as T. S. Eliot, Walker Percy, and Flannery O'Connor, reject the notion altogether. At the other extreme, the fundamentalist man in the pew also instinctively rejects it just as roundly. Yet we owe Arnold a debt for having located the problem rather accurately and for assessing the strain that it had already set up in industrialized Great Britain by the middle of the nineteenth century.

In any case, his suggestions about the role of poetry in modern culture are worth further exploration. They have, I would point out, a peculiar relevance to culture in the United States. Let me indicate why. In the first place, we are a pluralistic society encompassing a number of religious faiths and cultural backgrounds. In the second place, our constitutional separation of church and state forbids the teaching of institutionalized religion in state-supported schools and colleges; yet the problem of the inculcation of ethical standards and ultimate values becomes more and more urgent. It is intensified by such matters as the general breakdown of various traditions, the erosion of the family, the cultural rootlessness of much of our increasingly mobile population, and the growing secularism generated by a highly technological civilization.

So even if Arnold was wrong in believing that poetry could alone supply our culture with the proper goals, ends, and purposes, it may well be worth considering what poetry, and literature in general, can do. We are scarcely in a position to reject any available help from whatever source. Literature at least focuses attention on mankind's purposes, wise or unwise, and upon the values for which men and women had lived and died.

In fairness to Arnold, his task of analysis was more difficult than ours, for in his day the boundaries of science were not so clearly marked out as they have since become. One of the best concise statements on the limits of science appeared in an article entitled "The Frontiers and Limits of Science," written by Professor Victor E. Weisskopf, the distinguished physicist at MIT. He sums up as follows: ". . . important parts of human experience cannot be reasonably evaluated within the scientific system. There cannot be an all-encompassing scientific definition of good and evil, of compassion, of rapture, or tragedy or humor, or hate, love, or faith, of dignity, and humiliation, or of concepts like the quality of life or happiness."

In short, it is impossible for science to define for us the quality of happiness that Jefferson declared was the right of each of us to seek to attain. Each person will have to define that happiness for himself, using whatever guidance he can find. To have that choice taken away from us either by peer pressure, by the brainwashing of a totalitarian regime, or even by the seductions of our immense advertising industry is to lose some part of our humanity. Computers are programmed by human beings: but human beings move toward the state of computers when they allow themselves to be programmed by other human beings.

Accepting, then, the fact that we cannot expect guidance from the hard and objective sciences such as mathematics and physics, what do the humanities offer in the way of guidance? And in any case, how can they make any impression on a society that prides itself on being practical and getting down to the hard facts?

An answer to the second question might run like this: a world reduced to hard facts would thereby become a dehumanized world, a world in which few of us would want to live. We are intensely interested in how our fellow human beings behave—in their actions, to be sure, but also in the feelings, motives, purposes that lead them into these actions. The proof is to be found even in the situation comedies on television or the gossip columns in magazines and newspapers. We want to know the facts but we crave the whole story too—its human interest and what we call its meaning.

For example, consider a celebrated incident, the loss of the White Star liner *Titanic,* which sank in the north Atlantic when she struck an iceberg. How did the poet Thomas Hardy deal with the incident in a poem which he called "The Convergence of the Twain"?

Of many of the facts Hardy makes no mention at all. He does not tell us that the date of the disaster was April 15, 1912, and that it happened on the *Titanic's* maiden voyage; that she was at forty-six thousand tons the largest ship afloat; that over fifteen hundred lives were lost; that the ship, though warned of ice ahead, was traveling at high speed; or that she was regarded as unsinkable, with double bottoms and sixteen watertight compartments.

Hardy does refer to some of these facts early in the poem, but only obliquely—by references to the pride that the *Titanic* excited and men's confidence that they had at last conquered the sea itself with this mighty craft. What evidently most caught Hardy's imagination was that the ship and the iceberg had, with precision timing, arrived at the same spot at the same instant, just as if destiny had employed a split-second timetable for the whole affair; and he reminds his reader that while the liner was being built in the Belfast shipyard, nature had all along been preparing the mountain of ice far away on the coast of Greenland. Here are the closing stanzas of the poem:

> And as the smart ship grew
> In stature, grace, and hue
> In shadowy silent distance grew the iceberg too.
>
> Alien they seemed to be:
> No mortal eye could see
> The intimate welding of their later history.
>
> Or sign that they were bent
> By paths coincident
> On being anon twin halves of one august event,
>
> Till the Spinner of the Years
> Said "Now!" And each one hears,
> And consummation comes, and jars two hemispheres.

I remarked earlier that as human beings we want more than mere information. We want meaning and we want wisdom, but that elusive commodity is always in short supply. In the Book of Proverbs we learn that "wisdom crieth . . . in the streets" but it goes on to imply that "no man regardeth." If this was the situation several millennia ago, it remains so today. Secretly we may hunger for wisdom, but our overt craving nowadays is, of course, for information. Data banks are much in vogue and they are highly useful, but they are not equipped to pay off in the currency of wisdom.

A recent *New York Times* editorial matter-of-factly referred to ours as "the age of information." The poet T. S. Eliot makes much the same point but with a rather different implication.

Endless invention, endless experiment
Brings knowledge of speech, but not of silence,
Knowledge of words, and ignorance of the Word. . . .
Where is the wisdom we have lost in knowledge?
Where is the knowledge we have lost in information?

The first line quoted involves a serious pun. "Endless" invention and experiment means, of course, unceasing invention and experiment, but "endless" also means "without purpose, goal, or end," experiment conducted for its own sake, invention carried out merely to be inventive. In Eliot's verse the two diverse meanings actually support and emphasize each other. In this way poetry is often packed more richly with meaning than is prose.

Yet it is important that we understand how wisdom is mediated to us through literature. It had better not be presented didactically. In my boyhood days, as I recall, our scornful retort to an exorbitant demand was "You must want salvation in a jug." Salvation does not come in a jug, nor is wisdom a bottled essence. Of all people, the literary artist must not seem to be running an old-fashioned medicine show, entertaining us in order to persuade us to buy a product. John Keats, that remarkable poet and very wise young man, put it well: "We hate poetry that has a palpable design upon us."

In an all-too-well-known poem, Longfellow tells his reader that

Life is real! Life is earnest!
   And the grave is not its goal.
Dust thou art, to dust returnest,
   Was not spoken to the soul.

Such moralistic doggerel is not poetry, and it obviously does have a palpable design on us. Whatever the merit of that palpable design, the verse is tired, limp, and insipid. Jefferson was wise in these matters. He once remarked, "A lively and lasting sense of filial duty is more effectually impressed on the mind of a son or daughter by reading *King Lear* than by all the dry volumes of ethics. . . ."

In a poem entitled "Provide, Provide," Robert Frost has used a cunning device to remove any taint of the didactic. On the surface the poem, in sharp contrast to Longfellow's, seems to be giving his reader the same counsel that the villainous Iago gave to his dupe Roderigo: "Put money in thy purse." Wealth will solve all problems. The poem also seems blatantly didactic.

It begins:

> The witch who came (the withered hag)
> To wash the steps with pail and rag,
> Was once the beauty Abishag,

> The picture pride of Hollywood.
> Too many fall from great and good
> For you to doubt the likelihood.

A former movie idol has squandered or perhaps been bilked of her fortune and now ekes out her existence as a scrubwoman. Such things do happen to screen beauties, former heavyweight boxing champions, and even rock stars. But why does Frost name this woman Abishag? With a certain grim humor Frost went to the Bible for his movie star's name. When King David grew old and ill and, even when covered with bed-clothes, couldn't get warm, his servants and courtiers scoured the whole land to find a beautiful maiden to put into the royal bed to warm the poor old fellow up. The beauty's name was Abishag. But King David still "gat no heat" and was soon gathered to his fathers.

The poem continues with Frost's advice to the reader on how to avoid this modern Abishag's fate. But we had better take the whole poem into account for a proper understanding of just how seriously Frost is speaking when he says to his reader:

> Die early and avoid the fate
> Or if predestined to die late,
> Make up your mind to die in state.

> Make the whole stock exchange your own!
> If need be occupy a throne
> Where nobody can call you crone.

> Some have relied on what they knew
> Others on being simply true.
> What worked for them might work for you.

No memory of having starred
Atones for later disregard,
Or keeps the end from being hard.

Better to go down dignified
With boughten friendship at your side
Than none at all. Provide, provide.

"Go down dignified," "boughten friendship"—these very phrases are instinct with Yankee folk wisdom. Boughten friendship—store-bought friendship we would say in the South—is cold comfort indeed on one's deathbed. Not much warmth in that; still, it's better than nothing at all.

In spite of this outward show of worldly wisdom, the poet has hinted of other ways out. He reminds us that some have relied on "what they knew" and others on "being simply true"—on knowledge and integrity. Yet why does he throw into his poem this allusion to the philosophers and the saints only as a kind of afterthought—almost like a man saying: oh, by the way, I'll just mention this for the sake of the record, though I assume you wouldn't be interested? He does so because the cunning old artist knows that no emphasis often constitutes the most powerful emphasis of all.

Poems that nourish the human spirit can be as dry and witty as this one rather than exalted and sonorous like the poems of Aeschylus and Milton. The house of poetry has many mansions.

Yeats's "Prayer for My Daughter," a very different kind of poem, also contains wisdom, and even a strain of prophecy. But true to its title, it is content to be a troubled father's prayer for his child. Because of its prophetic character, it may be interesting to put it beside John Maynard Keynes's celebrated book, *The Economic Consequences of the Peace.* Keynes's treatise and Yeats's poem were, by the way, both published in 1919, the year after the end of the War to End All Wars.

Keynes foretold the disastrous consequence of the Treaty of Versailles, predicting what would happen under the peace terms to the economy of defeated Germany and the consequent ruin of the rest of Europe. Yeats's focus is on the future of his infant daughter, and he envisages the troubled years through which she must live. Yeats could not and did not specify the terrible happenings ahead, but he correctly sensed the dangers, and now it is easy for us to name them: the Great Depression, the rise of Hitler, the Second World War, the Cold War, and the threat of nuclear destruction.

As the poet paces beside the cradle that holds his sleeping child, he tells us

> I have walked and prayed for this young child an hour
> And heard the sea-wind scream upon the tower,
> And under the arches of the bridge, and scream
> In the elms above the flooded stream;
> Imagining in excited reverie
> That the future years had come,
> Dancing to a frenzied drum,
> Out of the murderous innocence of the sea.

In this context we are likely to associate innocence with the infant daughter, but the poet speaks of the "murderous innocence" of the sea. The phrase may be startling, but it is accurate. When we have in mind the destructiveness of a hurricane or a great earthquake, "murderous" seems a proper adjective, yet we know that there is no murder in the heart of nature—no motivation at all, mere senseless indifference. Indeed, the Good Book itself tells us that the rain falls upon both the just and the unjust, and so apparently do the showers of volcanic ash. We have to acquit all of them of guilt. They are innocent by virtue of their sheer mindlessness. Yet we have not done with the word *innocence:* late in the poem Yeats will set forth a third kind of innocence, the innocence which is not at all mindless, but the product of love and self-discipline.

What are the gifts which the poet prays his daughter may receive? Beauty, yes, but not so much as to make her vain and haughty. He wishes for her a "glad kindness" and courtesy. These hoped-for endowments are summed up in one concrete image:

> May she become a flourishing hidden tree
> That all her thoughts may like the linnet be,
> And have no business but dispensing round
> Their magnanimities of sound.
> Nor but in merriment begin a chase,
> Nor but in merriment a quarrel.
> O may she live like some green laurel
> Rooted in one dear perpetual place.

So, as a counter to the destructive wind, the poet proposes the laurel, hidden and sheltered from the blast and firmly rooted in its own "perpetual place."

Yet likening his daughter's thoughts to the songs of the linnet perched in the tree, especially when coupled with the father's petition that she may "think opinions are accurst," is probably calculated to affront every woman who reads the poem. Does Yeats want the girl to grow up to be a pretty little charmer without a thought in her head—to possess no opinion of her own?

By no means. Yeats knew his Plato well, and he is here following Plato's distinction between opinion and an idea. An opinion can claim at best to represent no more than probability. Absolute truth is to be found only in the divine ideas implanted in the soul and to be recovered by the deepest self-discovery. The later stanzas confirm that such is his meaning, for the poet will declare that the worst of evils is the "intellectual hatred" characteristic of an aggressive, opinionated mind, and that if the soul can rid itself of all hatred it will recover "radical innocence" and find

> that it is self-delighting,
> Self-appeasing, self-affrighting,
> And that its own sweet will is heaven's will;
> She can, though every face should scowl
> And every windy quarter howl
> Or every bellows burst, be happy still.

Here the earlier figure of the laurel tree, "rooted in one dear perpetual place," is still very much alive in the poem. Consider the phrase "radical innocence." For *radical* comes from the Latin *radix,* a root, and a radical innocence is not merely a basic or essential innocence, but one that is rooted deep in the soul.

In the concluding stanza, Yeats turns his thoughts to the kind of bridegroom he could wish for his daughter. He prays that whoever he may be, he

> will bring her to a house
> Where all's accustomed, ceremonious;
> For arrogance and hatred are the wares

Peddled in the thoroughfares.
How but in custom and in ceremony
Are innocence and beauty born?
Ceremony's a name for the rich horn,
And custom for the spreading laurel tree.

We miss the point and vulgarize this noble poem if we read the last stanza as a prayer for a wealthy son-in-law. The authoritative words are "accustomed" and "ceremonious." These qualities have nothing to do with conspicuous display, or even the mere possession of wealth. A word to which I would call your attention once more is "innocence." Beauty and innocence, which we usually assume are the random gift of nature, are in fact, so the poet here insists, born out of ceremony. Ceremony is the true horn of plenty, and the laurel tree which can withstand the storms of history is custom. This indeed is to invert our usual notions. For bodily beauty—Yeats again is borrowing from Plato—is the outward reflection of a beautiful soul. Yeats's innocence is the fruit of the disciplined soul that has come truly to understand itself. Such a person is incapable of harming anyone. So the term *innocence* is here neither the babe's lack of experience nor the blind indifference of nature, but the soul's clear-eyed mastery of experience and of itself. Perhaps this is the kind of wise innocence to which great literature may return us if we can learn how to read it.

In this magnificent poem every word plays its proper part and every image breathes life into an idea. For the poem is also a powerful humanistic document; not the bare skeleton of an abstract argument, but that argument fleshed out into an entity that possesses a life of its own.

Yeats's prayer for his daughter may not be at all your prayer. You are not asked to accept it as the truth, the whole truth, and nothing but the truth. But who of us could not find mind and imagination stimulated by it? The poem is not didactic in any schoolmasterish sense. Perhaps this is just the value of poetry and of literature in general: it lets us observe and overhear men and women as they choose, make decisions, or express their inmost hopes and fears. That in itself is a service of the utmost importance, for we can learn from the experience of others.

Such is the service rendered by great literature throughout history. It provides dramatic accounts of men and women in conflict with nature, and with other human beings, and often with themselves. This last conflict William Faulkner regarded as the greatest theme possible—the "human heart in conflict with itself." But though the phrasing is Faulkner's, the theme itself is found as early as in Homer's epics.

The conflict within the heart—the tug between two loyalties, two evils, or what appear to be two equally precious goods—is probably the most instructive of all. Sophocles' Antigone and his Oedipus, Shakespeare's Othello, Macbeth, and Mark Antony, are only a few of an illustrious company. They are not properly called role models, for they represent failure as well as triumph, and for most of us any direct imitations of them would be out of the question. But an acquaintance with them through literature provides something far better than simple imitation. The way they live and choose to die tests the human spirit to its limits. Through the magic of language their creators can pass on something of their experience to us.

The humanities cannot be eliminated from our culture, but they can be debased. They cannot be eliminated because as long as mankind remains human, his yearning for the song, the story, and the drama cannot be suppressed. People are interested in accounts of human behavior, in suspense and conflict of interests, in the expression of emotion, in motivation. If they don't have Shakespeare or Jane Austen or Melville to read, they will read something far less rewarding, too often utter trash.

Long ago someone said that when the true gods leave the scene, the half gods come out of the bushes, and I say that when the true muses retire from the scene, the bastard muses are ready to take over. Their names are Propaganda, Sentimentality, and Pornography. The shared trait that proves their sisterhood is this: all three are bent on distorting the human dimension. Propaganda does so by pleading, sometimes unscrupulously, for a special cause or issue at the expense of total truth. Sentimentality does so by working up emotional responses unwarranted by and in excess of the occasion. Pornography does so by focusing upon one powerful human drive at the expense of the total human personality. In short, the spurious muses offer partial and biased accounts of life in its fullness. Their productions do not nourish, but are debilitating.

With regard to human purposes and values in a technological age, mankind's need of guidance has not diminished but has actually increased. The evidence is everywhere. In the city in which I live I have never heard wisdom crying in the streets, but on Orange Street house after house exhibits neatly printed placards stating that counseling is to be had within. It would be comforting to think that in 1985 Dame Wisdom has simply conformed to the times and chosen a less primitive method of announcing her presence and marketing her wares. But I wonder. It is not for me, however, to say whether the counsel given on Orange Street is not worthy of that of Solomon. Perhaps it is. I mention the number of these counselors only as evidence of what is obviously a felt need. There is abundant evidence that many Americans yearn for guidance. Today we have a host of psychiatrists. There are certainly many in New Haven. Never have so many self-improvement books been published, or manuals offering instruction in how to conduct your marriage, or, if it is already pretty far gone, how to mend it; how to improve your face, or figure, or friendships; how to prop up your sagging psyche. For happiness, even for those possessed of adequate material means, continues to elude so many of us, and the pursuit of it proclaimed by Jefferson has often become an exhausting rat race. For some it may have become even worse: a race like that at the dog track in which the mechanical rabbit cannot possibly be caught.

If Jefferson could return to present-day America he would find much to marvel at and much to approve. How primitive would seem his own scientific efforts, and even those of the Dr. Priestleys of his day. Jefferson would doubtless admire our machinery, so powerful and intricate, machinery that has done so much to relieve human drudgery and extend the possibilities of human life. But I believe he would be shocked to find how many of us still cannot read, and even more shocked to learn what those who can read do read.

With reference to our schools and colleges, I wonder whether the proud founder of the University of Virginia might not say something like this: Though your students devote so much of their time and energy to securing the means by which to achieve for themselves the good life, I am puzzled that they should devote so little serious reflection on what a good life really is. They seem long on means; perilously short on ends. That imbalance might imperil democracy itself.

19

An Age of Silver

Contemporary American Literature

❧

American literature of the past few decades not only presents us with a great variety of themes and modes, but tends to overwhelm us with its sheer quantity. How best make this point vividly yet concisely? One might consider the *Harvard Guide to Contemporary American Literature*. It takes some six hundred pages to accomplish its task. It requires for poetry alone three solid chapters and discusses in some detail over 160 contemporary poets. What makes a commentator's task even more difficult is that a great deal of our recent literature is work of a high order—intelligent, sensitive, and carefully crafted. In fiction there is also a great plenitude of writers, though the *Harvard Guide* does not concern itself with the machine-made best-sellers. Nor shall I do so. Doubtless the writers and publishers of airport and drugstore fiction consider their rewards sufficient without demanding a pound of critical praise.

Confronted with such an embarrassment of riches, my only practical course will be to make wholesale omissions and to confine myself to a few representative authors. First of all, let me dispose of literary criticism. That brilliant poet of our time, the late Randall Jarrell, called our period an "Age of Criticism." He intended this as no more than a left-handed compliment, for he meant to *describe* the age, not to commend it for its preoccupation with criticism. We have indeed bred up a host of literary critics, and I have witnessed in my own lifetime the rise and fall of at least three or four reigning schools.

Yet I shall have nothing to say on the subject of criticism as such, and there are good reasons for the omission. First, I would have to raise too many technical issues—philosophical, aesthetic, and linguistic. Second, I am myself too much involved in criticism to appear as a plausible honest broker. Anything that I could say might well be regarded as self-serving.

Nor shall I say anything about American drama. A wise literary critic once remarked to me that American drama had, throughout this century, lagged behind American fiction and poetry. I believe that he is right, though I do not deny that some good plays have been written or that certain of our dramatists have a genuine flair for the theatrical. But the plays of some of our most highly regarded dramatists have not worn too well. I shall not be surprised, however, nor much disconcerted if others argue emphatically their fervent approval of our drama.

Yet, if I am correct in holding that our age has not proved the best nurturing ground for drama, such a weakness would seem to go back a long way. Victorian drama is not notably good, and to push back earlier still, the Romantic and neoclassical periods produced very few first-rate plays. The antidramatic force in Anglo-American culture is evidently deep-rooted.

The impress of our culture on contemporary literature also reveals itself in our fiction and poetry, though not always adversely. One way in which it reveals itself is in the recent movement away from a contemplation of history to a concern with contemporary manners. The literary masters of the early century—W. B. Yeats, T. S. Eliot, Ezra Pound, and William Faulkner, to mention only four—were steeped in history. One is tempted to say that they were even obsessed by it. It is not difficult to see why. The First World War had shattered the dream of universal peace and unlimited progress. That cataclysm made our writers furiously think— and feel as well. It is no accident that Eliot's *Waste Land* came at the time it did, nor that it took the shape it did—that is, a form that to its first readers seemed to reveal no pattern at all.

This concern with history hit the American writer peculiarly hard. Henry Adams provides a good instance, and in his own way, so does Henry James. The American writer found Europe wonderfully exciting precisely because the American had regarded himself as having cut his ties with the Old World. But in entering the New World, had he really been given a new start as a sinless and unfallen Adam? Was he or was he not implicated in the European cultural debacle? For, as Henry James had declared, to be an American was a complex fate, and the complexity was also a complicity: the American felt that he both was and was not a European. I think that it is significant that both Eliot and Pound were Americans living abroad, and that Yeats, as an Irishman, was also something of an outsider on the London literary scene.

With Faulkner the problem is taken one stage further: he felt that as a member of a conscious subculture, he was and was not even an American. In the more traditional and even provincial culture of the American South, the pressure of history was more immediate. The devastations of a war largely fought on its own soil were not something you read about in books, but matters that your grandparents had experienced and could tell you about viva voce. So we have Faulkner's characteristic use of history in his stories and novels, works in which the sense of history remains a powerful presence even in such novels as have their setting in the 1930s and 1940s.

Faulkner is not a special case. The novels of Robert Penn Warren and Andrew Lytle show something of the same pattern. The present had been shaped by historic events, and man was only partially a free agent.

In the rest of the country the situation was markedly different. The serious novelist had already turned his attention to present affairs in which a stress on history gives way to an emphasis on sociology and politics. For example, in the 1930s we got the protest novel or else accounts of the individual's struggle against a smothering society that respected neither intelligence nor sensitivity. Some of Willa Cather's early work and nearly all of Sinclair Lewis's will illustrate.

Of course, historical novels are still written, but nowadays they do not often occupy the serious writer. In the popular novel the historical background is ordinarily used only for romance and swashbuckling adventure. The aim is frankly to provide the reader an escape from what many people feel to be a dull and quotidian society. Novels of this sort show a close resemblance to the costume romances that Hollywood poured out through the 1920s and 1930s as popular entertainment.

Such a superficial use of history, of course, is actually a denial of history. For in a history reduced to the picturesque and the picaresque, the past as actually lived becomes irrelevant to us as moderns: it offers an occasion for self-congratulation that we live in such advanced times. Or the past becomes a dream world, one that it may be amusing to wander through in our imaginations but not a place that can provide intellectual nourishment to people like ourselves.

During recent decades, the writer's attention has turned, even for southern writers, from the past to the present. Walker Percy, for example, regularly sets his novels in the present day. If memories of the antebellum South and the Civil War obtrude themselves, the protagonist of the novel resolutely puts them aside. Thus in *The Last Gentleman* Will Barrett refers to "Lee's sad, useless victories"—sad because useless and useless because they could not stave off defeat in the war. Barrett does not fail to respond to the gallantry of his ancestors who fought for a lost cause, but in his scale of priorities the problems of the present are at the top.

For Percy, however, the most important problems are not merely present but eternal. They are philosophical and, more specifically, theological problems. In fact, so concerned is Percy with religion that his artistic problem will be how to keep his novels from becoming thesis-ridden. But if he has usually solved that problem, and I think that he has, it is in good part because he has such a sure grasp on the concrete detail of life and because he can render his characters credible. Thus, in spite of his repudiation of the stereotyped version of the southern novel—a repudiation that he has made in interview after interview—he is nevertheless one of the most intensely regional of our present-day novelists.

I want to be more specific still: he has proved himself to be an acute social critic—a sensitive novelist of manners, whose range pretty well covers the social scene of his region. In this area he is, of course, not alone. Peter Taylor and Eudora Welty do this sort of thing admirably. Moreover, the novelist of manners—if we extend the term just a bit—is to be found throughout the country.

Consider, for example, Saul Bellow. Bellow's novels have a wide range in social types and in atmosphere and tone. But it is fair to say that he has become a consummate novelist of manners. He is more fiercely scathing in some of his judgments than are most of his contemporaries. He indulges more fully in the absurd. But he clearly implies a moral center, and again like Percy or Welty or Taylor, say, he has his own special material, the well-to-do American Jew. Both *Mr. Sammler's Planet* and *Humboldt's*

Gift contain satiric accounts of the New York intellectual, of the Public Relations man, of the handsome young woman on the make, and of less flamboyant members of the American middle class.

Walt Whitman's America, in Bellow's novels, has got rich, corrupt, and a little zany. Even the members of the literary crowd are, for all their disdain of businessmen, also on the make, and very knowledgeable about money. One such character in *Humboldt's Gift*, Orlando Huggins by name, is described as "one of those radical bohemians who knew money," and the author goes on to comment, "In avant-garde New York everybody knew money."

I have already mentioned the element of the absurd in Bellow's novels. Consider the following scene. Humboldt, the failed poet, finally goes quite off his rocker with jealousy and "on Sixtieth Avenue, in front of Howard Johnson's," jumps on the young man whom he falsely suspects is his wife's lover. The young man is rescued by a group of lesbians, dressed up as longshoremen, who had just been having ice cream sodas together in the Howard Johnson's. They break up the fight and pin Humboldt's arms behind him. Then, "the women prisoners at the detention center on Greenwich Avenue [having been aroused by the noise of the fracas] begin shrieking from the open windows and unrolling toilet-paper streamers." The excuse for these absurd juxtapositions and comic confrontations, if any justification is deemed necessary, is the comically improbable nature of American urban society—at least as Bellow sees it.

The mode, then, is satiric and comic, but not wholly so. Even the failed poet Humboldt is allowed his due of integrity, and the narrator Citrine is allowed, for all his folly, an ability to distinguish between Good and Bad, the spurious and the genuine.

The moral center of Bellow's *Mr. Sammler's Planet* is even more clearly set forth. Dr. Elya Gruner becomes, in the eyes of Arthur Sammler, a quiet hero, and his death, the austerely noble death of a stoic, becomes a kind of high-water mark of fortitude in a world that has lost its standards and sunk into moral squalor. Mr. Sammler's own credentials for making such judgments are impressive. In his own lifetime he has seen much that is good and much that is obscenely wicked. He has himself narrowly escaped death in the Nazi extermination camps.

At the beginning of the novel he observes that "You had to be a crank to insist on being right," and at the end of the book he tells Dr. Gruner's spoiled and utterly corrupt daughter that "New York makes one think about the collapse of civilization, about Sodom and Gomorrah, the end of the world." In Bellow's novels there is much that is amusing, much that has to do with fun and games, but some of Bellow's characters, including perhaps Bellow himself, take a very dim view of the present quality of our society.

The contemporary American scene is viewed by the distinguished Negro novelist Ralph Ellison from his own special perspective. (I use the term *Negro* rather than *black* because Mr. Ellison has said that he prefers that term.) His celebrated novel *Invisible Man* remains the best single piece of fiction done from the Negro's perspective. The specific form of *Invisible Man* is that of the bildungsroman, the story of a youth's education and development into a man—a development not merely to the statutory age of adulthood but to a clear and unillusioned view of reality in mid-twentieth-century America. The most important knowledge of all gained by the narrator is the knowledge of how he appears to most of the members of the society around him. He is not seen as an individual human being; instead he is so hooded by a stereotype that his personhood becomes entirely unremarked. That is why he is truly an invisible man.

The mode of Ellison's book is that of a fictional autobiography, but the novel is not so personally centered that it leaves American history out of account or that it does not comment brilliantly and perceptively on the manners and behavior of society, white as well as black. Furthermore, though *Invisible Man* is an impassioned account of human suffering, it is much more than a protest novel designed to exhaust its impact with immediacy on one target. This novel seems to me quite as pertinent today as it was when it was first issued. The reasons for its permanence are easy to state: its basic issues are not topical but universal; it does argue for particular ideas, but its final concern is for universal truths. To cite only one example of the book's timelessness: Ellison gave us instances of "radical chic" decades before that term was invented.

Not the least significant feature of this impressive work is Ellison's techniques of narration and description. He manages to render his commentary on race relations in contemporary America through the behavior of his characters. To use Aristotle's terms, the "philosophy" which his book contains is embodied in the "history" that the book relates. The hero-narrator can comment on himself and his world as much as he likes, without ever seeming to be making a stump speech of it. Such a feat is obviously easier to describe than for many a novelist to perform.

John Updike is another brilliant commentator on the American social scene, though in much of his work the events recorded are outrageous and the juxtaposition of elements absurd. See, for example, the sex life of suburbia as described in Updike's novel *Couples,* or the literary life as described in *Bech,* or the heady mixture of the love of God and sexual love expressed in the confessions of a churchman and pastor in *A Month of Sundays.* All three of these works have an outlandish main character who seems to have come out of the theater of the absurd. Nevertheless, as critic after critic has pointed out, Updike has a serious moral interest that is reinforced by an informed interest in theology. What is the relation of the wit and comedy to Updike's underlying vein of seriousness? I confess that I do not always perceive it. About the wit, however, there can be no doubt. His novels bubble with it and are usually exuberantly written.

This observation applies to a great many of our serious novelists. Their fictions are thoughtfully constructed, and the writing is often superb: sentence by sentence their works are written up to the hilt. Not for a long time—perhaps never before—has there been a literary phenomenon quite like ours. Yet, whether carefully thought-out constructions and scintillating writing are, in themselves, enough to produce great novels may be debatable, though I have no intention of debating it here.

What is beyond debate is that ours is an age of highly sophisticated craftsmanship. One finds such brilliant writing in many of our novelists. John Gardner, for instance, is only one of the many recent writers who show it. One finds it even in some fiction writers who are dismissed as not serious, merely excellent entertainers. Yet a writer such as Peter De-Vries is a joy to read, and his comic wit never becomes mere sparkling froth.

There has been, then, in our fiction a shift away from history and the great epic themes toward commentary on a particular society—commentary with overtones of satire. One can observe a shift more extreme still: a shift to a concern for the individual and for his relation to the culture. This movement takes at least two forms: the first is to treat history from the perspective of the individual; the second is to disregard history altogether.

Some years ago the late Allen Tate argued very persuasively that the epic was no longer possible for us. Why? Because we lacked a general community of values, shared values that could be expressed in the tale of some hero, some truly representative leader, a man whose story could sum up the strengths and weaknesses of a whole people. Thus, Tate argued that there was no possibility of an American *Iliad* or a *Beowulf.* Archibald MacLeish's *Conquistador,* Tate pointed out, was, in spite of its epic sweep and magnificent language, finally a lyrical poem, not at all an epic. This story, told ostensibly as an account of the conquest of Mexico and the breakdown of a total culture, amounted in fact to a personal lament for the old conquistador-narrator's loss of youth and his marvelous experience as a follower of Cortez, an experience now reduced to fading memories. So also, Hart Crane's *The Bridge,* in spite of his splendid passages of description, did not really constitute an account of how America served as a bridge between an old world and a new world and so carried in its very being an almost infinite promise. Crane's poem was also at core a lyric, centered upon the poet himself, on his personal longings and his frustrations.

I think that Tate had hit upon a great truth about American poetry. This personal and lyric tendency was already well established in the nineteenth century. Whitman attempted to portray the "self" of universal democratic man through portraits of *himself.* One remembers that in his "epical" work on America, *Leaves of Grass,* the central poem was significantly entitled "Song of Myself." A generation or so later, Eliot wisely made of his *Waste Land* not an epic proper that should express communal values, but a poem about the loss of those values. Moreover, the very structure of the poem was one of no apparent structure. The poem itself became "A heap of broken images, where the sun beats."

Likewise, Pound's unfinished *Cantos* is fragmentary, though many of the fragments are eloquent. It is, in spite of its review of man's historic cultures, a record of Pound's own physical wanderings through Europe as an expatriate and his spiritual wanderings through the corridors of history. In short, as most of us now see it, Pound's hundred and more Cantos form an intensely personal poem.

When we turn to the last thirty years, we may ask whether there has been any essential shift from this pattern. I think not. Our consciousness is still suffused with the sense of past history and of the fact of cultural crisis. These ideas are widely dispersed throughout the poetry of the present age. If we want to find such consciousness in its most intense form I think that we should look into the poetry of Robert Penn Warren and of Robert Lowell. I shall postpone for the time any comment on Warren. At the moment I want to consider Lowell. His later poetry—the poetry of his *Notebook: 1967 to 1968*—is filled with a commentary on various historical persons and events. His attempt to reduce them to meanings that he and we can comprehend is audacious. I believe, however, that such efforts to take history by storm are less successful than Lowell's account of history when it is frankly mediated through personal experiences.

For example, his powerful "For the Union Dead" is indeed about our Civil War, but it derives its strength from the poet's sardonic view of contemporary America and particularly from his poem's being anchored to Boston, his birthplace. Lowell watches an underground parking garage being dug under Boston Common. The vibration is shaking a low-relief sculpture done long ago by Augustus St. Gaudens to commemorate the Colonel Shaw who died at Fort Wagner while leading his black infantrymen to the attack. After Lowell describes the scene portrayed by the sculptor he comments:

> Two months after marching through Boston,
> half the regiment was dead;
> at the dedication
> William James could almost hear the bronze Negroes breathe.
>
> Their monument sticks like a fishbone
> in the city's throat.
> Its Colonel is as lean
> as a compass-needle.

The poet implies that this city in which "giant finned cars nose forward like fish; / [in which] a savage servility / slides by on grease" is fully disoriented, having no regard for the direction to which Shaw's compass needle points.

Much of Lowell's poetry written about the time of "For the Union Dead" constitutes frank revelations of his early life, including his relation to his parents and his other relatives. The examples thus provided by Lowell, as we see now, looking backward, were a powerful impetus to what was soon to be known as "confessional poetry." It can scarcely be claimed that Lowell invented the confessional mode, for poets have been telling us about their inner lives from almost the beginning of time. Yet our recent decades have produced a spate of such poetry along with verse by poets who had little of interest to confess or whose confessions amount to little more than shrill and plaintive prose.

A further poetic mode that has become powerful in recent years is a poetry that is primarily concerned with the texture of sensory experience—the tang and savor of things, the weight and density and sensual quality of the data reported by the senses. In such poetry not only is history dismissed but statements of any kind. The poet is content if he can register the immediate impact of sensory experience.

This impulse was, of course, foreshadowed early in the century in the work of the Imagists. It was a special predilection of Marianne Moore, whose poems about birds and beasts and special landscapes became a pleasant feature of the first half of our twentieth century. Another powerful impetus to such "physical poetry," as the poet John Crowe Ransom was to call it, was provided by William Carlos Williams, with his often quoted dictum: "No ideas but in things," a notion that many of his own poems exemplify.

The tendency to write a poetry that stresses the concrete particularity of our world has been fed from many sources—as a revulsion from the poetry and doctrine of earlier masters like Eliot, as a rejection of all lingering traces of the metaphysical and the transcendental, as a final dismissal of nineteenth-century rhetoric, as a movement toward primitivism or toward non-Western philosophy. Anthropology, the religious rites of the American Indian, Zen Buddhism, and the mysticism of India have influenced it. One could illustrate such a conception of poetry from poets like Gary Snyder on the West Coast and Charles Olson on the East, and from literally dozens of American poets in between.

Eliot and Yeats believed that the poet could get at the transcendent only through particular images. The importance of the concrete and specific is firmly grounded in almost every twentieth-century conception of poetry. Yet the very dictum "no ideas but in things" implies that finally it is indeed an *idea* that the poet is to seek. Moreover, the very nature of language sees to it that any collocation of things tends to carry with it a symbolic aura, and once we have arrived at a symbolism, we are on the way to some kind of transcendence—we have literally passed beyond isolated and particular things. I think that a poetry without ideas is insufficient, though I have to agree that in literature we properly arrive at attitudes and ideas only through a presentation of concrete particulars.

"A Cold Spring" from Elizabeth Bishop's 1955 volume will furnish a good instance of what a poetry heavily tilted toward things can be. Even if this poem lacked its first line, in which the season is mentioned, the text itself would suggest the quality of spring—its typical landscape, its look and feel, its promise—even when it makes a chilly start. The poem is dedicated to a friend living in Maryland:

A cold spring:
the violet was flawed on the lawn.
For two weeks or more the trees hesitated;
the little leaves waited,
carefully indicating their characteristics.
Finally a grave green dust
settled over your big and sunless hills.
One day, in a chill white blast of sunshine,
on the side of one a calf was born.
The mother stopped lowing
and took a long time eating the after-birth,
a wretched flag,
but the calf got up promptly
and seemed inclined to feel gay.

The birth of the calf tells us something about spring and other such beginnings—their frequent ungainliness, their sometimes earthy realism—for example, the placenta swinging like "a wretched flag" from the cow's moving jaws—yet nonetheless a flag of triumph and a portent of future joy. Here is the rest of the poem:

The next day
was much warmer.
Greenish-white dogwood infiltrated the wood,
each petal burned, apparently, by a cigarette-butt;
and the blurred redbud stood
beside it, motionless, but almost more
like movement than any placeable color.
Four deer practised leaping over your fences.
The infant oak-leaves swung through the sober oak.
Song-sparrows were wound up for the summer,
and in the maple the complementary cardinal
cracked a whip, and the sleeper awoke,
stretching miles of green limbs from the south.
In his cap the lilacs whitened,
then one day they fell like snow.
Now in the evening,
a new moon comes.
The hills grow softer. Tufts of long grass show
where each cow-flop lies.
The bull-frogs are sounding,
slack strings plucked by heavy thumbs.
Beneath the light, against your white front door,
the smallest moths, like Chinese fans,
flatten themselves, silver and silver-gilt
over pale yellow, orange, or gray.
Now, from the thick grass, the fireflies
begin to rise:
up, then down, then up again:
lit on the ascending flight,
drifting simultaneously to the same height,
—exactly like the bubbles in champagne.
—Later on they rise much higher.
And your shadowy pastures will be able to offer
these particular glowing tributes
every evening now throughout the summer.

No one would want to deny the exquisite detail of the description. But we are getting much more than a heap of images piled up at random. We are learning something about our world and about the inner world of ourselves.

One could push the general point further still. Wallace Stevens, who has exerted so powerful an influence on the present generation of poets, valued the precise image as much as anybody. But he had a very real interest in philosophy, and one of his finest poems, a late poem in his own life, is entitled "To an Old Philosopher in Rome." It has to do with the last days of George Santayana, as they were spent in his nursing home at the Convent of the Little Blue Nuns in Rome. The nuns, the candlelight, the noises of the city's traffic outside, the books piled beside the old man's bed—these, all of them, are there in the poem, but Stevens makes them say something far beyond themselves. He celebrates Santayana as a kind of secular saint who has created out of his own unbelief in the Christian heaven a heaven which is nevertheless authentic and to which the old philosopher is an heir and which he is now on the point of entering.

Thus far I have said a good deal about schools and tendencies in modern poetry, and surely they are worth taking into account. Yet, when all is said and done the only distinction ultimately worth making is that between the poems that are authentic poems—whatever the school—and those that are not.

I am tempted to go on to say that most of the revolutions in poetry— not all, of course, but most—are really palace revolutions—mere seasonal alterations of the current slogans and catchwords and a changing of the guard of which masters are to be respected and imitated. In any case, the very best poems of any age are likely to incorporate a number of the current themes and pressing issues of the time.

Perhaps the best way to conclude my discussion is to bring forward such a poem. For this purpose I choose a poem from Robert Penn Warren's volume *Being Here.* I choose it because it is relatively brief, because it gathers up three of the themes that haunt so much of our current poetry—the themes of time, history, and personal identity—but most of all because I think it is a very fine poem in its own right.

The title of the poem is "Speleology," that is, the study of caves, and it tells of the author's exploration as a boy of twelve, armed with a flashlight, of a cave he had discovered six years before. Once he is deep inside the cave he tells us:

> I cut off the light. Knew darkness and depth and no Time.
> Felt the cave-cricket crawl up an arm. Switched light on
> To see the lone life there, the cave-cricket pale
> As a ghost on my brown arm. I thought: They are blind.
>
> Crept on. Heard, faintly below
> A silken and whispering rustle. Like what? Like water—so swung
> The light to one side. I had crawled out
> A ledge under which, far down, far down, the water yet channeled
> And sang to itself, and answered my high light with swollen
> White bursts of bubble. Light out, unmoving, I lay,
>
> Lulled as by song in a dream, knowing
> I dared not move in a darkness so absolute.
> I thought: *This is me.* Thought: *Me—who am I?* Felt
> Heart beating as though to a pulse of darkness and earth, and thought
> How it would be to be here forever, my heart,
>
> In its beat, part of all. Part of all—

The poets have throughout history likened time to a river. So it is in Warren's poem. The river he hears becomes the river of time flowing almost silently into the sea of oblivion which is here a sea of literal darkness as well as of death. The boy's own heart seems to him the only thing alive in this night of absolute darkness, and his heart, the center of his life, pulses in time to the rush of the dark river that has carved out this cave.

But the flashlight suddenly slips out of his hand and with a scream he wakes from the reverie into which the river's song has lulled him.

> But I woke with a scream. The flashlight,
> It slipped, but I grabbed it. Had light—
> And once more looked down the deep slicing and sluicing
> Of limestone where water winked, bubbles like fish-eyes, a song like
>   terror.

When the flashlight, burning once more, reveals the bubbles dancing on the rushing stream, Warren once again draws on his poetic heritage. Poets before him have seen a man's life as simply a bubble floating on the stream of time which bears all away. The bubble lives for only a moment as a separate entity and then winks out and becomes simply a part of the stream on the surface of which it had its brief existence.

With the recovery of the flashlight, the crisis is over, and presumably the boy had no great difficulty in finding his way out of the cave. But the experience evidently cut deep into his memory, and as the concluding stanza tells us, it has haunted him in later life.

Years later, past dreams, I have lain
In darkness and heard the depth of that unending song,
And hand laid to heart, have once again thought: *This is me.*
And thought: *Who am I?* And hand on heart, wondered
What would it be like to be, in the end, part of all.

And in darkness have even asked: *Is this all? What is all?*

This poem asks all the old, old questions that have renewed themselves with a special poignance in our secularized world. Who am I, I who was born, will die, and will subside into the world of matter, and yet am able to transcend it to the point of knowing as no other animal can know that I was once nothing and that I shall again be nothing as I sink back into general nature. Is my life in fact all that exists for me? What is the reality that encompasses me and yet which I can see beyond? The poem proffers no answers, nor perhaps can there be answers; yet to ask the questions in this fashion almost suffices.

It seems to me a magnificent lyric. If it does not gather up all our pressing themes, and it does not, it does put three intertwined ones with great authority. I wish for the sake of our epoch that I could say that it is a fair representative of our present literature. It is actually an especially fine example. But much of our poetry and of our fiction is good, very good.

Is it, however, as good as that of the first half of our century, which William Butler Yeats shortly before his death declared had produced more good poets than "any period of the same length since the early seventeenth century"? It is possible that Yeats exaggerated. In any case, I shall not claim that our recent decades constitute such a golden age as he suggests. But I shall not settle for anything less than an age of silver, and silver is a noble metal, not to be disdained. Moreover, our silver is of full weight, of a very high degree of fineness. The skill of our best craftsmen who work it is excellent, and at least we have a God's plenty of them.

20

Nature and Human Nature
in the Poetry of Robert Frost

What is the boundary line between nature and human nature? Does anybody know? And if there isn't any consensus, won't I be begging the question if I state in advance where that line is to be drawn? I think I must take that risk here in the interest of clarity, for in our time the line between nature and human nature has become so shadowy that some people are surprised if one attempts to draw any line at all. I think that the line must be drawn, and I want to stress the importance of the line before I begin to consider what Frost took to be the relation of man to nature.

Yet, instead of giving my own answer in so many words, as an abstract answer, let me quote a short poem by W. H. Auden, a fine poet himself, and a poet who admired Frost.

> As I listened from a beach-chair in the shade
> To all the noises that my garden made,
> It seemed to me only proper that words
> Should be withheld from vegetables and birds.
>
> A robin with no Christian name ran through
> The Robin-Anthem which was all it knew,
> And rustling flowers for some third party waited
> To say which pairs, if any, should get mated.

The plants and the birds have little or no choice. The robin can't vary his song: his musical repertoire is stringently limited. The flowers must wait on a "third party," a bee or some other insect, to consummate their marriage. Of course the plants and birds do not have or need words. The rustle of leaves, the hum of insects, the cry of birds, these are not speech— and since their utterances do not consist of words, the poet can refer to them as mere "noises."

> No one of them was capable of lying,
> There was not one which knew that it was dying
> Or could have with a rhythm or a rhyme
> Assumed responsibility for time.
>
> Let them leave language to their lonely betters
> Who count some days and long for certain letters;
> We, too, make noises when we laugh or weep,
> Words are for those with promises to keep.

That the creatures other than man lack the gift of words has its advantages, however. They cannot lie. They cannot make—and break—promises. They do not suffer man's sense of anxiety and guilt. In short, they cannot enter into the realm of good and evil, that peculiarly human realm of choice and responsibility. Auden often refers to this world as the domain of history as opposed to that of nature. Man, of course, lives in the domain of nature too, but he is truly amphibious. If his body is immersed in the sea of nature, his head—his consciousness—sticks out above the surface.

This difference between the human being and any other living creature is radical. Whether you call man a mortal creature who is nevertheless endowed with an immortal soul, or whether, more cautiously, you prefer to describe him as a mammal equipped with a consciousness that allows him to live in the past and future as well as in the present—in either case you have implied that the separation of human beings from the other natural creatures is sharp and decisive.

Where did Frost stand on this matter? Or, to put the question in its proper terms, where did Frost the poet stand? The evidence of the work clearly indicates that Frost made the line between nature and human nature sharp and decisive. A little later I shall take up for special consideration the one or two possibly ambiguous cases. But in poems such as "The Wood-Pile," "Range-Finding," "A Leaf-Treader," "The Birthplace,"

"The Most of It," "Come In," or "The Need of Being Versed in Country Things," the line is very clearly drawn.

For example, consider the last-named poem, in which the speaker, on a walk through the woods, has come upon a burned-down farmhouse. The poem contains a brilliantly circumstantial description of the scene. It speaks of human losses and faded hopes. It begets in the speaker a feeling of melancholy, a feeling encouraged by the mournful-sounding murmur of the phoebes, whose utterance seems "more like the sigh we sigh / From too much dwelling on what has been." Except for the circumstantiality of some of the description, Frost's poem might seem the equivalent of the typical Romantic poem of the late eighteenth or early nineteenth century. These poets were often moved to a not unpleasing melancholy on gazing at ivy-clad towers, desolate churchyards, deserted villages, or ruined cottages like that one so movingly described by the young Wordsworth.

But observe what happens in the last two stanzas of Frost's poem:

Yet for them the lilac renewed its leaf,
And the aged elm, though touched with fire;
And the dry pump flung up an awkward arm;
And the fence post carried a strand of wire.

For them there was really nothing sad.
But though they rejoiced in the nest they kept,
One had to be versed in country things
Not to believe the phoebes wept.

In these stanzas, common sense and perspicacious wit take over. Frost is really having it both ways: he feels the power of natural associations—he knows why Wordsworth could write as he did—but as for himself, he is a hard-bitten modern. If the Romantics felt an urge to project their own subjective feelings onto nature, or were so conditioned as to respond to certain scenes in nature with appropriate emotions—if they sometimes believed that man and nature were closely allied—that the same deep impulse throbbed through both—then Frost could sympathize and for a moment join in their belief. But in fact he knew all too well that nature was indifferent to man and was quite unaware that man even existed.

Now I must not press this issue too hard. A great Romantic poet like Coleridge sometimes seems to say that man is not really cut off from nature, and yet even Coleridge wrote at least one poem on the same theme as Frost's. In that poem, Coleridge tells us that though men commonly say that the song of the nightingale is melancholy—"Most musical, most melancholy," as Milton puts it in "Il Penseroso"—it is not really so. Men have merely projected their own melancholy feelings onto the bird. To Coleridge, the nightingale's song is actually a song of joy, for it was his faith that everything in nature is joyful. Coleridge's poem "The Nightingale" is not really a very distinguished poem, but it is worth recording the fact that 175 years ago he was aware that men often wrongfully interpret nature by projecting their own moods upon it.

Keats was another one of the Romantics who was aware of the fallacy of a sympathetic nature. His poem on the nightingale—unlike Coleridge's effusion, a very great poem indeed—approaches the matter from another direction, but if I read the poem correctly, Keats also insists on the chasm that separates man with his burden of consciousness from the spontaneous and unconscious natural creatures. The poet longs to be like the nightingale, which lives in a timeless present unaware of the fact of death. It is not weighed down with anxieties. Indeed, it is so deeply immersed in nature that its song seems the voice of nature itself—the divine nature that knows no death. The poet would happily enter the nightingale's realm, but the burden of human consciousness bars his entrance. However attractive nature may appear to human nature, it is bound to remain that paradise of innocence, the gates of which were locked against man long ago.

Other Romantic poets, however, did hope to find in nature an answering voice—a spiritual force corresponding to the human spirit itself. Wordsworth, in some of his poems, including the finest poems he ever wrote, asserts such a link between nature and human nature. There is in Wordsworth's early poetry a strong element of pantheism, and Frost, though no pantheist, was fully aware of this Wordsworthian doctrine. In a poem entitled "The Most of It," the human yearning for an answering response from nature becomes quite explicit. The poem begins with the "I" of the poem thinking that "he kept the universe alone." The only answering voice

> . . . he could wake
> Was but the mocking echo of his own
> From some tree-hidden cliff across the lake.

But that is not enough. What the speaker of the poem wants "Is not [his] own love back in copy speech / But counter-love, original response." But there is no such response. He hears, to be sure, a noise on the other side of the lake, but the source of the noise turns out to be nonhuman—only a great buck that swims the lake and, landing on the shore, ". . . stumbled through the rocks with horny tread, / And forced the underbrush and that was all." The animal is just as oblivious of Frost's observer as was ever Keats's nightingale of the young listener on the moonlit lawn at Hampstead.

John Lynen in his excellent and too little known book, *The Pastoral Art of Robert Frost,* states the meaning of the poems very precisely. In this poem, he writes,

> the poet shows us [in bold outline] the gulf separating man from nature . . . , and this is probably why the poem has been generally ignored. The picture he presents is certainly not cheerful, much less pretty. It is impressive. It demonstrates how exalted an idea of the human mind and how awesome a view of reality the contrast between man and nature expresses.

Yet Frost is not at all scornful of the human yearning to bridge the gap between man and nature. In "Two Look at Two," the members of one of the mated pairs are human; the other pair are a buck and a doe. When they meet across a tumbled wall of stone, the doe does not take fright, and in a moment "passed unscared along the wall," to be followed in a moment by the antlered buck, who sees the human pair, views them a moment "quizzically with jerks of head," and then also passes "unscared along the wall."

This poem, in theme at least, represents Frost at his most Wordsworthian; and yet even here Frost qualifies very carefully. The lovers do feel that nature is responding to them with something like human love. That they should feel this is, in the situation described, thoroughly understandable, but the poet does not venture beyond saying they felt "as if . . . earth returned their love."

Yet, one may well ask whether Frost did not find—"Two Look at Two" would be a good instance—analogues to the specifically human experience in nature? Indeed he did; but this discovery is the kind of exercise of the human spirit that long antedates the advent of the Romantic movement and, one predicts, will long survive it. In fact, it will continue as long as human beings continue to be recognizably human. Men have from the beginning found analogies for the human in the workings of nature. To go no further back than the Middle Ages, men wrote elaborate bestiaries and allegories; and the Renaissance produced emblem books. Thus long before René Descartes separated the heart from the head and thus unwittingly stimulated the necessary countermovement to this severance, the movement that undertook to reunite head and heart, idea and emotion, science and poetry—in short, the Romantic movement—men had always used natural objects and processes as vehicles for the metaphors by which they attempt to describe their human experience.

One reservation may be usefully offered at this point. I find in Frost's treatment of nature something quite different from Emerson's treatment of nature. Though the young Frost learned from his mother Emerson's notion that "the world is a temple whose walls are covered with emblems, pictures and commandments of the Deity," and though he always considered himself a symbolist, Frost resisted the tendency to reduce nature to a mere expression or reflection of man's imagination. This aspect of Romanticism is illustrated in its most extreme degree by William Blake and by the New England Transcendentalists. But Transcendentalism proved to be an intellectual diet too rich for Frost's blood.

Thus, I find nothing in Frost's poetry that corresponds to Emerson's notion that nature may be merely a "divine dream from which we may presently awake to the glories and certainties of day," or that the "whole of nature is a metaphor of the human mind." Frost was too earthbound for that, as his poem "To Earthward" will testify.

Along with Emerson's insistence that matter was subservient to mind—in fact not much more than a shadow of the mind—went Emerson's rejection of evil. The Puritan element in Frost could not accept so optimistic a view of reality. Frost's official biographer, Lawrance Thompson, quotes G. R. Elliott as having told him that "While loving Emerson, [Frost] *always* criticized Emerson's lack of perception of evil and sin."

Indeed, I would argue that Frost's indebtedness to Emerson has usually been much exaggerated. A radical difference between them has to do with their different ways of describing the relation between nature and human nature. With Emerson, the distinction has all but disappeared. Nature amounts to not much more than an extension of human nature, a lower and more gross aspect of spirit. Frost, on the other hand, is still in the mainstream of the Classical-Christian tradition. He has been touched by the Romantic movement and he is aware of the impingement of modern science, but his own perspective has not been seriously altered by either of these impacts. Can one say, however, that Frost's view is still recognizably Christian? Thompson makes a good deal of Frost's essentially Christian position, though scarcely in terms of dogma or of any connection with institutional Christianity. On this point, what is the evidence of Frost's poems? Do they yield any pertinent evidence?

What was the orthodox version of the classical tradition as absorbed by Christianity? At the risk of seeming obvious—though how obvious to most people today?—let me set it forth in simple—even oversimple—terms. God, the transcendent Being, had fashioned nature and the creatures that inhabit nature, including man. But to man he gave an immortal soul, a gift that involved memory, language, responsibility, and choice. Each of these gifts, it ought to be plain, implies the others. The primal man fell and was expelled from the Garden of Innocence, but was to be given another chance, the opportunity to find a recovered innocence; but first he would have to suffer death, the experience that befalls all other natural creatures. It may be interesting, in this connection, to look back at a poem that I alluded to earlier—Auden's "Our Lonely Betters"—and to put beside it Milton's *Paradise Lost*. Both are garden poems—and both refer to a realm of lost innocence—lost, that is, to the human being.

I want to add to these another garden poem in order to provide a more telling brief example of what is essentially an orthodox example of the Classical-Christian tradition. It is Andrew Marvell's poem entitled simply "The Garden."

The "I" of the poem, hot and dusty from his vain pursuit of love and glory in the bustling and competitive world outside the garden wall, enters the garden and feels at once refreshed, calmed, cooled, and restored. As for love, the green of the foliage of the trees seems more "amorous" than any lady's "white and red." As for fame, the garlands that the trees spontaneously offer make the victor's chaplet or the warrior's circlet of oak leaves suddenly look vulgar, ostentatious, and not quite worth the sweat required to win them.

Thus, in these opening stanzas nature judges the life of struggling humanity and finds it wanting. The vision it offers is Arcadian—the happy and innocent world of the golden age. This is the most classical part of the poem, something like Saturn's peaceful realm, though it is reminiscent of Eden's garden too. But Marvell's garden does more than remind the observer of the past golden age: it also looks forward in its peace and joy to eternity. In fact, the body is so filled with quiet joy that the soul can afford to leave it for a moment. The moment is literally ecstatic—for, as you know, ecstasy means "a putting aside," and this is just what the soul does:

> Casting the Bodie's Vest aside,
> My Soul into the boughs does glide:
> There like a Bird, it sits, and sings,
> Then whets, and combs its silver Wings;
> And, till prepar'd for longer flight,
> Waves in its Plumes the various Light.

That "longer flight" is, of course, the flight to heaven that the soul will take when it casts the body's vest aside forever.

These closing stanzas constitute the more specifically Christian part of the poem, though Marvell keeps them urbane and witty, even in a curious sense "worldly." For Marvell wrote in a period in which one might still be witty and urbane and yet Christian.

In Marvell's "The Garden" we see that nature may comfort man and may even prefigure his eternal rest in heaven. Yet in this poem there is no question either of worshiping nature as if it were God or of imagining that man can create nature out of his own head. Nature is not God, it is the creation of God; and man is not, by virtue of his imagination, a god, or even a demigod. He is a creature too, created by God, and, though created in the image of God, he can only in a very remote way imitate God's creative power. In Marvell's seventeenth century we are still far away from Blake's insistence that man's creative imagination is divine, or from Hart Crane's belief that the poet can literally create his world.

One further point: the garden experience as interpreted by Marvell is a temporary respite, an incidental refreshment. The person who speaks this poem is obviously not going to retire to a hermitage in the wood, or assume the lotus position and meditate for the rest of his days. We may be sure that next week he will be carrying on his political duties as a member of parliament, as Marvell himself did, or pamphleteering for his political party, as Marvell did, or even writing another poem, as Marvell did—or, if you insist on a more serious program for him, resuming his life as an active wayfaring Christian, as Marvell did. In short, he will be striving, if not for "the Palm, the Oke, or Bayes," then for that immortal garland that Milton says was not to be won without dust and heat.

I think that—granted the differences between the seventeenth and the twentieth centuries—we may find some general similarities between Marvell's orthodox Christian stance, as exemplified in "The Garden," and some of Frost's nature poems.

But here I think I ought to interrupt the course of my argument. I interrupt it to answer those who are saying to themselves: Really, is it necessary to bring in so many poets other than Frost? We came to hear a tribute to Frost, and here you are invoking the whole tradition of English poetry. What's the point?

The point is just this: at this date, one hardly needs to celebrate Frost's power as an artist. How skillful he is! How cunning in his manipulation of tonal effects! How brilliant in his control of idea and emotion! Even less needful at this time is more praise of Frost's portrayal of the humors and manners and folkways of the older New England. That achievement requires no further emphasis. Indeed, it was for a long time stressed somewhat too much—even to the hurt of Frost's reputation as an artist and as a man concerned with universal issues.

A more useful service to Frost, it seems to me, is to place him squarely in the Classical-Christian tradition, where I think he belongs. He still needs, as Thompson has indicated, to be freed from entanglements with New England's transcendentalism, and his relation to the Classical-Christian tradition ought to be made much clearer. On this latter point Thompson, in spite of his two monumental volumes of biography in which he makes many references to Frost's conservative religious beliefs, does not show how they appear in Frost's poetry. That, I think, is worth doing, and I know of no more effective way to accomplish this aim than to cite examples of the traditional view of the relation of nature to human nature as illustrated in earlier English poetry. In short, I have wanted to establish the traditional intellectual background against which to present Frost's own position.

Before I can take up Frost's typical handling of this problem, however, I want to mention one more poem, though this time one by way of contrast. The poem I have in mind is Thomas Hardy's "In a Wood." Like Frost, Hardy had behind him the Classical-Christian heritage, but Hardy's faith had been knocked out by Victorian science. "In a Wood" is not one of Hardy's best, but it does focus precisely on the issue that I want to raise here.

The poet has retreated to a woodland in search of peace and nature's calming power, but as he looks at the trees he cannot help seeing that they are in ruthless competition with each other.

> Great growths and small
> Show them to men akin—
>   Combatants all.

The poet has evidently lost not only his Christian faith, but his Romantic faith as well. Nature is not, as Coleridge believed, joyous. It is as bad as man—even worse, for it lacks man's occasional goodness. So the speaker sadly concludes:

> Since then, no grace I find
>   Taught me of trees.
> Turn I back to my own kind,
>   Worthy as these.
> There at least smiles abound,
> There discourse trills around,
> There, now and then, are found
>   Life-loyalties.

It is a cautious and carefully qualified tribute to human nature. But a tribute it is. And Hardy is insistent on the chasm separating nature from human nature.

Suppose we set in contrast to Hardy's poem a poem by Frost. This poem is also about trees. It is, by the way, one of my favorite Frost poems, one that I think is too little known.

> I have been treading on leaves all day until I am autumn-tired.
> God knows all the color and form of leaves I have trodden on and mired.
> Perhaps I have put forth too much strength and been too fierce
>   from fear.
> I have safely trodden underfoot the leaves of another year.
>
> All summer long they were overhead, more lifted up than I.
> To come to their final place on earth they had to pass me by.
> All summer long I thought I heard them threatening under their breath.
> And when they came it seemed with a will to carry me with them
>   to death.

Another year is dying; the falling leaves mark one more autumn passed, and that fact obviously brings a certain relief to the speaker. He tells us (in line 3) that he has perhaps been "too fierce from fear." Fear of what? The fear of joining the falling leaves in this seasonal death of the year.

Now in his relieved complacency, he can afford to expatiate a bit on his triumph over this year's leaves. He has indeed withstood their challenge and their threat. Yet in spite of his present playfulness, he had apparently taken their threat seriously: "And when they came it seemed with a will to carry me with them to death."

With the last stanza, however, there is a change in tone. Man is, like the leaves, a mortal creature. How does the Prophet Isaiah put it? ". . . we all do fade as a leaf; and our iniquities, like the wind, have taken us away." The Psalmist takes up the same theme: "As for man, his days are as grass: as a flower of the field, so he flourisheth. For the wind passeth over it, and it is gone."

The speaker knows that in one sense he is no better than a leaf—and knows further that there is something in his own spirit that makes the final subsidence into death somehow attractive: The leaves "spoke to the fugitive in my heart as if it were leaf to leaf. / They tapped at my eyelids and touched my lips with an invitation to grief." But then occurs a second bold shift in tone. The speaker is not a leaf. He is a human being; and so he pulls himself together and becomes for the moment at least, the stubborn, even roguish little boy who, when the children in the yard next door are called in by their mother to get ready for bed, taunts them with his own temporary freedom: "But it was no reason I had to go because they had to go."

But then the tone suddenly changes a third time: the speaker is fully aware that his present triumph is only temporary. If he has successfully stayed on top of the leaves rather than having them bury him, his struggle is never ending. Can he stay on top of the snow, which will soon be falling? "Now up, my knee, to keep on top of another year of snow."

Frost's attitude toward nature is quite different from that of Thomas Hardy. In Frost's poem, nature is not really hostile to man even though Frost's speaker pretends that the leaves threaten him. Moreover, Frost's poem is spirited, even playful, and though the issues treated are serious enough, the note struck has nothing of Hardy's somber meditation. Matthew Arnold, one suspects, might have regarded "A Leaf-Treader" as lacking the "high seriousness" that he demanded of all great poetry. But "A Leaf-Treader," slight as it may seem, has a high-heartedness that has its own value, and it does deal, Matthew Arnold notwithstanding, with a serious subject: with man's courage and willingness to endure. If man is a creature like the grass of the fields or the leaves of a season, consigned to death, still he must live out his time as a man and meet his death as a man.

Frost could treat the same basic situation in a more lyrical mood. Consider his poem "Come In." This poem is rather close to the situation of John Keats listening to the song of the darkling nightingale.

As I came to the edge of the woods,
Thrush music—hark!
Now if it was dusk outside,
Inside it was dark.

Too dark in the woods for a bird
By sleight of wing
To better its perch for the night,
Though it still could sing.

The last of the light of the sun
That had died in the west

Still lived for one song more
In a thrush's breast.

Far in the pillared dark
Thrush music went—
Almost like a call to come in
To the dark and lament.

The poem begins simply enough. A man is out for an evening walk. He means to get clear of the trees so that he can look at, let us say, the summer constellations. But his attention is attracted by the song of a wood thrush, and as he listens, gradually the plaintive music woos him toward a mood of melancholy. As the bird's song issues from the dark woods beside the road, it might well be the voice of nature herself inviting man to join her in a lament for what Virgil long ago called "the tears of things."

The situation is much the same that we found in "A Leaf-Treader," where the dying leaves appealed to the fugitive in the man's own heart. He and the thrush are frail creatures living in what seems an indifferent world. They are both mortal and soon to perish.

But in "Come In," as in "A Leaf-Treader," the poet suddenly does a *volte face*. After all, he is a man with his own designs and purposes. He had planned to look at stars—not to listen to thrush music—least of all to lament. "But no, I was out for stars: / I would not come in." But then suddenly he remembers his manners, and so he adds: "I meant not even if asked," and then as common sense reasserts itself, he makes one further addition: "And I hadn't been."

That little natural creature, the thrush, singing out of its instinctive life, is not singing to him, does not even know he exists, and great nature itself is just as oblivious to mankind. As with the murmur of the phoebes in "The Need of Being Versed in Country Things," so the song of the thrush here is sung with no reference to any meaning but its own.

The poet is not, let me hasten to say, daunted by that realization. He loves nature in spite of the fact that she is oblivious to him. He can derive something valuable from nature. But he has his own value because he is unique in nature—Pascal called man a reed but a "thinking reed."

"Stopping by Woods" repeats this same theme, though in its own way.

Perhaps it is the best poem with which to conclude, for it is so well known that I don't really need to quote it, and yet it contains all the aspects of the problem I have been discussing.

For example, there is the attraction of the woods by which the man in the sleigh has stopped: "The woods are lovely, dark and deep. . . ." So they are, just as the phoebe song is filled with a poignant melancholy, and with something of the attraction of the thrush's song which had seemed an invitation to come into the dark and lament. There is something in nature that does quietly urge man to give over his struggle and accept what Keats called "easeful death."

Further, in this poem Frost defines man, that strange amphibian who is a mixture of calculation and emotion. The man in the sleigh, moved by the beauty of the scene and by the nameless hunger that it feeds, pauses by the woods. The owner of the woods, however, would probably be puzzled by anyone's stopping there in a snowstorm. Why is the man stopping? Has he designs on this piece of property? Practical calculation can make nothing of pure contemplation. Nor can the little horse make anything of it either. The animal has been conditioned to pull the sleigh, and if he isn't pulling it, he wants to be home in his warm stall, eating his dinner of oats. No wonder he "gives his harness bells a shake / To ask if there is some mistake."

The man in the sleigh finally does drive on, not because he fears that the owner of the woods will catch him looking at this land, and not because of the restlessness of his horse. Why then? Because he has "promises to keep." Man is the aesthetic animal, and that is why he has stopped to look at the woods. Their beauty affects him as it does not affect the horse. But man is also the ethical animal. What he has promised to do may not in fact be very important, but a promise is a promise, and a commitment to be kept. The horse cannot make promises any more than Auden's birds and flowers can make promises. But man can. That is why he has to be either better than the beasts or else worse. He cannot simply be a happy "innocent" creature along with all the other creatures. The line between nature and human nature is radically deep. Though perhaps Frost would disagree with Matthew Arnold's assertion that "Nature and man can never be fast friends," surely Arnold is right in saying that man has more than nature has, and in "that *more* lie all [man's] hopes of good."

21

Walker Percy

In Celebration

*F*rom almost the beginning, Walker Percy has elicited questions and called attention to all sorts of exciting problems, some of them highly contemporary problems, and problems not easily solved—indeed, perhaps, insoluble.

He has often been interviewed. Some of the questions put to him have had to do with matters of personal affairs—with Percy's own life, his family background, his modes of writing, and so forth. But nearly all of the questions get quickly into more general matters: the South, old and new; questions having to do with race, with religion, and especially with the relation of science to secularism; and the state of our present culture. Topics like alienation and loneliness, and the breakdown of the older institutions, such as marriage, the family, and the cohesive social community, have come in for a good deal of questioning. One can think of a number of people in the United States who share his concerns with the problems of our culture and who recognize their seriousness, people whose notions of what needs to be done bear some resemblance at least to Percy's own. But they rarely command Percy's audience, in size or in the special quality of his mind.

Percy is a highly interesting man. He pursued a scientific course of study in college and capped it with an M.D. from the medical school of Columbia University. He is a Roman Catholic convert. He is an artist, a literary artist, and more particularly a novelist. It is rare to find a person so widely informed about scientific and artistic matters, and so well equipped to deal with the prestigious matters of the hard sciences, as well as psychiatry and semiotics.

To describe Percy in such terms as these, however, is to risk distorting the man and thus gravely falsifying the kind of human being that he is. In spite of his solid learning and his deep convictions about mankind and man's position in the universe, Walker Percy is no sharp-featured dogmatist who peers out on our world with a grim and austere gaze.

On the contrary, he impresses one as the most amiable of men, courteous, pleasant, and civilized. He puts the visitor at ease at once. So it was on my first meeting with him in the early 1960s, soon after the publication of his first novel.

I remember well that first visit to his pleasant house just outside the little town of Covington, Louisiana, across Lake Pontchartrain from the city of New Orleans. He and his wife—who always went by her nickname, Bunt, just as my wife, a New Orleans girl, always clung to hers—had found what seemed an ideal retreat, though it also could serve as an excellent observation post on the great world outside.

Their house looked out on a sleepy little bayou. Their lawn lay within a grove of trees. The air was warm but fresh. It seemed a place capable of calling forth good talk and good stories. The Percys abounded in both.

In view of some of the things I mean to say about Percy in what follows, I want to ask my reader to put aside certain falsifying notions that abound in American thought: namely, that a religious man who is happy doesn't take his religion seriously; that to hold transcendental beliefs implies that one has evaded the great intellectual issues of our day; and that to be able to see stable relationships among serious events means that one lacks an adventurous mind. Percy is in his own terms a very serious man; yet, nevertheless, he is witty, easy, and gracious.

Percy is especially concerned with the state of American culture, which he finds in very bad state indeed, not that he is hopeless about America or Western culture, but he is completely aware of the difficulty of restoring it to good health. He is intensely interested in what is happening to our culture under the pressure of ideas of great power, though ideas, he would say, much misunderstood and misapplied. One might argue that his real problem as a novelist is to keep the novel, under his constant emphasis on the idea, from leveling out into a tract.

The most captivating aspect of Percy's work is the sheer enjoyment of reading his account of the life around him. But such reading is not at all a matter of sorting through a bag of sugarplums. What we are shown is verifiable but we must get much more than a comforting sense of how very true all of this is. The observations derive from a point of view—what might even be called a plan of attack. They may appear to be casual and desultory but they are not merely random. They have been carefully aimed.

Consider, for example, an episode from Percy's first novel, *The Moviegoer*. The "impression has been growing upon [Binx Bolling] that everyone is dead." Soon after this intimation has come upon him, Binx meets his friend, Nell Lovell, who has just finished reading a celebrated novel which takes a somewhat "gloomy and pessimistic view of things." She is angry because she believes that the novel gives a radically wrong view of life. She, herself, doesn't "feel a bit gloomy." Indeed, she tells Binx how happy she is and how pleased she is with her values, yet the episode ends with "We part laughing and dead."

Take another instance: Binx's account of his Uncle Jules, who is "as pleasant a fellow as I know anywhere." Uncles Jules "has made a great deal of money, he has a great many friends, he was Rex of Mardi Gras, he gives freely of himself and his money. He is an exemplary Catholic, but it is hard to know why he takes the trouble. For the world he lives in, the City of Man, is so pleasant that the City of God must hold little in store for him."

In these episodes, Percy develops his criticisms of a society that has always made much of life, liberty, and the pursuit of happiness, and especially of a society that as it has matured has come to conceive of these goals in purely secularistic terms. Binx, in spite of his social connections, his friends, his healthy body, and his good job, is bored, anxious, and desirous of an escape. For him, the world of the moving picture has become more real ("significant") than the world outside it.

Percy's novels have an attractive quality, though one so obvious that its importance is easily overlooked. It is the quality of his writing: a lively, sharply perceptive prose that mirrors the scenes that he presents with sufficient faithfulness to validate their accuracy as a revelation of the American scene but that also gives authority to Percy's criticism of the way in which we are living out our lives. Percy can be very funny, aware of the little giveaways that witness our boredom, or our pretentiousness, or our solicitude for the American dream as it is set forth by our politicians and our advertising agencies and by the unconscious turns of our own daily language. The reader knows what Percy is talking about, even when forced to view it from an angle that exposes its hollowness.

Percy's language is the kind of instrument that any good satirist must have at hand. Lacking it, criticism of the society and its behavior dwindles into a dreary sociological tract or else into an excoriation, even into a hellfire sermon. Comedy, parody, witty allusions—these are the satirist's proper modes.

Yet the satirist must do more than carry us along as he gives our world a proper dressing-down: The emptiness, the fatuity, the deadening and crippling malignancy must be shown as such. A clever literary artist can render any situation slightly ridiculous, for all our situations, however highly regarded, have in them elements that provoke laughter.

If the satirist does have serious concerns and if the culture is truly infected, his style must do more than to keep the reader happy as he coasts along. The particular descriptions, characterizations, and observations must bear upon the problem and show that its banality or silliness or viciousness is potentially lethal.

A satirical job of this sort is much harder to do. It will not be enough to tick off an oversight or peccadillo; such might be sufficient to elicit a smile. On the other hand, sharp condemnations move away from satire to direct moralizing. The satirist, even a Jonathan Swift, must be careful not to preach.

A number of readers have sometimes demurred at the way in which Percy's novels usually end. His conclusions do not seem to conclude. Will the marriage of Binx Bolling and Kate be a happy one? The signs are good, but Kate's recovery from her illness is still tentative and the author has been very frank about the problems that still confront Binx. Percy seems to have his own ideas about what constitutes a truly happy ending. It has to be earned—achieved. It is rarely if ever simply given. Percy's concern is to get the problem dramatized and his hero tested by his ability to cope with it.

Percy prefers to let his stories end quietly: a gesture, a minor incident, a brief word that indicates that something of importance has happened, but that the problem of the culture has not thereby been solved and the seeker himself has not reached necessarily a final destination. Thus *The Movie-*

goer ends, not with all of Binx's confusions neatly sorted out and his way perfectly clear. The reader must be content with Binx's final conversation with Kate, now his wife. That conversation includes a request, a reassurance, a pledge that he will be always helping her, and ends with a tenderly spoken command. The language is simple, even commonplace, but it fully implies what Binx has to say to her: Face reality; I am trying to face it myself; and I will try to help you to do so.

So a muted, even workaday conclusion of the novel does not show Binx, the searcher, as having succeeded: it signifies that he is on the right path. The reader will have to be content with that.

Percy's second novel, *The Last Gentleman,* becomes, among other things, a commentary on the folkways of a secularized culture. Will Barrett, who has returned to his native South after several years in New York City, thinks he has fallen in love with Kitty Vaught. Kitty is as confused as Will himself. She and her siblings represent all the problems and possibilities of choosing to live a good (that is, decent, proper, successful) life in the American century: Percy uses them well to set up Will's problems as he tries to discover what is wrong with himself and what, if anything, is right about his advanced technological world.

What happens at the end of *The Last Gentleman*? Does Will Barrett go back to Alabama and marry Kitty Vaught or does he not? As most novels go, such would have to happen. While Will's attempt to describe the happiness of a "normal" married life with a position in his father-in-law's automobile business suggests the romance may not yield much happiness after all, the hints remain hints, and it is not until many years later, in *The Second Coming,* that we find out Will did not, in fact, marry Kitty. In this novel, Will is fiftyish and the widower of a wealthy northern woman. He still does not know what to do with himself and is on the road to new and strange encounters.

I confess that when I first read *The Last Gentleman,* I was thrown back hard upon myself by what didn't happen. I felt the story had made an important point and that the Will who had been a bemused and confused observer of the human scene in his earlier days in New York had become a rather different man because of what he had seen and experienced. In short, my interest in the novel went far beyond the mere satisfaction of the outcome of the plot.

When Will Barrett returns to his native South, things have changed. "The South he came home to was different from the South he had left. It was happy, victorious, Christian, rich, patriotic and Republican. The happiness and serenity of the South disconcerted him. He had felt good in the North because everyone else felt so bad."

Walker Percy knows as much about how the people of the Deep South act and speak as anyone that I can think of. He knows what is limited, narrow-minded, and even grievously wrong in the social fabric of the Old South. But the New South is not necessarily a better South. If it has made its improvement and has redressed certain wrongs, it has lost also some of the old virtues the region once possessed and is now in grave danger of accepting uncritically the values offered by "Americanism."

Percy is concerned to observe not merely the qualities of his native region but those of the country generally and, even further, the character of Western civilization. Percy's basic virtues then are grounded in commitments much deeper than those that define, for example, the conventional newspaper editorial on the state of the country. Percy's basic material, however, is southern, drawn from the society that he personally knows best and in which he prefers to live. A society closely affiliated by all sorts of relationships and social ties is not only a society in which a great many unusual things happen, it is a society that still likes to talk, that notices the little personal details through which men and women express themselves and which eventually generate sharp, often witty, nearly always personal talk. The twentieth-century southern artists have greatly profited from this fact. Walker Percy knows precisely how to use such talk.

There is no letup in his wonderfully good talk from the first of his novels right on through the rest of them: *Love in the Ruins, Lancelot, The Second Coming,* and with its release in 1987, *The Thanatos Syndrome.* From this last volume, for example, here is a commentary on one of the most important instruments in our American culture: "TV has screwed up millions of people with their little rounded-off stories. Because that is not the way life is. Life is fits and starts, mostly fits."

Or Dr. More on his profession: "There is a slight unpleasantness about doing a psychiatric consultation in a small general hospital. Here a psychiatrist is ranked somewhere between a clergyman and an undertaker.

One is tolerated. One sees the patient only if the patient has nothing else to do."

Or another comment from Dr. More, on the pursuit of happiness: "It is not for me to say whether one should try to *be happy*—though it has always struck me as an odd pursuit, like trying to be blue-eyed—or whether one should try to beat all the other jay-birds on the block. But it is my observation that neither pursuit succeeds very well. I only know that people who set their hearts on happiness either usually end up seeing me or somebody like me, or having heart attacks, or climbing into a bottle."

Is this observation on the pursuit of happiness very un-American (even subversive) or thoroughly American? In any case, it is typical of Percy's Dr. Thomas More and I should think typical of Walker Percy himself. It is the kind of thing that gives his novels their special character and makes them a sheer enjoyment to read.

22

The Real Importance
of the Humanities

*O*ne of the things that I want to talk about is the marvelous language that we have inherited. You can do almost anything with it. You can express almost any mood. It can be made to run off the tongue as smooth as silk or as rough and prickly as a porcupine's back. To take an extreme instance of this almost furry softness that the language is capable of, listen to that world-weary poet, Swinburne, in one of his most world-weary moods.

> From too much love of living,
>   From hope and fear set free,
> We thank with brief thanksgiving
>   Whatever gods may be
> That no life lives forever;
> That dead men rise up never;
> That even the weariest river
>   Winds somewhere safe to sea.

If there is such a thing as a death wish, this is a very seductive statement of it. The words, the closing simile, and the rhythm all cooperate to lull one into a kind of acceptance of the final sleep of death.

At the other extreme is a short piece from Robert Penn Warren's wonderful novel *All the King's Men*. The political boss and demagogue, Willie Stark, has just picked up the telephone to get a message when his hard-boiled secretary, Sadie Burke, bursts in. She's got important news to give the governor and, of course, Sadie's not in the least awed by him.

"What's up?" the Boss demanded again.

"Judge Irwin," she managed to get out with what breath she had after the rush.

"Yeah" the Boss said. He was still lounging against the wire, but he was looking at Sadie as though he might be preparing to do a sketch of her.

"Matlock called up—long distance from town—and he said the afternoon paper—"

"Spill it," the Boss said, "spill it."

"Damn it," Sadie said. "I'll spill it when I get good and ready. I'll spill it when I get my breath. If I'm good and ready and if you—"

"You're using up a lot of breath right now," the Boss said with a tone of voice which made you think of rubbing your hand down a cat's back, just as soft.

"It's my breath," Sadie snapped at him, "and nobody's bought it. I damn near break myself down running out here to tell you something and then you say spill it, spill it, before I can get my breath and I'll just tell you when I get good and ready, when I get my breath and—"

Well, the question is not whether you admire Sadie or the Boss or whether you think their conversation is particularly edifying, but the language that they are speaking is electrifying. Take the way in which they pick up on this word *breath* and run it through every question and retort they make. Like seasoned tennis players who hit the ball back and forth across the net, quickly and professionally.

The language we have inherited is indeed a great language and capable of so much. Consequently, it is a pity to see how ill-used it is and how many people, including a great many college students, say "you know," with every *breath* that they take. "You know" is becoming an almost meaningless grunt. What it really is saying is "I can't tell you and therefore I hope to goodness that you *do* know because I can't tell you myself."

Somebody conducted a poll of college students recently to find out why they had come to college, and a vast number of them, I think the actual figure was 80 percent, said that the reason they had enrolled in college was to learn how to make money. Now money is a very important commodity, and if you had lived through the Great Depression as I did as a young man, it would have been burned deep into you. You'd never forget just how important it is to have some money.

Nevertheless, if your motive for going on to further college work is only to make money, you're not interested in a college education. What you're really after is a training school. There's nothing wrong with training schools. Whether you are eager to be a first-rate artisan, or a good carpenter, or a mason, or to get into one of the learned professions like medicine. More power to you. Training is essential. But this is only one side of college life and in some ways not the most important side. The sad thing is that we live in a society that is in danger of losing the very concept of a liberal education.

Why liberal? What is "liberal" about it? Some knowledge of our language can help us here. A liberal education originally meant the sort of education that you gave to a free man. (*Liber* in Latin means free.) A slave needs to acquire only certain skills. That is true not merely of a chattel slave but of the wage slave and even of the wealthy man who is completely enslaved to his business. Our democracy proudly insists that all its citizens are or ought to be free men. If so, each of us deserves a liberal education—one that helps us not merely to make a living but to *live* a fully satisfactory life.

How does a liberal education do that? Well, one of the ways in which it liberates us is by providing us with much ampler living room. Each of us is born in one little corner of this world and in one narrow segment of time. It doesn't matter too much whether it's in Hicksville, Nebraska, in 1901 or in Flatbush, Brooklyn, New York, in 1843. Either will prove rather cramped quarters if that is all we ever know. But history and literature can liberate us: they can make us acquainted with the rest of the world and with all of the past experience of humanity itself.

I'm well aware that the jet plane has allowed us to conquer space and has given us at least a tourist's view of the rest of the globe. But all airports are alike and all luxury hotels are alike, and if you know nothing of history, all the palaces, all the cathedrals, and all the castles soon come to look very much alike. Also, unless you know some history, just scampering around the globe does not give you much further information or stir the imagination. It is the opening up of the past that is really important, telling you about human beings of thousands of years ago and providing you with a valuable perspective on our own age. We are not the only superpower to arise. The story of mankind is rich and interesting and can contain wisdom.

Small wonder that history, literature, and philosophy have long been regarded as what we call the humanities. All of them make use of language, and indeed language is crucial to their activities. Here I shall be concentrating on literature and especially that most condensed and intense kind of literature that we call poetry. I shall do so for good and sufficient reasons. I know more about literature than I know about history and philosophy, and I can use more examples if I draw them from poetry. Whether the poems I quote provide any help in articulating and making choices of human values, you will have to judge for yourselves. But you may be quite sure that such knowledge as they offer is very different from "scientific" knowledge and that it is offered to the reader in poetry's own and very special way.

Let me begin by considering some poems about love. All three of the following are addressed by a man to a woman he loves. Anyone who has tried to write a love letter has discovered how difficult it is to say anything that seems fresh and genuine and even sincere—how difficult it is even to express your own feelings. So you ought to be interested in what these poets have done.

The first one, entitled "Go, Lovely Rose," is literally addressed to the flower that the man is sending to his sweetheart. Ostensibly he is simply dictating the message that the rose blossom is to convey, but of course he secretly hopes that the girl, by looking at the flower, will get the message. In any case the flower is only a go-between. Indeed, in this instance the old-fashioned language of flowers is taken up to its highest notch.

> Go, lovely rose!
> Tell her that wastes her time and me,
>   That now she knows,
> When I resemble her to thee,
> How sweet and fair she seems to be.
>
>   Tell her that's young,
> And shuns to have her graces spied,
>   That hadst thou sprung
> In deserts, where no men abide,
> Thou must have uncommended died.
>
>   Small is the worth
> Of beauty from the light retired;
>   Bid her come forth,

Suffer herself to be desired,
And not blush so to be admired.

Then die! that she
The common fate of all things rare
    May read in thee;
How small a part of time they share
That are so wondrous sweet and fair!

"Go, Lovely Rose" is a graceful, tender, and an altogether charming appeal to the young woman to accept the lover's plea—to overcome her shyness and to allow herself to be an object of amorous devotion. "Suffer herself to be desired" is the way the poet puts it—for beauty does not last and love's springtime is brief and should be enjoyed.

Andrew Marvell's poem on the same general subject is bolder, more direct, and far more realistic in its terms—almost savagely realistic. The first part of the poem is devoted to the praise of the woman's beauty. To do justice to her body's charms would require centuries, and he would happily spend whole lifetimes in such praise of her manifold attractions. Yes, he would gladly devote

An age at least to every part,
And the last age should show your heart.
For, lady, you deserve this state,
Nor would I love at lower rate.

Talk about the poet who writes a sonnet to his mistress's eyebrows! This one declares that he would outdo them all and the lady can be as coy as she pleases. She deserves a courtship that goes on for centuries. That, however, is not the point. The poet and his mistress simply do not have centuries at their disposal. "Time's wingéd chariot [is] hurrying near." He hears it constantly, and it is hurrying both of them into no green and pleasant land, but as he puts it, into "deserts of vast eternity."

He becomes more specific still, telling her, when your body lies in its marble vault, you won't be able to hear my echoing song of praise to your beauty, and

        . . . then worms will try
That long preserved virginity,

And your quaint honor turn to dust,
And into ashes all my lust. . . .

Therefore, since we can't halt time and what time will do to our bodies, let's not wait for him to devour us slowly as he will. The poet goes on to chart a course of action that outdoes the old adage, "If you can't beat them, join them." For he proposes that they beat time at his own game: live so fast that time will be hard put to catch up with them. His plea thus ends in this proposal, that they should seize on their pleasures greedily

And tear our pleasures with rough strife
Through the iron grates of life:
Thus, though we cannot make our sun
Stand still, yet we will make him run.

It is a passionate poem, a plea to live intensely in the present, and yet for all of its emotional violence, it is witty, beautifully organized, and as tightly put together as an exercise in logic: if the circumstances were these; but clearly they are not; therefore, let us act thus.

A good poem is best likened not to a bouquet of carelessly gathered spring flowers but to a cantilever bridge. No wonder that when the French poet Baudelaire wanted to compliment Edgar Allan Poe he described him as a great literary engineer.

Yet this same Andrew Marvell also wrote a poem which seems to be the complete antithesis of "To His Coy Mistress." It is entitled "The Definition of Love." The lovers in this instance will never be able to consummate their love. We are not told why. One can imagine various situations that might render their union impossible. What our poet was interested in, however, was evidently something else: how the lovers could answer up to this apparently desperate situation.

The lover bravely begins by stating the hopelessness of their situation:

My Love is of a birth as rare
As 'tis for object, strange and high;
It was begotten by Despair
Upon impossibility.

The poet then runs through a set of paradoxes in which lean, implacable despair shows herself as generous and even magnanimous. But hope, which most of the poets celebrate as indomitable and strong beyond strength, is labeled "feeble."

> Magnanimous Despair alone
> Could show me so divine a thing,
> Where feeble Hope could ne'er have flown
> But vainly flapped its tinsel wing.

Presumably the poet is saying that the love that he and his mistress have for each other is too ideal ever to hope for realization, and its very ideality removes from it any trace of self-interest, personal aggrandizement, desire for dominance over another, or any other of the elements which appear in so many love affairs and marriages. The poet does not, however, spell out any such reasoning in the poem. He prefers to present it through the mythology he has chosen to use: with personifications such as despair, impossibility, and in the ensuing stanzas, fate.

Thus, the poet accounts for the problem of the lovers only in the most grand of terms: fate in desperation has forbidden their union in order to preserve its own existence. The poet's argument runs like this: if any love truly perfect could occur in this time-ridden world of contingency and blind fate–driven lives, the realm of eternity would have arrived. Time would be no more and with it fate would have perished. Fate's opposition to the union of the lovers is thus an act of self-defense. Fate's very existence is at stake.

Yet the speaker does not rest his case on logical statements alone. He uses analogies, though analogies drawn from such exact sciences as mathematics and spherical geometry. Jealous fate has indeed pushed the lovers "poles apart," but how cleverly the lover who speaks the poem develops the image. The earth, we say, turns on its poles, but so does the whole world of love turn on these two perfect lovers, because, though pushed poles apart, their ideal love provides the end points of human love and in the perfection of their own love comprehends all the possibilities of genuine love that lie between these extremes. In short, their perfect love provides a measure by which all lesser loves can be judged, valued, and fitted into a total scheme. As for the lovers never being allowed to touch each other, the answer again is to be found in the perfection of their love.

So thoroughly do they match each other that, like truly parallel lines, they can never meet. For their inability to do so arises not from defect but from their complete spiritual likeness, in which one is parallel at every point to the other.

I find this poem deeply moving: it is a gallant compliment made to the lady, this "object strange and high," and it is a brave statement, putting the best face on a hopeless situation, with absolutely no whining and no self-pity. But even readers who are not moved by it—if there are any such—will have to admit that it is a brilliant tour de force. In any case, don't forget that the situation described here touches a deep chord in the general human psyche. The lost love, the love that cannot be fulfilled, is in some ways the most poignant love of all. The Arthurian romances were full of it though written centuries ago. In our own time American movie audiences have wept into their popcorn many times over the fate of the little Viennese shop girl who has fallen in love with the student prince, and he with her. But affairs of state have forced him to give her up since custom forbids their marriage. And what about the ending of perhaps the most popular movie of our time, *Casablanca.* When Rick insists that his true love, Ilse, join her husband, the freedom fighter, on the plane which will take her to America and out of his life forever, the audience has no trouble in sensing his feelings: honor demands that he give her up. But the sacrifice deepens and intensifies his love for Ilse and hers for him.

Which of these two poems by Marvell gives the truer view of love and therefore is the sounder and wiser? A natural question, but before I attempt an answer let me make this observation: each poem pushes the case to its extreme limit. The first urges the fulfillment of love's pleasure without regard to any other consideration. If obstacles or inhibitions exist they are of no special account. The lady's coyness is all that seems to matter here. But "To His Coy Mistress" no more recommends that lovers consummate their love than "The Definition of Love" urges on lovers a strictly platonic relationship as more valuable and rewarding. The wisdom that resides in poetry (if indeed wisdom does reside in poetry) is not typically contained in "thou shalts" and "thou shalt nots." It is to be found in the way in which poems can express our feelings and depict our actions and often render or at least imply their consequences.

The virtue of genuine literature is the creation of a better understanding of our inner natures through an honest portrayal of reality as human beings actually experience it. In short, literature presents us with a store of vicarious experiences which have been organized for us and at least implicitly evaluated.

Human beings of our day are more and more preoccupied with the knowledge of processes and means, but when it comes to the matter of ends, we get mighty thin nourishment. Poems provide a much needed supplement, especially when we are allowed to compare accounts of different values and are forced to make our own judgments of their relative worth.

Somebody may, however, still want to ask, "But what did Andrew Marvell actually believe?" I respect the question, though my argument is that for a profitable reading of his poetry it doesn't finally matter. I do not know that Marvell ever had a coy mistress, nor is there any evidence that he ever entertained a hopeless love, which became the more precious because it could never be fulfilled in the flesh. Marvell's other poems would suggest that he often pondered the strange relations between the body and the soul—often speculated on their seemingly contradictory commands. He wrote some very beautiful, thoroughly Christian poems, and he was obviously deeply versed in Christian theology. But he knew well the pagan poetry of the ancient classical world. He was a man of affairs and a member of parliament. He was a minor official in Cromwell's government, but later he was well acquainted with personages in the dissolute court of Charles II. So far as is known, he never married. But he evidently was able to enter into many different states of mind and to express them sensitively and convincingly. His poems can make accessible to us various human responses to various circumstances and make it possible for us to discipline our emotions and perhaps improve our own responses.

I have touched upon only a few items in the vast treasury of love poems written in English—not to mention the countless others written in other languages. In this great library we can find poems that render sensitively and honestly all sorts of love—not only romantic and sexual love but the various other types and kinds of affections.

I trust that you have noticed the precision with which these poets have expressed not only the main features but even the delicate shadings of different kinds of love. We think of science when we think of precision tools and measuring instruments, but the literary artist has his own precision instruments also, and though he deals with emotions his poems and novels are full of headwork too. But further illustrations of this point can be found in poems that treat topics other than love—war and battle for instance.

Here is a short poem by the author of the great novel *Moby-Dick*. It is entitled "Inscription" and commemorates an action in the Civil War battle of Fredericksburg. I have visited that battlefield. Ambrose Burnside, the commander of the Union forces, had got his men across the Rappahannock River and attacked the Confederate forces under Lee who were entrenched on Marye's Heights overlooking the river. The Confederate positions were practically impregnable. But one small Union detachment did break through temporarily before being crushed. Here is Melville's poem:

To them who crossed the flood
And climbed the hill, with eyes
Upon the heavenly flag intent.
And through the deathful tumult went
Even unto death: to them this stone—
Erect, where they were overthrown—
Of more than victory the monument.

Those soldiers in being overthrown actually set up, "erected," a testament recording something greater than any mere victory. The truly brave and truly dedicated man is willing to die for a cause he cannot win. Somebody has erected a stone on the battlefield to commemorate this event and it displays a poem. But not Melville's. Our government is not at its typical best when it comes to choosing poems.

Here is another poem about soldiers, this time mercenary soldiers. Mercenaries—soldiers who fight for pay—are not in good odor and usually are not counted praiseworthy by poets or anybody else. Hence the following poem by A. E. Housman, which is frankly called "To an Army of Mercenaries," is something of an oddity—maybe worth looking at because of that fact alone. Here is the poem.

These, in the day when Heaven was falling,
    The hour when earth's foundations fled,

Followed their mercenary calling
  And took their wages and are dead.

Their shoulders held the sky suspended;
  They stood, and earth's foundations stay;
What God abandoned, these defended,
  And saved the sum of things for pay.

I have been told that Housman wrote this poem in praise of the small British professional army that finally stopped the German advance through Belgium in World War I; the Kaiser had dismissed them as "that contemptible little army." But many readers have taken the meaning of the poem more broadly: those praised are the realists in general, who don't talk much about high ideals and lofty motives, but when push comes to shove, stay in there and get the job done.

In any case, I don't see how the poem can be taken literally. You can hardly persuade a man to die just for money—certainly not when the money involved is a typical GI's pay. There are always other motives: love of adventure, genuine patriotism, esprit de corps, manly pride, hope for glory. Nevertheless, one can sympathize with the poet's willingness to exaggerate in his praise of those who, with no pretense to pure motives and high ideals, perform the difficult and dangerous tasks that others take for granted but which they are paid to perform.

To judge from another of Housman's poems, a poem that is simply entitled "1887," Housman did believe that men could die for patriotic reasons. The year 1887 marked the fiftieth anniversary of Queen Victoria's reign, and the exact day was celebrated all over England. That night the beacons had been lighted, and in the pubs and other meeting places, people were singing the national anthem, "God Save the Queen." The beacon, by the way, was an ancient form of early communication. Stacks of wood were kept on platforms of stone on high hills all over the island. If a hostile fleet was sighted in the English Channel, that night the coast beacons were lighted; people watching in the next district saw the flame and lighted theirs. So the news of danger could be carried across hundreds of miles in a few hours.

As part of the anniversary celebration the villagers in the county of

Shropshire have lighted their beacon, and so the poem begins on a note of happy jubilation.

> From Clee to heaven the beacon burns,
>   The shires have seen it plain,
> From north and south, the sign returns
>   And beacons burn again.

> Look left, look right, the hills are bright,
>   The dales are light between,
> Because 'tis fifty years tonight
>   That God has saved the Queen.

The last line introduces something of a jarring note. "God Save the Queen" is a ceremonial phrase, but here it is being treated as an ordinary grammatical statement; and worse is to come. Some of those who helped save the queen never came home. Indeed, in a following stanza we are told

> The saviours come not home tonight,
>   Themselves they could not save.

The very phrasing reminds us, and clearly is meant to remind us, of Christ, the savior of mankind, as he hung on the cross. "He saved others; Himself he could not save" was spoken of Him in mockery.

Some of the queen's soldiers died in Africa and Asia in the far-flung British Empire. The patriotism of her soldiers is not being questioned here. Presumably her living soldiers are now joining in the patriotic song.

> "God save the Queen" we living sing,
>   From height to height 'tis heard;
> And with the rest your voices ring,
>   Lads of the Fifty-third.

Evidently the Fifty-third was a Shropshire regiment.

The poem assumes a sincere patriotism on the part of the "lads of the

Fifty-third," and the poem ends with an assurance that God will save the queen. But the poet specifies a condition.

> Oh, God will save her, fear you not:
>   Be you the men you've been,
> Get you the sons your fathers got,
>   And God will save the Queen.

Again there is the ironic note. Isn't the poet saying in effect: God has nothing to do with the matter? If England continues to produce sturdy men, willing to fight for England, England and her symbolic head of state will endure? Maybe so, though the poet might answer: Do not expect God to perform miracles in your behalf. You yourselves concede that God uses human instrumentalities to achieve his purposes. If you think that you can simply save the queen, or anything else, by sitting idly by and asking God to do all the work, you are badly mistaken.

One would not, I grant, try to make a case for "1887" as a fervently Christian poem or a poem in praise of the Christian god. Furthermore, there *is* indeed a great deal of irony in the poem; but the proper question is: at what is the irony directed? Not at the young British soldiers who let themselves go out and get killed; nor is it an antiwar poem as many people have conceived it to be.

I would say that the irony is directed at the thoughtlessness with which we utter so many conventional phrases. In short, the poet is bent on attacking not patriotism but the shallowness of those who make glib declarations without taking into account the human cost.

Years later, when Britain was faced with "saving the king" (and more important, England's independence), Churchill warned the British people that it would cost them "blood, sweat, and tears" to do so. Important decisions always cost something. I find nothing in Housman's poem that would conflict with Churchill's speech. As for the sheer rhetorical brilliance of Housman's poem, it is most successful. It gets our attention and it hits hard.

Does this brief examination of a few poems tell us about what literature can do for us? I think it does. First it can help us articulate our own feelings and emotions, getting them up from our unconscious; it provides us with a better understanding of reality as human beings actually experience it and so it helps us not only understand the world outside us but also understand our own inner selves. When we try to express our true feelings, we don't have to keep mumbling, "you know," "you know." *We* will really *know* what we feel and be able to put it into words that enable other people to know what we feel. We will also have widened our own experience by having lived at least imaginatively the experiences of many other people, including people in distant lands who lived hundreds of years ago. Thus, in making our own choices we will have so many more possibilities from which to choose. "What know they of England, who only England know," wrote an English poet, and we may ask what do we know of our own country who really know only one little patch of it as it exists in one little span of time?

Literature cannot settle the problem of values for us. Obviously, it cannot substitute for science. Those who believe it can take the place of religion are, I think, clearly wrong. Nor is the job of literature that of social engineering. The misguided folk who take that view usually end up by turning literature into propaganda. Nowadays that tendency is very strong.

Literature has its own job to do, and I have tried to suggest what that job is and why it is important, and why it is of special importance today. For the greatest literature, we may even make the claim that it possesses wisdom. Wisdom is a certain kind of knowledge, one that is never mere information, for it involves judgment as well. It enables us to make considered decisions. In a time that boasts itself an age of information, it is ridiculous to rely simply on what we call gut feelings. Important decisions ought to come from a higher center than the gut: the brain and also the heart ought to be involved.

If literature is a valid source of wisdom, no wonder that thoughtful men and women have derived solace, comfort, enjoyment, and wisdom from reading what the most articulate members of our culture have had to say about life. William Butler Yeats, perhaps the greatest poet of the twentieth century, called such writings "monuments of the [soul's] magnificence" and in his own later years found a strengthening power in contemplating them.

I ought, however, to let Yeats speak for himself. He writes,

An aged man is but a paltry thing,
A tattered coat, upon a stick, unless
Soul clap its hands and sing, and louder sing
For every tatter in its mortal dress,
Nor is there singing school but studying
Monuments of its own magnificence. . . .

Earlier in the poem Yeats had called the great works of the mind and spirit "Monuments of unaging intellect." One can see why. The body ages; but intellect does not. Truth does not age. Great art does not wither. These things are impervious to time. As the Latin poet put it long ago: *vita brevis, ars longa*.

Yeats as an aging artist is thinking of art as the special recourse for age. But a poem is not merely something like a long-term bond that pays off only many years later. John Keats at twenty-four knew better than that. He was very early studying in this singing school of the soul, making use of these "monuments of [the soul's] magnificence" and joining in with his own voice.

In promoting the values of literature and of the humanities generally, I do not see myself as the salesman for a kind of spiritual Geritol, a medicinal compound good for soothing the aches and pains of the elderly. Great literary art provides substantial food for all of us. The truth of the matter is that it is the elderly who are most likely to misconceive matters. I am thinking of the businessman who is desperate for something to do when he retires because without his business he is lost, or the woman who, with her husband dead and the children grown up and gone, may be completely at loose ends.

All of which reminds me of a poem by Robert Southey entitled "The Old Man's Comforts and How He Gained Them." Southey was one of Britain's nineteenth-century poets laureate, but the poem from which I shall quote is not one of his best efforts. It begins with a young man's praise of old Father William and with enquiries as to how, at his advanced age, he can remain so hearty and cheerful. Here are the last four stanzas.

You are old, Father William, the young man cried,
And pleasures with youth pass away;

And yet you lament not the days that are gone,
Now tell me the reason, I pray.

In the days of my youth, Father William replied,
I remember'd that youth could not last;
I thought of the future, whatever I did,
That I never might grieve for the past.

You are old, Father William, the young man cried,
And life must be hastening away;
You are cheerful, and love to converse upon death,
Now tell me the reason, I pray.

I am cheerful, young man, Father William replied,
Let the cause thy attention engage;
In the days of my youth I remember'd my God!
And He hath not forgotten my age.

It's pretty awful stuff, isn't it? Note that my quarrel is not with the ideas expressed so much as with the way they are expressed. The sanctimonious piety of Father William's replies is obviously self-serving.

The author of *Alice in Wonderland*, Lewis Carroll, was amused at, but also probably annoyed by, this lip-smacking recital of personal virtues and thought it fair game for parody. Here is the way he chose to deal with the conversation between Father William and his youthful questioner.

"You are old, Father William," the young man said,
"And your hair has become very white;
And yet you incessantly stand on your head—
Do you think, at your age, it is right?"

"In my youth," Father William replied to his son,
"I feared it might injure the brain;
But now that I'm perfectly sure I have none,
Why, I do it again and again."

The devastating parody continues for a half-dozen more stanzas and deals a knockout blow to this unctuous sermonizing. We can always, by the way, safely leave it to the poets themselves to keep their house in order and sweep out the trash.

What I have been talking about hasn't anything to do with the utterance of pious truisms. Homer, Dante, and Shakespeare, or to come down to our age, Yeats, Eliot, Faulkner, Warren, and Welty, are not spooning out soothing syrup for children or pap for the aged. They are providing wisdom for an era badly in need of it. They are offering truth about the ends and purposes of life, truth that is supremely important, though it does not come out of a scientist's laboratory and cannot be detected by the most sensitive microscope. It is not the kind of truth that tells us how to make a living but the truth by which we can live.

Index

Acknowledgments

The essays in this volume are reprinted by permission of the original publishers or copyright holders as indicated.

"In Search of the New Criticism," reprinted from *The American Scholar* 53, no. 1 (winter 1983–1984), copyright © 1983 by the author, and "John Crowe Ransom: As I Remember Him," reprinted from *The American Scholar* 58, no. 2 (spring 1989), copyright © 1989 by the author, by permission of the publisher.

"The Primacy of the Linguistic Medium," "The Primacy of the Author," and "The Primacy of the Reader," published by *The Missouri Review* as *The Rich Manifold*, copyright © 1983 by the Curators of the University of Missouri. First presented as part of the Paul Anthony Brick Lecture Series, University of Missouri–Columbia, April 1982.

"The Crisis in Culture as Reflected in Southern Literature," from *The American South: Portrait of a Culture*, edited by Louis D. Rubin, Jr. (Baton Rouge: Louisiana State University Press, 1980), used with permission.

"Religion and Literature," *Sewanee Review* 82 (winter 1974), and "The New Criticism," *Sewanee Review* 87 (fall 1979).

"Frost and Nature," from *Robert Frost: The Man and the Poet*, edited by Earl J. Wilcox (Rock Hill, S.C.: Winthrop College, 1981). Originally presented as a lecture at the Winthrop College Major Modern Writers Symposium, 1980.

"*The Waste Land:* A Prophetic Document" and "Episode and Anecdote in the Poetry of Robert Penn Warren," *Yale Review.*

"Faulkner's Criticism of Modern America," *Virginia Quarterly Review.*

"English Literature: A Subject Matter? A Discipline? A Special Amalgam?" *Bulletin: International Association of University Professors of English*, spring 1973. First presented as an address at a meeting of the English Association at McMaster University, Hamilton, Ontario, Canada, February 7, 1973.

"Science, Religion, and Literature," *Arts and Letters*, January 1987. First presented as a lecture at Bryan College, Dayton, Tennessee, April 15, 1982.

"T. S. Eliot and the American South," *The Southern Review.*

"The Past Reexamined: *The Optimist's Daughter*," *Mississippi Quarterly* 26, no. 4 (fall 1973).

"The Past Alive in the Present," from *American Letters and the Historical Consciousness: Essays in Honor of Lewis Simpson,* edited by Gerald Kennedy and Daniel Mark Fogel (Baton Rouge: Louisiana State University Press, 1987).

"Literature in a Technological Age," presented as the Jefferson Lecture, sponsored by the National Endowment for the Humanities, May 8, 1985.

"An Age of Silver: Contemporary American Literature," *Quarterly Journal of the Library of Congress* (winter 1982). First presented as a lecture at the Library of Congress on the occasion of the thirtieth anniversary of the Gertrude Clarke Whittall Poetry and Literature Fund.

"Nature and Human Nature in the Poetry of Robert Frost," from *Robert Frost: Read and Remembered,* edited by Margaret G. Trotter (Decatur, Ga.: Agnes Scott College, 1976).

"Walker Percy: In Celebration," *Humanities* (May/June 1989).

"The Real Importance of the Humanities," the last lecture prepared by Cleanth Brooks before his death in May 1994, was delivered before the Davenport College Fellowship, Yale University, March 1994.